ROSALIND MILES

Rosalind Miles is the award-winning author of fiction and non-fiction, including *Women and Power* and *The Rites of Man: Love, Sex and Death in the Making of the Male*. Educated at Oxford University, she later studied at the Universities of Birmingham and Leicester. She founded the Centre for Women's Studies at the University of Coventry, and became the youngest J.P. in the country at the age of 28, a position she held for ten years. She has lectured and broadcast all over the world, and her other books include a highly acclaimed biography of Ben Jonson and the historical novel *I, Elizabeth*, the story of Elizabeth I. She is a contributing editor to *Cosmopolitan* magazine and a consultant on women's career development and equal opportunities issues. In 1990 she was appointed a Fellow of the Royal Society of Arts. Married with two children, she lives in Kent.

ROSALIND MILES

The Children
We Deserve

Love and Hate in the Making of the Family

HarperCollins*Publishers*

For my dearest children
who taught me all I know.

HarperCollins*Publishers*
77–85 Fulham Palace Road,
Hammersmith, London W6 8JB

This paperback edition 1995
1 3 5 7 9 8 6 4 2

First published in Great Britain by
HarperCollins*Publishers* 1994

Author photograph by Jerry Bauer

ISBN 0 586 09231 5

Set in Sabon

Printed in Great Britain by
HarperCollinsManufacturing Glasgow

Contents

In ancient shadows and twilights
Where childhood had strayed,
The world's great sorrows were born
And its heroes were made.
In the lost boyhood of Judas,
Christ was betrayed.

AE, 'Germinal'

It is up to us as adults, depending on how we treat our children, either to turn them into future monsters or to allow them to grow up into feeling and hence responsible human beings.

Alice Miller, *Banished Knowledge* (1990)

Foreword

EVERY COUNTRY, it is said, gets the government it deserves. The same principle could be applied to marriage. I believe it to be even more true of children.

I wrote this book to complete a trilogy that has occupied me for over ten years now. The first book, *The Women's History of the World*, set out to answer a question that had haunted me since schooldays: why are there so few women in history? In answering that, I found I had embarked on a wider task, that of explaining the origins of the female sex worldwide, and the forces that have made us what we are. The international success of *The Women's History* showed me how many others, male and female, had wondered about this too.

That book had an unexpected consequence in the form of numerous requests from both women and men: why don't you do the same for men? Clearly there was no need for a history: all history as we have it is the story of men. But only of the famous few, self-selected by their skill in politics, war, or the public world. Why not a book asking then, as *The Women's History* did, where do men come from, and what makes them what they are? So was born *The Rites of Man*, more provocatively published in the USA under the subtitle of its British edition, *Love, Sex, and Death in the Making of the Male*. And who, as a producer on CNN drily asked me, would not be interested in that?

It has been the writer's dream come true to receive some of the letters these two books have brought me from all over the world. (I discount those that begin: '*Bitch!!! It's women like you who* . . .') On the saner side of the blanket, men and women of all ages and cultures have written to say 'your book made me proud to be a woman' or 'now I understand what it is to be a man.' These letters almost invariably concluded as the others had, 'Why don't you do the same for blacks/Asians/lesbians/gays', or almost any other of the groupings that make up our world. Yet no one ever said, '*What about children?*'

What about them? you may think. Never has the public been more conscious of children all over the world: pick up any newspaper on any day and you will find reports of treatments to promote fertility, genetic engineering to ensure healthy birth, improved infant survival rates, new developments in school curricula or programmes of child care. Daily too we get the darker news: of youth gangs in Mozambique, child carpet-weaving slaves in India, street orphans in Rio, school suicides in Japan, and from this we may comfort ourselves that our own children are not so bad.

But the West has its own brand of distress. Here there is an uneasy sense that the children of today are very different from the young of times past: more sophisticated yet less responsible, more out of hand yet more demanding, more sensation-seeking and more drug-abusing, more delinquent and more dangerous than ever before. The classic adult reaction to everything from anorexic daughters to joy-riding sons is to ask, '*What have we done to deserve this?*' Yet could not these children make the same demand of us, with even more natural justice?

For some, the case has already gone beyond an easy answer. In the part of the world that calls itself advanced, some fear that we are in fact sliding back to a new Dark Age. The public debate is gripped by a strange terror – fed on a daily diet of crack dealers of 14, child-mothers of 12, killers of 10 and 7, we clutch each other and wail, '*What are they coming to?*' But in all this moral panic, where do we hear the still small voice that asks, '*How have we let it come to this?*'

There are other questions too. A newborn baby is a perfect miracle of nature, beautiful and unspoiled. We were all like that once, at the morning of the world. Most children are born to parents overwhelmed by the sheer wonder of that new life, and determined to do their best to live up to the humbling, terrifying responsibility for that smallness, that innocence, that truth. Most babies enjoy an upbringing good enough to enable them to grow up into people who will be good enough parents in their turn. Most growing children are never more than averagely troublesome at the level we all understand and can manage. *They are not the problem.* It is time to look more deeply into those who are, and those responsible for making them so. What happens in the course of growing up that turns some children into hardened mini-adults, and leaves some adults as the damaged children passing for grown-ups that so many are today?

Or was it always so? All childhoods are unhappy, whether we know it or not, said Dostoevsky. Can this be true? If it is, how do we bear it? And why do we let it go on?

I wrote this book to address these questions and to work towards some answers. It was clear from the outset that there are no easy solutions. But it is equally clear that nothing will change until we are ready to devote a great deal more thought, time, attention and political will to the plight of children and the demands of parenting than we have done for some time.

For children in recent years have been getting an increasingly raw deal. From the Sixties revolt against authority which for the first time in history gave adults the right to become or remain children, to the emphasis of the Seventies on self-expression and self-discovery, through the 'Me-decade' of the Eighties on into the grim survivalism of the Nineties, *the preoccupations of adults have dominated the agenda and the needs of children have been pushed to the back of the queue*. With increasing evidence of children's domestic rebellion and public disorder, their educational difficulties and emotional distress, the time has surely come to accept that children must come first. They must be placed at the centre of all our calculations, seen as the heart and core and *raison d'être* of every family, not as the 'lifestyle adjunct' of those who want to have it all, but not necessarily together, or even with their child.

The time has come for children in another important way, too. The modern wave of the Women's Movement which began around 25 years ago necessarily concentrated on the abuses and discriminations women were suffering then. With the acceptance that in this struggle the personal truly was political, the second stage inevitably shifted the focus to men, seen now not as representatives but as fellow-victims of patriarchal oppression in all its forms. So far from 'sleeping with the enemy', many women came to feel that we were sharing a world with a race of walking wounded from 17 to 107, any or all, in fact, who had been subject to the violence of 'the rites of man'. And more and more men, it is now clear, were feeling this too.

Any rapprochement of male and female in the age-old sex war, any progress for feminism towards achieving full humanity for both sexes, is to be welcomed with an open heart. Within this generation, the Women's Movement has won some immeasurable gains for women, while also building bridges and opening many doors for men. Yet men and women do not stand alone in the world. Now we are poised to embark on a new and crucial third wave of feminism in which we can reclaim the world for children, too. The rights of children must be the last frontier in the fight for freedom for us all, a consideration of their needs the last territory to be won back from the age-old tyranny of patriarchy and the casual brutality of its domination.

Today's men and women may not have won all the battles for freedom and understanding, but at least they have identified the battlegrounds and accepted the scale of the task. Of all human groups, only children continue to suffer what Betty Friedan dubbed 'the problem that has no name', the routine denial of their right to autonomy, the equally routine insistence that their situation is 'natural' and 'normal' and 'the way it has always been'. If feminism cannot look at the way we are treating the children of the world and repeat on their behalf the demand of its founding mother, '*Is this all?*', then no force on earth has the power to do so. For feminism, the plea for women's rights, is nothing less than the demand for full human rights, rights which must in due course be extended to children, the majority of whom, as females, will be the next mothers of the next children all over the world.

I believe passionately with the poet William Blake that the voice of the children should be heard in the land. But children cannot speak for themselves. Who then speaks for them? This book is an attempt to do so. Like its two predecessors, *The Women's History* and *The Rites of Man*, it does not pretend to be any more than a personal journey, drawing on informal material and anecdotal experience as much as on academic research and official statistics. My aim was to examine the whole process of bringing a child into the world and preparing it for life, from the moment of conception through to adulthood, looking at what may go right or wrong for our most precious resource, the young. It is not a 'How-To' book, not an addition to the many books on child-rearing, not another 'Bringing Up Baby'. It does not purport to discuss anything that lies within the remit of the professional paediatrician or child psychologist. Instead it attempts to reflect on the children of today and to reassert some values and techniques of parenting for today's committed, concerned, and often wholly unconfident parents. For that, I suspect, is what most of us are.

We are also all members of our communities, work-places, corporations, churches, clubs and schools, and the countless other organizations which we fear may be threatened by the rise of a lawless, alienated youth. The prevalence of today's news stories about criminal children, abused children, children out of hand, however much they smack of newspaper hype and moral panic, point to a genuine, growing, and justified concern.

For these are, to put it no higher, children in great need. And when they grow up, what happens to them? To their children? In all today's confused political rhetoric and golden-age nostalgia, we have to look to the present, not pine for the past. Past and future are in any case already foreshortened in our world: in no time at all the 10-year-old thug becomes the 15-year-old killer, the sexualized 9-year-old the 14-year-old child-mother. Every child not getting what it needs right now is a ticking time-bomb, waiting to explode.

The concern of adults with this problem, from my neighbourhood policeman to the President of the Royal College of Psychiatrists, has been evident in the tremendous help I have received in the preparation of this book. Parents of children of all ages also shared their opinions with me and allowed me access to some of their most private experiences. My grateful thanks are due, too, to all the teachers, doctors, lawyers, priests, social workers and child-care professionals who so freely gave me their time and the benefit of their expertise.

Above all, simply being with children, learning from them, was the most rewarding aspect of this project. Two above all, my daughter and my son, have taught me as much as I have taught them and more, since the moment they were born, and this book is a recognition of that.

Where individuals are quoted in the text, their words are taken from personal interview. Other sources will be found cited in the notes and references at the end of the book. The use of both forename and surname indicates the real name of the speaker. Single names indicate a pseudonym.

My highest hope now is that we can begin to 'feed the children', as the psychologist D. W. Winnicott once memorably advised the carers of the millions of displaced young after the Second World War. For too long in this generation, the adult world has fed its own hungers at the cost of theirs. We all accept that it is time for change. We all want our children to grow up to be happy, good, and free. Let us see then what can be done to help all children to become the kind of people that society wants, needs, and can value. That way, and only that way, will we get the children we deserve.

Rosalind Miles
December 1993

Introduction

'What kind of a childhood did you have?'
'Short.'
    Clint Eastwood, *Escape from Alcatraz* (1979)

IT WAS IN GEORGETOWN, Texas, but it could have been any hotel room in the world. As the TV news flickered in the corner, the story emerged: a 2-year-old boy lost by his mother in a shopping mall in the north of England, and subsequently filmed by security cameras in the act of being taken away.

Within hours these raw moments of blurred video had flashed round the globe. A French friend called from the heart of the Charente: 'The little boy who has been stolen away – did you see it?' Everyone saw it, from Melbourne to Murmansk, and back again to Main Street, USA.

What was it about the abduction of James Bulger that captured the conscience of the world? He was an ordinary child from an ordinary family in Liverpool, a city that, even in England, had seen far worse than this. One week in New York or Bogotá could outdo it in horror a thousandfold. The video of the incident on 12 February 1993 was so poor as hardly to be worth screening. The figures of the abductors could scarcely be made out. And in a universe plagued with wars, death, disease, crisis and despair, where did one lost 2-year-old rate in the grand scheme of things?

Was it because this was the first abduction ever to be seen 'live on TV', recorded as it was actually taking place? Or was it because we all knew that the child was going to die?

Police investigators in Britain saw a blend of both these factors. 'This must be the first live abduction ever captured on video,' said a senior officer. 'When you watch a replay and see him taken away like that and you know he is going to be brutally murdered, it is a uniquely chilling experience.' This overlooks one even more chilling factor about the Bulger case. For if the victim was only a child, so were the killers. Both James's murderers proved to be no more than 10 years old.

•••

Children as young as 10 may legally be charged with
murder. But it has to be shown that they knew what they
were doing.

British Home Office statement after
the James Bulger killing

•••

For James Bulger, it should have been just another day. Countless
other toddlers out shopping with their mothers that Friday came
home safe that night, as he had done a hundred times before. But
when his mother's attention was distracted, James wandered off.
Moments later, security cameras at the shopping mall picked him up
in the company of two other boys. Trustingly holding the hand of
one of them, the little figure trudges out of view.

Within seconds, he was missed. But as his distracted mother ran
one way, James was led away the other. Under the uncaring eye of
the cameras, James was seen being taken from the mall, and once
again in the street outside. By the time his mother had raised the
alarm, he was nowhere to be found.

As his life ticked away, James was glimpsed several more times.
Looking frightened now, he was picked up by another security video
camera on a construction site some distance from the shops. Later
that afternoon a woman noticed him distressed and weeping, with
cuts and bruises to his face and head. Challenging the two boys with
him, she was told they were taking him to the police station. After
one final sighting at 4.45 that Friday afternoon, silence fell.

Despite intense police activity, James's body was not discovered
till the following Sunday. A post mortem revealed 'horrendous' injuries: the little boy had suffered 22 bruises, splits and grazes to his
face and head, and 20 other wounds on his body. Paint had been
thrown in his eyes, he had been kicked in the face, his underpants
had been removed and the foreskin of his penis pulled back, before
he was beaten to death. Afterwards his body had been thrown on
to a railway line, where it had been cut in half. Those who found it
had no words for what they saw.

Still the idea persisted that the killer had to be some unknown
madman, a psychopath who had happened on James after the other
boys had abandoned him. The two abductors, even on the evidence

of the poor-quality video recording, were just a couple of lads, too young to kill, it seemed. *Surely not these children*, was the unspoken prayer. *Surely not . . .*

That hope died four days later when two boys, both aged 10, were arrested and charged with the killing. 'My belief is that James came by the fatal aspects of his injuries early on the Friday evening,' said Detective Superintendent Kirby, the CID officer in charge of the case. No one else was believed to have been involved. All the same, the authorities proceeded gently with the accused, said the Detective Superintendent: 'You have to remember that they are only ten years old.'

This was to prove difficult to remember, yet impossible to forget. Denounced on the one hand as monsters of evil, defended on the other as children who themselves must have suffered evil beyond imagining, the two boys triggered a panic of self-examination unprecedented in modern news coverage: 'A youth crime wave is striking at the heart of the nation,' pronounced the *Sunday Times* one week after James's death.

'James Bulger's murder was a watershed,' says Professor Masud Hoghughi, the controversial former director of the Aycliffe Centre for disturbed children and Professor of Psychology at the University of Hull. 'It made the nation wake up to the fact that the children at the margins of our society are out of control.' After the instant sensation subsided, the death of James seemed to have a deeper resonance for the whole of the advanced world. 'Just as we look darkly at maleness when another woman is raped, so this tragedy has made us look askance at the nation's children,' mused the British commentator Christina Hardyment in the wake of the event.

Such child-watching has become almost a reflex in recent times. Never have the children of the world been subjected to a more critical scrutiny at every turn. And who can be happy with what they see? From both sides of the Atlantic the evidence seems to be piling up that our children are more and more deviant, more delinquent, more out of hand:

- The number of youth crimes in Britain has soared by 54 per cent in the last ten years, with school arson alone costing around £300 million a year.

- Drug addiction among British under-18s has increased fourfold in the same period.

- Illegitimate births have increased sixfold, while abortions have also increased by the same factor among teenage girls.

In the US, the same story prevails:

- The homicide rate among American children leaped by 252 per cent between 1980 and 1988.

- Of Americans aged 12–25, 2 per cent are using cocaine, almost 4 per cent crack, 13 per cent are taking cannabis, 13.2 per cent use hallucinogens and over 20 per cent regularly abuse alcohol.

- The number of illegitimate births and abortions to American women under 20 have both almost doubled in the last twenty and fifteen years respectively.

Delinquency used to be the province of 'naughty boys'. As these figures show, girls are now likely to be involved in antisocial activity too, from mugging to drug-taking. And the delinquents are getting younger: British police records for 1992 include an 8-year-old car thief and a professional burglar of 7. Across the water, Americans have the right to bear arms, at any age, it seems: New York police reported a 6-year-old found in possession of a loaded revolver and a Brooklyn 3-year-old armed with a .25 automatic pistol.

'A SICK SOCIETY', moan the headlines. 'CHILDREN OUT OF CONTROL', 'EVIL BEYOND BELIEF.' Masud Hoghughi made a characteristically sombre assessment of the situation:

> Crime committed by young people is burgeoning, not only in numbers, but in range, intensity and quality. As a group youngsters now commit the most burglaries and car thefts for joy riding and burning. They are also probably responsible for a third to a half of all sexual offences against children. The numbers of children found guilty of rape, arson and aggravated robbery has risen significantly. Many more young people display a sense of hopelessness and anger which makes them implacable.

And crime is only one measurement of child activity, a crude and sensational indicator that does no more than grab headlines and make news. Criminal children after all are only those who have been caught – how many more are acting out the pressures that they all feel and share? Lawlessness is only one end of a spectrum on which all children are located. The forces that make some young people criminal are undoubtedly operating on all the others too.

Hence the anxiety. The small handful of children who are in prison do not worry us as much as all those who look as if they could be, maybe even should be there, the disaffected youth we see around us every day. 'Are our children spinning out of control?' asked the British journalist Jonathan Margolis, 'towards some kind of spiritual abyss?' One by one the sacred institutions of civilized society seem to be under attack from its uncivilized young: the family, private property, and even motherhood have quite lost the value which our parents and grandparents never thought could be questioned, let alone undermined.

Clearly our forefathers had an easier time of it in some ways, for they knew where to lay the blame. The good, the great and the godly of earlier generations had no doubt that the evil spirit is born in a child along with the spark of conception. Christianity crystallized this concept as the doctrine of Original Sin. Thus encouraged, the Spanish Inquisition of the 16th century burned and garrotted heretics of 12 and 14, while the English judiciary as late as the 19th century hanged and transported felons of 10 and 12.

But can we truly apply the concept of evil to young children? Or are we simply stigmatizing them out of our own childish urge to make ourselves feel better by insisting they are worse – *it's not us, it's them* . . .

'We have to demolish the idea that these children are monsters, the hairy black underbelly of the nation,' says Masud Hoghughi. 'To us they are children deserving the best care.' To call a child 'evil' reads perilously like creating scapegoats for our own sins. Is it not simply more tolerable for the adult world to pass on the blame, than to confront and examine what these events make us feel?

'When in doubt, blame the children,' says journalist Beatrix Campbell. '"Dangerous" children, "killer" children – they have become the enemy within. Childhood has become a metaphor for a country that is out of control. The country hides its shame and self-hatred by regarding its young victims as culprits. It is as if we have become obsessed with the threats *from* children, rather than the threats *to* them. *None of the politicians who have called for a crusade against children's crimes has complained about crimes against children* (italics inserted).'

• • •

Crimes against children represent the most frequent of all types of crime.

Alice Miller, *Banished Knowledge*, 1990

• • •

As in the killing of James Bulger, is it not possible that children might be both offenders and victims? If we shift the perspective to look at the world around us through the eyes of a child, what do we see?

- Violent crimes in the adult population of Britain have soared from a 1961 level of 24 in every 100,000 of the population to 523 today; in the US the figure rose from 1.3 million to almost 2 million in the last 10 years.

- Divorces in this country have quadrupled in the last 30 years, making four times as many children now the victims of split allegiances and broken homes.

- In the last 20 years the number of one-parent families in Britain has soared from 500,000 to 1,500,000, in the US from just over 3 million to over 7.5 million.

- Families below the UK state poverty line have risen from 82,000 to 360,000 in the same time: in the US the number of children in poverty increased from 2.7 million in 1979 to 12.7 million in 1990.

- Reported cases of child abuse in Britain are three times more numerous today than in 1970.

- The percentage of child victims of murder in the US between 1980 and 1988 rose from 18 to 41 per cent.

- Numbers of British children in psychiatric hospitals have risen by 65 per cent in the last five years.

- Suicide among US children aged 15–19 rose from 3.5 per cent in 1960 to 11.3 per cent in 1988.

If children are indeed the barometer of the welfare of the wider society, what does this say about how we value them? Statistics are clear, but cold. In human terms they mean children violated in body and mind, bruised and betrayed even before they have grown old enough to learn the meaning of the word 'trust'. Children are born innocent, both harmless and powerless. If they become confused and ignorant, violent and depraved, destructive and self-destructive, then the society that produces them must be so too.

And we are not talking about the cruelly abused minority. This is not the one child in ten who is being viciously battered, sexually perverted, or deliberately starved of food and love.

This is 7-year-old Jason, whose mother regularly shuts him in the coalhouse overnight when he is 'a little bastard'. This is Lucinda, gravely anorexic at 13, clutching a picture of herself taken before her parents' divorce and crying, 'That was when Daddy loved me.' This is privately-educated Sarah, doing cannabis at 13, a heroin addict at 17. This is Peter, 15, eldest of an abandoned family of seven, walking into the sea, 'to make Mum come home'.

Even within a 'normal', 'happy' family, young children may suffer traumas that leave scars for life. They are also all liable to punishments that the law has long ago deemed 'cruel and unusual' when applied to the full-grown. No man or woman in our society now may legally be subjected to the deliberate infliction of physical pain, deprivation of food or sleep, incarceration in dark or confined spaces, or being locked out of shelter at night. *All these things are regularly happening to children everywhere without intervention by the adult world.*

'I'd like to have people stop and realize that kids are fragile, and they absorb feelings from the time they are conceived.' This is the hindsight of Barbara, mother of a 17-year-old son who killed his father after a lifetime of being told, 'You were a screw-up as a kid, you're a screw-up now, and you'll be a fuck-up for the rest of your life.'

'These are clearly children in need,' says Dr Fiona Caldicott, President of the Royal College of Psychiatrists. 'And there is clear evidence that more problems are coming to light. The implications are very serious.'

• • •

> Life for children got worse in the 1980s. However you slice it, the nation as a whole has moved in the wrong direction for kids.
>
> Judith Weitz, project co-ordinator for the US Center
> for the Study of Social Policy

• • •

'The problems are *piling up* . . .'

Dr Benjamin Spock, lifelong champion of the child, is insistent that we recognize how far conditions for children have worsened in the past decade. 'Society has become extraordinarily stressful,' he says. 'Families are experiencing unprecedented strains. The health of children has deteriorated. Lead poisoning has gone up, deaths in children under a year have gone up, child abuse has gone up so much, and is a very good example of how out-of-sorts our whole society is.'

How did it get like this? In public debate and private conversation the same explanations emerge: the loss of family values, the decline in education, permissiveness, feminism, the recession. 'What is not realized is that all "causes" are linked in an interdependent ecology of deviance of which detected and prosecuted crime is only one aspect,' insists Hoghughi. At a deeper level many sense a dark communal malaise, a breakdown in parental morale, a failure of the will. It is as if we have given up: as if we no longer believe we can bring up loving, kind, well-behaved children capable of cherishing us and all that we hold dear.

And where vision fails, in its place comes an increase in furious rhetoric and hollow bluster, seeking to fill the void of understanding at the nation's heart. Who thunders louder about family values and the alienated young than the divorced politician who has slipped the reins of a 25-year marriage to take up with a 23-year-old? Who is harder on the 'amoral selfishness' of young offenders than the judge whose own eminence is the result of an unwerving dedication to his own interests? And what is more reassuring, as we look into the mirror of our children's antisocial acts, than to see our own wrongs and injuries reflected there at twice their natural size?

If we look into any mirror, should we not try to see what is truly there? Above all, see ourselves reflected as we are, not sifting through the ever-shifting images in the search for someone else to blame?

Where to begin?

At the beginning.

When a child is born.

* * *

We can and must turn this round if our children are to enjoy, and to be, a civilization.

Professor A. H. Halsey, Nuffield College, Oxford

* * *

I

THE PRIMAL SCREAM

My mother groaned, my father wept,
Into the dangerous world I leaped:
Helpless, naked, piping loud,
Like a fiend hid in a cloud.

William Blake, *Songs of Experience* (1794)

CHAPTER 1

To Be Or Not To Be

of the dark past
a child is born
with joy and grief
my heart is torn

James Joyce,
Poems (1917)

MARY IS A PUPIL at the Convent of the Sacred Heart in the north of England, she is 15 and she is pregnant. Born into a devoutly religious family and named after the Blessed Virgin Mary herself, when she fell in love she found herself too Catholic to use contraception but not too Catholic to screw. When she became pregnant, she was also too Catholic to consider abortion. And there was no question of marrying the baby's 15-year-old father, like her still at school.

Shanice dropped out of her high school in Washington DC around the time when the authorities installed metal detectors to prevent the students from bringing in guns. She does not believe in any of that religious stuff. First pregnant at 13, she is already two kids up on Mary at the same age. No, she doesn't mess with rubbers. But what's it to you? She can take care of her kids like her mother took care of her. Butt out!

Jean-Paul has worked for Club Med as a 'GO' (Gentil Organisateur) since he left school five years ago without his *baccalauréat*, the French school-leaving qualification. In summer he finds himself somewhere hot and horizontal, and in winter he skis his way through those of the GMs (Gentils Membres) who are susceptible to his French accent, his Mickey Rourke stubble and his joints. He will use a *capote* (condom) if the girl has one or if she makes a big deal out of it. Otherwise not. 'It don' feel the same.'

Dave is unemployed; in the town where he lives there is no work. His life consists of hanging around with the boys and getting laid whenever he can. Sure he's got condoms, but y'know, they break or you lose 'em or you can't find 'em, and after a few beers, what the hell, you forget about 'em, y'know how it is. Sure he's heard of AIDS, but he doesn't go with those kind of girls. It's not his fault if a girl gets 'plugged': 'That's what she came for, ain't it?'

The father of Mary's child passed through her life and was gone in less than three months. Shanice's only memory of the baby-makers who came and went is a faint shrug. No-goods. Who cares? Mary does. She prays every night that her baby will get to know its father one day.

In the meantime, she frets about what kind of life she can give her child. Like Shanice, Jean-Paul and Dave, she has no qualifications, since she had to leave the convent school when she became too big to sit behind her desk. She has no job, as there is no one to mind the baby: her own mother already works full-time. Inevitably, she has no money. This also she shares with Shanice, Jean-Paul and Dave.

'Dick-wit boys and fuck-wit girls,' broods Howard Steiner, a London-based economic analyst for the World Bank, 'we've bred a generation of the *unaccountable*. We've given them freedom from previous social and religious restraints without teaching them any other kind. They can't even use the mechanical barriers that are available!'

'*A baby is the world's greatest wonder*,' runs the Turkish proverb, '*and its heaviest curse*.' How many of today's parents are ready for parenthood, emotionally or financially? We speak of 'the maternal instinct' and encourage young couples to 'build a family'. But behind the social rhetoric lies a different reality. One in four children in Britain alone is destined to cruise the poverty line all its life, according to the charity Save the Children. Almost 36 million of America's 251 million people are officially classified as unable to provide for the children they have. Hundreds will have to go into care, thousands will spiral down into drink, drugs or delinquency. In the global recession, child pornography remained one of the few boom industries along with child abuse. Why do we bring children into the world, knowing what lies in store?

The first step towards getting the children we deserve must lie in having the children we want. 'Every child a wanted child' – was this Sixties slogan of the Family Planning Association ever more than an impossible dream?

•••

We all feel that the world is in a state of crisis. Sooner or
later we will reach the point of no return.

Sir Francis Graham Smith, vice-president of the Royal
Society and chairman of the 1993 World Population
Summit in New Delhi

•••

Mary's priest tells her that God will provide. What her God will not
provide for Mary and for millions like her worldwide is a reliable,
cheap form of birth prevention to reduce at least some of the pregnancies that are neither wanted nor desired, a reduction that our
overcrowded globe desperately needs. While Mary undergoes an
average eight-hour labour, more than 80,000 other women worldwide will be labouring at precisely the same time. While I write
this sentence, twenty more babies will be born. Before this book is
published, another population the size of Jean-Paul's France will
have come into being. Ninety-seven million tiny terrestrials now
make landing on Planet Earth every year, three every second, more
than 10,000 an hour. Allowing for the natural death rate both of
the aged and the newly-born, the world population will increase by
250,000 every 24 hours.

Why?

And what can we do to halt it?

Clearly the doubling of the world's population in the last 40 years
has contributed to the crisis of the environment and the degradation of
the earth. At the 1992 Earth Summit in Rio de Janeiro, Britain and other
countries attempted to put pressure on the Roman Catholic Church to
change its opposition to artificial birth control. If there is a right to free
speech, even a 'right' to bear arms, the argument runs, surely afford-
able and accessible contraception is a basic human right, too?

For the Vatican, however, nothing supersedes the right to life, even
the chance of the right to life at all times. 'It's disgusting,' Mary's
mother says now. 'You show me anywhere in the Bible where God
says "Thou shalt not use condoms".' But God does not need to,
when the Cardinals and the Monsignors and all the hosts of the
faithful will speak for Him. In the preparatory conferences before
the summit, a coalition of Catholic countries succeeded in removing
references to 'unnatural' forms of contraception from the 800-page

document Agenda 21, which set out the programme for the 'green' government of the world's future. 'Sadly,' commented the Prince of Wales at the time, 'it seems that certain delegations are determined to prevent discussion of population growth.'

In response, the Catholic hierarchy strongly defended its opposition to artificial birth control, especially in developing countries, where 96 per cent of the world's population growth is taking place. 'The priority,' explained Father Patrick Jewell SJ, 'ought to be to eradicate poverty, not to eradicate life. It's poverty that encourages people in these countries to have more children, as a combination of unpaid labour force and insurance against their old age.'

Non-Catholic commentators including the Prince of Wales accept at least part of the Church's argument. While regretting the blanket ban on any discussion of contraception at the Earth Summit, the Prince has repeatedly warned that the future health of the world can only be guaranteed if population growth and poverty are tackled together.

To many Catholics and non-Catholics alike, the stress on population growth as a cause of environmental disaster itself evades the issue of where the real responsibility lies. 'One person in the industrialized West consumes more of the world's non-replaceable resources than several families in South America,' says Clive Ponting, author of *The Green History of the World* (1991). Leading Catholics endorse this position without reserve. 'Over-consumption by the rich nations is sucking the life-blood of the poorer members of the world's family,' states Father Philippe Azar, a French priest who has been active in the Third World. A senior member of Opus Dei agrees: 'This forces poor families into producing children as their only means of sustaining non-industrial production.'

Catholics also stress that their ideology alone is not responsible for our exploding planet. 'Catholic countries would have a higher population growth than anywhere else in the world if these arguments were true,' says Mark Topping, spokesman for the Catholic Fund for Overseas Development. 'But it doesn't work out that way. The Philippines and Bangladesh both have similar population growth.'

'So let us at least reduce what we can,' counters Karl-Jurgen Meier, a Hamburg-based activist for the Greens. 'Every unwanted child not born today increases the world's chances of a better tomorrow.' Others are not afraid to lay the challenge at one particular door.

'The Pope will have to give way on this sooner or later,' predicts journalist and family health specialist Lynne Miller:

> Look at what's happened in Holland – the priests there have been telling the Dutch Catholics it's a matter for their own consciences for years now. It's one thing to keep generations of women in miserable enslavement to their bodies – it's quite another when they're holding the whole world to ransom. They're going to have to work hard at digging themselves out of the hole they've got themselves into. But they can't be allowed to pull the rest of us down with them. They'll have to accept modern forms of contraception in the end.

Never, says Mary's priest, the Pope will never sanction artificial birth control. This view received official backing with the publication of the 1993 papal encyclical, *Veritatis Splendor* (The Splendour of Truth), which restated the Church's teaching and demanded unswerving obedience to it with a dogmatism that reduced even committed Catholics to despair. 'The temptation will be to see it not as an honest search for the truth but as a desperate attempt to justify the position adopted by the hierarchy,' wrote the Roman Catholic writer and journalist Robert Nowell. 'But then the last thing the present papacy wishes to face up to is the fact that the church has got it wrong.'

Others were less circumspect: 'One of the great papal mistakes', a 'syllabus of errors', and 'the latest in the historical catalogue of papal bloomers' were some of the reactions in Britain and the US. Like Mary's priest, the Church remained sublimely impervious throughout to all voices of dissent. Their truth in all its splendour was not up for debate. What happened and what happens is the will of God.

•••

> As a man is, so is his God: this word
> Explains why God so often is absurd.
>
> Giles & Melville Harcourt,
> *Short Prayers for the Long Day* (1978)

•••

Studies of surviving Penitentials, the rules governing the performance of penitence for different transgressions, have shown that the

Catholic Church regarded contraception (*coitus interruptus* or the rhythm method) as the most grave sexual sin as early as the 6th century, worse than sodomy, rape, or even incest. In China, where draconian measures have been adopted for the last twenty years against a population growth which has to be revised upwards at every census, the struggle is against a belief system which was already old when Saint Peter was young. Without a son to perform his father's last rites, a man's soul will wander for ever unburied, so pre-Confucian philosophy taught. Today, when China's population stands at almost 2 billion and official birth control policy prohibits more than one child per couple, the Chinese people repeatedly break their own laws, either to have another 'accidental' pregnancy if a son does not come, or more coldly still, to abort or murder the babies who prove to be that dreaded thing, the unwanted girl.

And this despite severe, even savage penalties, for while female infanticide is widely condoned, breaking the 'one-child rule' is not. In a 1991 case widely publicized throughout the country, 50 couples in the south-western province of Sichuan, China's most heavily populated region, were arrested for exceeding their quota of one child. Ten subsequently refused to go through with the abortions enforced on the remainder. The offending husbands were stripped by party officials and caned on their bare buttocks, one stroke for each day of their wives' pregnancies, until they capitulated. One husband had providentially absented himself from the round-up, so his pregnant wife was ordered to take her husband's punishment. She agreed to abort her baby before the first stroke could be given. The *Ninxia Legal Daily* described the affair as 'a complete victory against the die-hard elements of Chinese society'.

• • •

The course of liberalization is irreversible. Yet Mao's face still stares down over Tiananmen Square.

Jung Chang, *Wild Swans* (1991)

• • •

For reasons of both history and culture, China remains peculiarly resistant to any counsels other than its own. With terrible, almost incalculable results: according to a projection in *Demography Journal* as long ago as 1986, when the world was first waking up to the implications of 'the China solution', 48 per cent of today's

Chinese boys will have no hope of finding a wife when they reach marriageable age. Brute emphasis on birth control, therefore, shorn of a wider social policy, can help to create problems as intractable in their own way as the original challenge.

Yet if it is properly considered, planned, implemented and delivered, who can doubt that the prevention of unwanted pregnancy should be among the highest priorities of all international concerns? Actress Susan Hampshire has helped to promote the work of Oxfam for over twenty years, making gruelling trips to locations from Bangladesh to Hong Kong. Now she complains that the charity is failing to promote birth control to those who pay for its neglect with their lives. 'I have seen for myself the suffering of women who get pregnant every year and die in their 30s,' she says. Dr John Guillebaud, medical director of Europe's biggest family planning clinic, the Margaret Pyke Centre, and a former adviser to Oxfam, strongly supports Hampshire's attack. 'It is possible to buy something as nutritionally useless as Coca-Cola and Pepsi in every corner shop in Africa,' he comments, 'when you can't get condoms or pesticides.' American obstetrician John Potts, president of the US organization Family Health International, attributes this inaction to an 'outdated' fear of offending powerful interests by imposing Western ideas. For him this is simply an inverted form of post-colonial cultural domination, racism in reverse: 'I have held women in my arms as they died from illegal botched abortions, and I am angry about the Western arrogance that stops us from giving women in developing countries the same rights as we have here.'

Potts's 'here' must refer to North America rather than to Europe. On this side of the Atlantic the battle for contraceptive rights is far from over. In Poland, as in the Third World, Roman Catholic bishops have been steadily increasing their opposition to birth control with every step the country has taken along the road to freedom from the chains of Communist control. In a well-orchestrated campaign, they have also succeeded in toughening legislation against abortion until it now carries a jail sentence of *up to two years* for any doctor who performs an abortion and all who assist, except in cases of rape, incest, or urgent medical necessity. Now even these exceptions are under fire. And the fight goes on. In what is perhaps one of the most ludicrous and painful cases to come out of Ireland even in the history of that strife-torn country, a Dublin court fined the Irish Family Planning Association £400 in 1991 for selling two condoms from a Virgin Megastore. One witness was a haemophiliac unwittingly contaminated with AIDS-infected blood during transfusion: he pleaded for the free sale of contraceptives in the Republic for the chance to make love to his wife without infecting her. He died before the case was finally concluded.

On appeal, the ban was upheld and the fine raised to £500. Any further offence, the IFPA was warned, would result in fines of £5,000 a time, with accumulative fines of £200 per day for any continuance. Contraceptives now are available in Ireland only from a limited number of controlled medical outlets for strict family planning purposes, and continue to be denied to AIDS sufferers or any others whose lives may depend on them. Up country, in Ireland's remote rural interior, they are not to be found at all. Even in the capital, the 1993 case of a woman trying to open a shop who was turned down by 38 Dublin landlords as soon as they knew she planned to sell condoms, shows that ignorance, fear and superstition still continue to dog this issue in Ireland, despite the best efforts of the enlightened few.

•••

Ireland is the old sow that eats her farrow.

James Joyce,
A Portrait of the Artist as a Young Man (1916)

•••

Yet there is more to this whole issue than either handing out contraceptives or leaving entire populations to the monthly round of Vatican roulette. For the very concept of controlling fertility is relatively new in human history, and when first introduced struck even educated and forward-thinking members of industrialized societies with horror. The daughter of the Victorian Prime Minister William Gladstone, for example, was disgusted by her Liberal father's support of something which so violently 'flew in the face of nature and God's ordinance'.

Many people alive today were born to parents who may have tried not to have as many children as their Victorian grandparents did, but who otherwise had little concept of 'planned parenthood', with carefully judged intervals between each child. Many women today, with or without the guidance of religion, still prefer to feel that children somehow choose of their own volition to 'come along'. Of the two women closest to me, one has had five pregnancies by three different men. The other has had 'three contraceptive errors and one mistake'. Each has had four children without planning any of them. But neither would change what happened for anything.

Because 'unplanned' does not mean 'unwanted', as we may be tempted to believe. Nor does it mean that the couple is somehow 'out of control'. Most children are born to married couples or to partners who regard themselves as in a stable relationship. Yet most of these babies come into the world without their parents ever asking themselves the long hard *why*. Why do we plunge so unthinkingly into the most difficult task in the world, bringing up a child? And why is it that this question is never even asked?

•••

> I remember the flash of insight I had in 1940 as I recalled
> my professor of psychology's explanation of why women are
> less productive than men. He had referred to a letter written
> by Harriet Beecher Stowe in which she said that she had it in
> mind to write a novel about slavery, but the baby cried so
> much. It suddenly occurred to me that it would have been
> much more plausible if she had said 'but the baby smiles
> so much.'
>
> Margaret Mead,
> *Blackberry Winter: My Earliest Years* (1972)

•••

Why do we bring children so unthinkingly into the world? One answer must lie in the powerful appeal of the very young, a call so strong that childless women speak of their sides, their very guts literally aching for a baby of their own. 'Earth hath not anything to show more fair,' rhapsodized the poet William Wordsworth one pearly dawn on Westminster Bridge. The unmarried poet had clearly never seen a newborn child. He should have seen mine. As any mother could have told him, even the plainest baby will beat the view from a bridge for beauty, any dawn of any day.

The birth of a baby is the one everyday miracle that overwhelms even professionals in the field. 'It is no exaggeration,' observes veteran 'people-watcher' Desmond Morris, 'to say that the human infant is the most remarkable life form ever to draw breath on this planet.' Small, vulnerable and speechless though the baby may be, Morris insists, it is 'power-packed' with all the potential for human communication needed for its life ahead.

How do parents brave the challenge of this potential? How do we even visualize it?

Over the centuries, the model of the newborn child has undergone staggering variations. From the Early Christian Fathers' concept of Original Sin, that grim obsession with the child as a mini-Adam down-loaded with all an adult's capacity for evil, the pendulum has swung to the opposite extreme. In this century, 'the century of violence' as Lenin called it, we have perversely invested the infant with the innocence we have destroyed, recreating the image of the child as purity itself, the proverbial 'blank slate'.

Yet even as the century turned, the ideas of Freud seemed to be harking back to the older model of the child as very far from innocent. To many ears, Freud's theories of child sexuality spoke of Original Sin all over again. This was our old friend 'the Devil within' in another form, or rather in the oldest form: for it was in the shape of the great serpent that Eve was tempted, and through the sexual toils of that erring female that Adam fell . . .

Either way, the baby was perceived as an object, even as something less than human, as Morris points out:

> In the past, adults have sometimes wrongly looked upon the baby as a 'blank canvas' on which anything can be imposed, or as a little lump of insensitive flesh, barely reacting to the outside world. One Victorian commentator summed up this condescending attitude with the remark 'Here we have a baby. It is composed of a bald head and a pair of lungs.' In similar vein an insensitive priest defined a baby as 'a loud noise at one end and no sense of responsibility at the other.'

We now know that the 'loud noise' of the infant is as meaningful as a Mozart overture to those who can give ear to its music. We have learned that the newborn child is highly sensitive to sounds, smells and sensations, and poorly equipped to deal with many of the routine experiences of its daily life without the constant protection, care and control of as many concerned adults as can be enrolled in the task. But too many babies are still born to those who have not progressed beyond the unquestioning assumption that 'having a baby' is the next inevitable stage of life's journey after leaving school, getting a job, and getting married. *We have to question this inevitability as another key step towards achieving the children we deserve.*

•••

> My mother was not a woman who wanted children. She
> was not a mother mother. She was a woman who bore
> children.
>
> Tina Turner

•••

'What do you mean, think about it?' says Penelope, currently working her way up a major law firm. '*Of course* I thought about it! I planned it exactly, to get pregnant after I was confirmed as a manager, and before I needed to push for a partnership. I don't think anybody could have decided it more carefully than I did.' But like almost all of those who are confident that they thought the whole thing through, Penelope is talking *when*, not *if*. And least of all, *why*.

Why do any of us bring a child into the world without thinking, planning, looking ahead, counting the cost? How can we be so blind to the difference between the idealized image of motherhood and the reality of taking on a responsibility never to be laid down? Parents and friends pressurize a young couple into parenthood from the moment they walk down the aisle. How many of these would-be grandparents ever make the opposing demand: *have you done your sums, can you afford it? Or if you can, are you ready to pay the price of being a parent?* – a cost infinitely greater in every way than money alone can ever meet?

Let's talk money first: this is the sales pitch that parents-to-be never hear. You'd like a baby? That'll be £45,000. Of course that's only the price of the basic economy model: nappies and clothing alone cost around £2,000 in the first two years, according to the market research organization Mintel in 1991. For the couple who want any extras (playgroup, private tuition for sports, hobbies or music, school trips, family holidays), we're looking at upwards of £60,000. The luxury version, the AB1 model that goes all the way to college yet stays at home for over twenty years, let's start at £100,000, shall we?

No one is ever told in advance that a baby costs so much. Social convention and commonsense 'wisdom' conspire to minimize the economic impact of these transactions, just as they brush aside the expense of marriage: 'Two can live as cheaply as one.' 'It goes without saying that you should never have more children than you have car windows,' observed Erma Bombeck: that must be why it is never said. And the expense is delusive, simply because it is cumulative. The money spent on food, clothing, heating, lighting, holidays, a larger house and larger car, all the hidden expense of having another member of the family, is spread over so many years that few ever stop to keep count. But as research studies from the Child Poverty Action Group and actuarial statistics in both Europe and America show, it all mounts up to the kind of sums most of us can hardly imagine. 'You could have had a Porsche instead of me?' queried my car-mad 14-year-old son. 'How did I ever get *born*?'

Of course a baby is not just another consumer durable. But it's not just the rosy cuddly bundle of dreams either. 'Too many young women are in love with the idea of having a baby, and nobody wants to burst that balloon,' says family therapist Dr Joni La Bessard of Daytona, Florida. 'But babies, like kittens, are only cute for an amazingly short time. Then you have to live the reality. You can't send a two-year-old back like a hi-fi system when you can't keep up the payments.' So flush all the gooey sentimentalities down the gurgler where they belong, advises Joni, and think of size 10 shoes or 30AAA bras, skateboards and school exchanges, and one more car on the road in twenty years' time for every new driver you bring into the world. Then think of paying for it all.

And the price of having a child is not just for equipping, keeping and feeding it. Actuarial statistics of industrialized countries show that there is also a huge 'cash opportunity cost' to every woman who becomes a mother. This is the money that she will lose through taking time out of her working life or career. On average, says London University economist Heather Joshi, mothers of two children lose nine to ten years of full-time employment, while many women lose twenty or more full-time years, since they only ever return to work part-time.

Those 'lost woman-years' can cost a couple dear. The cost in lost earnings of having one child was set at £122,000 on 1986 figures, when the woman in question was assumed to be earning only £6,000 a year. Multiply that by a modern salary to arrive at the real cost in today's terms. Another guideline, according to Heather Joshi, is that the 'money lost to mother' costs are around *double* the direct cost of having a child. And these costs take no account of others, like the loss of pension or health care rights that follow any loss of salary, nor of the other imponderables that will affect a woman's career after childbirth: the loss of experience inevitable after taking 'time out', the loss of promotion and progression in comparison with colleagues with a more complete work record. 'Once a woman takes a career break, her value is reduced,' says John Swiffney, a Human Resources manager with a major US retail network. By 33 then, a mother will be earning on average one-third less in salary than any woman who has stayed in work.

Can this be avoided by deferring childbearing until the woman's career is well-established? Timing the career break makes no difference, says Heather Joshi: 'The estimates suggest that both early and late childbearing are slightly "cheaper" than starting at 25 or 30, but the difference is minimal.' Does it make a difference to limit your family? Not really: the situation is 'front-loaded', Heather says: 'The cost of the first child is about three times that of any subsequent children.'

And the cost is not purely financial. The birth of a baby has the most fearful and sometimes fatal impact on the parents' relationship. 'It's a terrible irony,' observes London marriage guidance counsellor Judy Simonides, 'that you choose your partner because you want to be with them, and them alone, more than anyone else in the world, and then you do the very thing to make that impossible for the next twenty or thirty years. After a baby, your relationship, like your body, can never be the same again.' The psychic change from being 'lovers' to becoming 'mummy and daddy' is enormous. 'When you have a baby you set off an explosion in your marriage,' says the American writer Nora Ephron. And each of the partners makes this journey alone, with entrances and exits distinctly marked 'his' and 'hers'.

And all this falls, it's worth stressing, within the parameters of normal parenthood – and also within the expectation that both parents will always have enough money, love, patience, health and strength to get through it together. What happens when things go wrong? How well is any of us equipped to deal with a less-than-perfect child?

• • •

The first half of our lives is ruined by our parents, and the second half by our children.

Clarence Darrow

• • •

There are more than 40 common defects of birth from cleft palate to club foot, from Down's Syndrome to spina bifida, cerebral palsy and autism, or even the relatively mild dyslexia. 'Nature doesn't care about the individual baby, she's only interested in numbers,' the great British obstetrician Professor McLaren once observed. 'She can play some pretty cruel tricks.'

Dr Eleanor Barnes, director of the Family Fund which distributes over £10 million a year to the parents of children with special needs, would agree. 'Most people [in the field of special needs] think there is a more severely disabled population now. The availability of superb neo-natal care means that babies which would have died, don't. The cost of caring for handicap is enormous in money terms, but what it does in human terms can't be measured.' Unlike nurses, Dr Barnes points out, mothers are not on shifts. 'Not only are the parents crippled by what it takes out of them, but the other children are too. The more noble the family, the worse it is, because they have nothing left over for themselves. Many break up under the strain.'

All the world loves the story of the 'miracle baby', the tiny premature infant whose frail life is saved by the wonder of modern technology in all its splendour of plastic tubing, computerization and gleaming chrome. Yet saved at what cost? Half of all children born at 25 weeks or less suffer multiple handicaps, and may be blind, deaf, brain-damaged and epileptic, on a scale unimaginable to parents. 'Usually, once a child is born, its parents will agree to anything to preserve it,' says Dr Martin Bax, a consultant in disability at the Westminster Children's Hospital. 'One severely affected spina bifida baby looked absolutely gorgeous. I couldn't get the parents to understand that he would never be continent because he had no nerves to the bladder. They were convinced they could train him.'

Peter and Jill felt that way about their first child. When the very premature baby boy was born, they admit to 'pressuring' the doctors to keep him alive at all costs, so determined were they that he should survive. Even when the extent of his disabilities began to emerge, the future still looked hopeful. He was an adorable baby, they were young, they could cope, they would have more children and build the family around him, they would surround him with love.

'But we never got hold of the idea that Benjy could never be any more than a baby, however big his body grew,' says Jill. 'And we didn't foresee how totally he would dominate the needs of the whole family. We have to spend more time on him than on all the other three put together, and it's not just that they resent it. The truth is, we all do.' Peter takes up the story. 'With hindsight, we should have let him die when his body wanted to. We kept him alive for ourselves, not for him. We never once asked ourselves what kind of a life he'd have. If you can call it a life.'

No one, Peter now argues, has the right to sentence a child to a lifetime in the world if they can't even spend twenty minutes putting some thought into what they'd do if they were less than 100 per cent lucky in that great lottery, the miracle of birth. Marie Louise Hirsch, a family therapist working in Paris, agrees. 'You say people want a child because it's the obvious next stage? The pressures are at least as much psychological as social, and there are many, many narcissistic people around. I have worked with parents who wanted a baby like a grown-up version of a toy or a doll, even as a designer accessory or a photo-opportunity, living proof of the success of their lives. They literally never seem to think of the child as another human being, capable of pleasure and pain – still less as another adult in their lives in less than twenty years.'

Those hesitating about parenthood, Marie Louise suggests, should ask themselves this: forget the sweet and cuddly baby you dream of, how ready are you for a 4-year-old who refuses to be toilet-trained? For a 6-year-old who kicks out viciously, roaring 'I hate you, I wish you were dead'? A 12-year-old who takes your last pair of tights and uses up all your tampons? An 18-year-old who writes off the family car, gets drunk, gets pregnant or does drugs, a child-adult who long ago stopped being your heart's desire and became a pain where the ulcers grow?

When young marrieds are contemplating parenthood, their own parents are rarely honest with them about what lies ahead. Neither is anyone else, says the Child Poverty Action Group's Carey Oppenheim: 'The cost of having children is not met adequately in our society.' And the cost of this denial is enormous. Most of us think of the Save the Children Fund as doing grand work thousands of miles away among the starving poor of Africa and Asia. In fact one-third of all Save the Children's work is carried out in Britain, where there are more than 40 family centres and more than 100 on-going projects. 'Our work here goes all the way through from infancy to young offenders,' a spokeswoman explains.

And it remains a full-time job, to save these children, or even to give them any childhood. One Nottingham 14-year-old known to the CPAG works all night in a sock factory, then goes straight on to school. Children as young as 11 and 9 in poverty-stricken families are known to be working illegally throughout the country to bring in a little cash. The damage is measurable and widely apparent:

- Edinburgh University's Alcohol Research Group shows that 75 per cent of Britain's youngsters start drinking between 9 and 14, and by the age of 18 alcohol abuse is 'widespread'.

- Anorexia is also reported by the Royal College of Psychiatrists to be 'widespread' in Britain now in girls under 10.

- Incidents of child abuse reported to the Criminal Injuries Compensation Board rose by *47 per cent* in 1990.

- The Children's Legal Centre has been set up to help today's rising tide of young victims.

Figures like these can be replicated from all round the world. In America, rising alcohol consumption is implicated in over half the teenage fatalities every year. One University of Michigan study showed that 30 per cent of high school students and 43 per cent of college students had indulged in binge drinking (sessions of six drinks or more in one sitting). Among girls, the *Congressional Quarterly Report* showed that over 16 per cent of 5th to 8th grade students admitted to binge eating and bulimia, and over 8 per cent were anorexic. In the younger age groups, reported cases of child abuse rose from 785,100 in 1980 to 2,025,200 by the end of 1987.

And every one of these was a baby once. Without adequate, unopposed access to birth control for all, and without a greater readiness to question the fixed belief in parenthood for all, their sufferings are doomed to be repeated in every generation. Children as yet unborn are already sentenced to a life below the poverty line, physical, mental, emotional, social and financial. Is it any wonder then that some of them become the children we don't deserve?

To reverse this trend, we must:

- Ensure that free contraception, freely available, becomes as much of a human right as life, liberty and the pursuit of whatever we choose to pursue.

- Restore one of the key demands of the women's movement as an international right and imperative, abortion on demand.

- Educate the young to the reality of parenting, and to the cost, emotional and financial.

- Establish parenthood as an election, not an obligation, guiding each individual towards taking full responsibility for becoming a parent.

- On an overcrowded planet, relegate the 'right to life' rhetoric to the dustbin of history as a luxury the new millennium cannot afford.

Of course there will always be those who long for a baby, cherish its life as the most precious achievement of their union, and tenderly raise it to a useful and fulfilled adulthood. Watching a daughter skipping round the Mixed Infants' maypole on May Day or buckling down to a demanding course at college, or a son appearing as the Third Shepherd in the Nativity Play or making a solo hike across America from sea to shining sea, will give most parents the surging joy and pride only weakly indicated by the conventional phrase, 'It's all worth it.'

Similarly, most parents do not even attempt to put into words the delight of welcoming into the world the baby who has been hoped for, longed for, planned. Many women trace the bond with a wanted child from the moment they feel it stir. For me, the first sight of that newborn face, the first dawn of recognition in those bright, unclouded eyes, brought on a feeling so strong that I could hardly breathe. When my second baby was on the way, I feared that it would not be possible to love another child as much as I loved his sister. But on first sight again the connection occurred, and he brought his own world of joy with him. I could never work out how I could love them more every day, since I loved them both with all my heart from the very beginning.

This is not strange, since it happens to so many. But deciding, thinking and planning in advance do not constitute a betrayal of all this, still less a downgrading of real and loving parenting. *Calculating the cost of a child does not mean that we do not know its value.* On the contrary, we show the value that we place on every child by putting our consideration for its future above our own romantic fantasies and emotional needs. And that must be the most honest and humble recognition of how hard it is to be worthy of such a priceless blessing, such a gift of endless love.

•••

> Like a great storm
> the two of us shake
> the tree of life
> down to the most hidden
> fibres of its roots
> and you appear now,
> singing in the leaves
> of the highest branch
> we reached with you.
>
> Pablo Neruda,
> 'Our Child'

•••

CHAPTER 2

Mommie Dearest

Mother, I love you so.
Said the child, I love you more than I know.
So she laid her head on her mother's arm
And the love between them kept them warm.

Stevie Smith

There's a lot more to being a woman than being a
mother, but there's a hell of a lot more to being a mother
than most people suspect.

Roseanne Barr

WHEN THE American evangelist Jim Jones formed his bizarre
religious cult in the 1970s, he insisted that all his followers call him
'Dad'. But when he led them all to one of the greatest mass suicides
of history in the jungles of Guyana, his last scream, recorded for
posterity on the camp's public address system, was 'Mother'.

In the mind of a child, every mother has this enormous, primeval
power over her offspring, a hold which is normally lifelong. It may
even become a metaphor for the raw female principle: the hero of
Philip Roth's novel *Portnoy's Complaint* saw his mother as 'The
Most Unforgettable Character I've Met', 'so deeply embedded in my
consciousness that for the first year of school I seem to have believed
that each of my teachers was my mother in disguise.'

'All I am, or all I hope to be, I owe to my angel mother,' said
Abraham Lincoln. The importance of the primal bond is recognized
in other ways, too. When children go astray, the mother is the first
to be blamed: a mother's place is in the wrong. *If children are to go
right, the mother's influence must be the base from which we build.*
Yet how much help and support are given to new mothers as an
essential stage in producing the children we deserve?

'If motherhood is an occupation which is critically important to
society the way we say it is, then there should be a Mothers' Bill of
Rights,' US senator Barbara Ann Mikulski has said. Is there any

likelihood of this? Is a mother ever thought of as having 'rights' of any kind, when her rights over her own body are so regularly under attack? Or does the myth of motherhood drown out the reality, so that many of us are left floundering at the time of our greatest need?

One of the most powerful and damaging myths of motherhood lies in the overwhelming rhetoric of conception, childbirth and mothering as 'natural' processes. It is true that pure biology normally sees to it that an impregnated female will in the course of nature deliver a child. But human beings departed from the biological baseline over 200,000 years ago. There is far more to mothering than the physical ability to reproduce, and the mother's confidence in herself is vital. Despite the power she may have later over the mind of her child, few mothers feel powerful in any way, especially at the beginning.

'I remember leaving the hospital thinking, "Wait, are they just going to let me walk off with him? I don't know *beans* about this! We're just amateurs",' says the American novelist Anne Tyler. In today's world, the sophistication of childbirth technology combined with the inevitable ignorance and fear of a new mother means that having a baby now can feel more like incubating a life-threatening disease than bringing a new human being into the world.

And if motherhood is so 'natural', why is it often so difficult? At the age of 15, Rosemary stopped menstruating for almost a year when her mother died. Later her doctor prescribed the Pill 'to regulate her cycle'. Nearly fifteen years later she is still struggling to re-establish her fertility.

She is not alone. In contradiction to the media stereotype of the feckless teenager who becomes pregnant so casually that she does not know the father of her child, there are legions of women who, for a variety of reasons, cannot become mothers when they choose. Worldwide, one couple in six proves to be infertile. Although the cause does not always lie with the female, as was almost invariably assumed in the past, in Britain alone, following the world trend, there are over five million women at any one time trying in vain to conceive, in the US almost ten times that number. For many women, including the former First Lady of the United States Jacqueline Kennedy, the disappointment of a miscarriage or a period of infertility will be followed by a successful pregnancy. For many more, it will not.

•••

When will you come, my child, my love?

Federico García Lorca, *Yerma* (1934)

•••

The best and happiest children come from mothers who have freely and happily chosen this role. Sadly, most women are never in a position to choose. If motherhood is *natural*, the argument runs, it must be *inevitable*, women's highest function and destiny. Bearing a child has been held up as the apotheosis of womanhood throughout history: the Quran teaches that only motherhood can redeem a woman from the taint of Eve: 'When a woman conceives by her husband she is called in Paradise a martyr, and her labour in childbed and her care of her children protect her from hell fire.' Today, becoming a mother makes women out of girls, it gives employment to the unemployed, and for the religious and non-religious alike it offers a focus and a *raison d'être*, even a justification for female existence.

The overwhelming pressure upon women to become mothers at all costs is nowhere more apparent than in the treatment of those who fail. No woman would willingly be excluded from the one great freemasonry that is exclusive to our sex. Yet is motherhood an inevitable, inalienable right, duty or necessity in every case?

Infertility has been with us as long as fertility itself, from time immemorial. Elizabeth, whose plight is described by Saint Luke, is one of the many 'barren' women recorded in the Bible. In other societies and at other times, Julius Caesar's wife Calpurnia, Napoleon's Josephine, the consorts of England's Edward the Confessor in the 11th century and Richard II in the 14th, 'Bloody Mary' Tudor in the 16th, and Charles II's queen Catherine of Braganza after the Restoration were all childless, despite desperate attempts to bring forth the much-needed heirs.

All these women knew that the continuance of their line, even their survival, depended entirely on the fruits of their womb. As Anne Boleyn observed when her failure to produce the longed-for Tudor prince for Henry VIII cost her her head:

The King has been very good to me. He promoted me from a simple maid to be a marchioness. Then he raised me to be Queen. Now he will raise me to a martyr.

Yet without the dynastic imperative, is it essential in today's world that every infertile woman be manhandled into productivity? Today the grief of accepting childlessness as the will of God has been replaced by the new anguish of treatments which may in themselves be an added torment, both in their painful and humiliating processes, and in the uncertainty of success. For in the fifteen years since the world welcomed its first test-tube baby, conditions have not improved for the unhappily infertile. Childless women now find themselves queueing up for medical attention and competing with others for scarce resources in the debilitating fight against time and the ever-louder ticking of the biological clock.

As waiting lists grow longer, costs soar. Speaking at the Sixth World Congress on In Vitro Fertilisation and Alternative Assisted Reproduction in Israel in 1989, IVF specialist Dr Bernard Lunenfeld estimated that the 'potential market' for fertility drugs in the industrialized world amounted to 10 million women, a figure which was set to rise by 700,000 a year. One course of one drug alone costs around £1,000: three courses are routine, six common and ten not infrequent.

Clearly only those willing or able to commit thousands of pounds to the quest can even consider treatment. Part-time librarian Pattie Barker and her husband Geoff, a retail grocery manager, have so far spent almost £15,000 on two exploratory operations, five episodes of major surgery, and three attempts at IVF (in vitro fertilization), all so far unsuccessful. 'I only want what every woman wants,' Pattie says, 'a baby of my own.'

A baby of my own . . .

In one of the most painful paradoxes of our divided world, while couples in China may be tortured for over-producing, in the industrialized West unfortunates like Rosemary and Pattie will torture themselves to produce in the teeth of nature's resistance. And their men will too. 'There are lots of tests that involve sitting in a nasty little bog and wanking into a bottle with some tacky magazines to help,' was the bitter comment of one husband. From the male partner miserably masturbating in a hospital cubicle, to the female undergoing a painful and humiliating overhaul of her entire gynaecological system, the treatment is without question worse than the original condition.

But childless women rarely drop out of a treatment programme once they are accepted, says London infertility consultant Peter Bateman. 'They've usually had to wait quite a long while, even if they've got the money to pay, and they're painfully conscious of the passage of time. Often they've had a year or more of persuading their husbands to take part – most men are hugely sensitive to the implication that they may be the partner responsible – and the wives know their chances are reducing every minute. But no matter how bad it gets, they simply grit their teeth and get on with it. I'm constantly amazed at their courage and determination. These women could climb Everest!'

In this climate of compulsory motherhood, Londoner Tricia Lewis reveals something of the pressures driving childless women on: 'My mother desperately wanted grandchildren. When she died I was devastated, I felt I had failed her.' Years after embarking on the grim round of tests and surgery, Tricia feels her chance of motherhood slipping away with the passage of every month. 'Now our only hope is the Suzi technique (sub-zonal insemination). But the success rate is very low, about 5 per cent.' And the struggle is taking its toll:

Sex? there's nothing to say. I gave it up a few years ago now. Cruel as it may sound, I feel no need for it, with no chance of me getting pregnant. Maybe I should seek help with this later, but at the moment there are more pressing things. Sometimes I feel as if I have the whole world on my shoulders, especially when Richard is not supporting me. But every time I reach breaking point, he seems to change and catch me as I fall. I hope he never leaves it too late.

Is the struggle for a child worth any sacrifice, any price, even this? Or does the drive to motherhood risk obliterating all loving, all humane, all sane thinking in these women's minds? How would it be if, instead of immediately reaching for the medical/surgical armoury of tests and solutions, childless women and their partners could be offered a course of counselling to lay before them the costs, financial and emotional, of this perilous quest, and the likelihood of failure at the end? Or is motherhood for all so axiomatic that the possibility of simply accepting childlessness is the one option that is never offered? Too 'unnatural', perhaps?

•••

The woman with happiness inside her.

Ancient Chinese ideogram for a pregnant woman

The tiny madman in the padded cell.

Vladimir Nabokov's description of an unborn child

•••

Even for the woman who has no difficulty in conceiving, the process of becoming a mother is generally far less 'natural' than we are led to believe. Giving birth to a child involves a whole series of hidden costs that a mother is usually left to discover for herself, and to suffer alone. No one ever tells a young and childless woman the truth about pregnancy – the loss of selfhood, the loss of autonomy and control as she becomes not an individual but what Tolstoy's wife Sonya called 'a vessel', the changes to her breasts, stomach, thighs, ankles, bladder, even to her expanding ribs and exploding fingers, changes that ensure her body will never be the same again. And all this is without any consideration of the humiliating ordeal of the monthly antenatal examination, or the hundred and one frightening and distressing complications that fall within what the professionals call a 'normal' pregnancy.

Labour even more is surrounded by a conspiracy of denial among women and professionals alike. No antenatal class ever prepares a woman for the quality of the pain. ('We don't call them pains, dear, we call them *contractions*' is the standard reproof/reassurance handed out to the nervous mother-to-be.) Not one of the busy midwives, doctors or nurse-tutors ever explains truthfully what an induction means, a forceps delivery, or an episiotomy ('it's just a little cut' for me meant 26 external stitches in addition to the internal repairs), or that labour may entail all or any of these.

Because birth is a dangerous and violent process, with nothing natural about it except the great blind life force itself at its most urgent and destructive. 'Nature doesn't care about mothers,' remarked the British obstetrician Professor Hugh McLaren, 'she tears great holes in them.' And afterwards? Anything from the collapse of the lower bowel to a malfunctioning urinary tract to a backache that lasts for five years – but no one ever prepares a mother-to-be for the aftermath of childbirth, either.

Why the conspiracy of silence? 'You don't want to frighten a young girl,' was the shocked reproof of one older woman to this challenge, 'you might put them off for life!' Surely any young woman contemplating the life-changing possibility of motherhood is entitled to the truth? Isn't it far more frightening to be gripped and shaken in the teeth of a pain like a tornado, to lie screaming in fear and the fear of fear, or rigid with the dread of losing control? Or does the real motive lie in the final words, 'you might put them off'? Do women know that if they told the truth about childbirth to their daughters, hardly any of them would ever ascend to the blessed sanctity of grandmotherhood?

• • •

It's still the biggest gamble in the world.

Gilda Radner, US actress and comedienne

• • •

The loss of self – the loss of confidence – the fear – these are what new mothers remember vividly even 25 and 50 years on. Especially the fear. 'I was afraid that if I took my eyes off her for a second, she would stop breathing, I was so young and ignorant,' says Linda, who had her first baby at 21. But Jo-Anne, a first-time mother at 38 after a high-powered career in financial management, reports exactly the same anxieties. 'First-time motherhood is the pits, whatever age you are!' she says cheerfully, 'It's called "maternal anxiety", and there's not a damn thing you can do about it!'

It's hardly surprising, then, that young mothers find themselves at the mercy of 'experts' confident they know more about any baby than its own mother could ever be expected to do. Traditionally, too, the powers-that-be were far more interested in getting mothers to toe the offical line than in empowering them in their own right. One name to be forever execrated for the narrowness of his vision and the cruelty of its effects is that of the pre-World War II paediatrician Dr Frederick Truby King, 'the guru of baby experts', whose insistence on the value of breastfeeding became the cornerstone of a system that seems designed to destroy the skill of mothering, not enhance it.

In the London 'Mothercraft Training School' which he established after launching his scheme successfully in New Zealand, Truby King taught that 'feeding and sleeping by the clock' were the only methods of establishing 'perfect regularity of habits and the ultimate foundation of all-round obedience'. Babies were to be fed on the dot of the appointed hour, never before, and never at night. If they cried, they were to be left to 'cry it out': the exercise was good for their lungs. This experience was guaranteed to foster self-reliance and that quintessence of all the virtues, the British stiff upper lip.

The Truby King baby was further 'toughened up' by being kept outdoors, lightly clad, in all weathers. Potty training, the young mother was told, should begin at three days old, when 'the cold rim of the pot should just be allowed to touch the child's anus' to 'establish a reflex'. Kissing and cuddling was to be avoided since it made the child a 'weak, dependent character' in later life. Playing with a baby of less than six months was out of the question: it led to 'overstimulation'. Thumb-sucking was only marginally less bad than masturbation, and both were to be punished without hesitation.

One young mother recalling her early days with her baby for a BBC TV series on parenthood gave this poignant account of the Truby King regime:

> It was rigid, it was to the minute of the clock almost. And you really didn't give the cuddles and the love and affection, you fed her, you changed her, you pushed her up the garden and that was it. Oh, it was naughty, wasn't it, when you come to think of it? I not only deprived my baby of all the love and cuddles, I deprived myself. She grew up withdrawn. She often seems to me to be rather bottled up, and I would say that this is a direct result of the training she had as a baby.

When they needed support and encouragement, these new mothers received bullying and intimidation. One young Londoner, terrified of 'breaking the rules', left her child outside until it developed pneumonia and nearly died. Another, beside herself in the attempt to follow Truby King's instructions to ignore her crying child, finally insisted on a medical examination which showed the little boy had been in constant pain for months. When he died of this congenital condition, the mother could never forgive herself.

The Truby King experience endured from the time of the First World War until well after the Second. Only with the advent of Dr Benjamin Spock, who published the first version of his *Common Sense Book of Baby and Child Care* in 1946, did the pendulum of opinion begin to swing against this vicious regimentation. From the mid-to-late 1950s, then, a new generation of mothers learned to feed a child 'on demand', and to encourage the development of its own physical and mental rhythms of control.

But the reign of the expert was far from over. From Truby King's absolute prohibition against maternal tenderness sprang a reaction to the opposite extreme, a new ideology of mothering in which only a mother's tender hand would do. The name of another guru, John Bowlby, author of *Child Care and the Growth of Love* (1953) can still make some 1960s British mothers froth with indignation. 'He made us feel so guilty,' recalls Midlands teacher Jennie Wise. 'All that stress on "maternal deprivation" if we didn't take care of our babies ourselves every minute of every day. Not a word about the father, of course, he could do what he liked. As long as we gave up our jobs, our freedom, our entire lives to bond with the baby, everything would be hunky dory!'

• • •

In the sheltered simplicity of the first days after the baby is born, one sees again the magical closed circle of two people existing only for each other.

Anne Morrow Lindbergh, *Gift from the Sea* (1985)

• • •

How did the women of the past manage without 'expert' instruction in the art of 'bonding'? 'Bonding' with the mother has been one of the most powerful of the 'expert' myths of our time which can tyrannize new mothers at the time of greatest need, and make us feel like failures. If mother and baby are left to themselves, Dr Fiona Caldicott, President of the Royal College of Psychiatrists, points out, bonding is a natural instinct which needs no interference from outside parties, still less 'expert instruction'. But the American writer Laura Shapiro gives a humorous account of 'the theory that quickly turned into a demand' during the 1970s and early 1980s:

Unlike the oid-fashioned way of getting to know one's baby, mother-infant bonding had to happen right away in hospital. And strangely, it was a more precarious relationship than plain old love. *Bonding required full-time maintenance by a mother at home* [italics inserted].

Where bonding did not occur, the experts warned, all manner of mischief followed. 'In that first year,' urged one of the fathers of the 'bonding' theory, US child-care guru T. Berry Brazelton, 'the child gets a sense of being important. And the kids that never get it, they'll make everybody angry, they'll become delinquents later and then they'll become terrorists.'

Just like that. And all for the want of a little total full-time self-sacrifice by the mother. Amazing.

Rubbish, says University of Pennsylvania psychologist Diane Eyer: 'I would like to urge the impossible,' she writes, 'that we discard the word entirely.' The whole concept is 'a scientific fiction', Eyer maintains. At best it is no more than 'a metaphor', and should never have become an imperative, for children can never be influenced by mothers alone. Mothers and fathers, families, schools, television, food, neighbours and neighbourhoods – all these together make our children what they are. Let us attend to these, Eyer argues, instead of looking for one simple solution to all the world's ills. And the one simple scapegoat for our children going wrong: the mother. *To have the children we deserve, we have to empower mothers, not intimidate them: offer the warmest help and support, not bullying and blame.*

● ● ●

> Life is the first gift, love is the second, and understanding the third.
>
> Marge Piercey

● ● ●

Fear of not 'bonding' with our babies certainly gave some of us bad times that could well have been avoided. Far more pernicious and ill-judged was the instruction given in the same post-Sixties era to generations of young mothers, that they should put their babies to sleep lying face down. This was supposed to strengthen babies' muscles as they strove to push themselves up and turn over, making them healthier, and accelerating their development. But I remember seeing my six-pound daughter flopping around mewing with distress in this position as soon as the nurse had put her in it, and thinking, *'This just can't be right.'*

Through the efforts of one woman, Australian paediatrican Susan Beale, we now know that the so-called 'prone' sleeping position was seriously, even fatally wrong. For Beale has proved that this has been a major factor in causing a catastrophic increase in Sudden Infant Death Syndrome, the so-called 'cot death', where a mother puts down her baby to sleep, and returns to find it dead.

The explanation for this is cruelly simple. In the 1960s, nurses and medical researchers observed that premature babies fared better and developed more quickly if they were nursed lying on their fronts. At this, says consultant in public health medicine Sarah Stewart-Browne, the medical profession broke its own 'golden rule':

> The golden rule states that it is wrong to extrapolate the results of studies on small sickly sub-sets of the population to formulate policy for improving the health of the population as a whole. It is a tribute to the enormous power that doctors wield that they could in such a short time and on such slender evidence influence the care of normal babies so profoundly, and to such devastating effect.

According to one of the leading proponents of the 'prone' position, consultant paediatrician Peter Fleming, it 'never occurred' to anyone that full-term healthy babies were any different from their immature, undersized premature counterparts. Stewart-Browne is one of hundreds and thousands of women with every reason to regret this oversight. As a young medic, she diligently followed her colleagues' advice to lay her baby face down. At two months old, her daughter became another 'cot death'.

Once convinced of its terrible error, the medical profession worldwide took action to reverse its previous advice. In Britain the government's Back To Sleep campaign, led by television presenter Anne Diamond (whose own son Sebastian was a cot-death victim), saw an immediate drop in British cot-death fatalities of almost 50 per cent, from 912 in 1991 to 456 in 1992. Stewart-Browne has said that she does not feel bitter: she only wishes that she had listened to her mother rather than to her paediatrician.

Yet women's wisdom ('old wives' tales') rarely holds its own against 'scientific fact'. And any young mother can bear witness with Stewart-Browne how hard it is to defy 'expert' opinion. Standing above baby after baby floundering face down in obvious discomfort, hopelessly trying to turn its head towards its mother or any source of sound, I tried again and again to persuade friends to put themselves in the baby's position and see how unnatural it was. So far from

'strengthening the muscles', the prone position seemed to me calcu-
lated to instil frustration, even fear or panic, by taking away from
the baby what limited physical control it already had.

I never succeeded in getting even one of them to 'break the rule'.
It remains an outstanding wrong to the bereaved parents, and an
outrage against motherhood itself, that so many mothers were afraid
to challenge the 'expert' opinion about their own babies for so long.

Another 'expert' shibboleth thrown down – how many more to
go?

•••

> There is one taboo that has withstood all the recent efforts
> at demystification, the idealisation of mother love.
>
> Alice Miller, *The Drama of Being a Child* (1987)

•••

Throughout the centuries 'expert' advice has proved itself to be as
rooted in the dogmas of its own age as any other form of authority.
But how do women learn how to handle their babies if they cannot
trust the experts? The other great source of information and in-
spiration for every woman must be her own mother. Yet how often
are we ever encouraged to question this constructively, to re-examine
our own mother's mothering, in the same spirit in which we should
receive any other 'expert' or established source of advice?

Of course we would turn to our mothers, because mothers are
wonderful, runs the commonsense agreement on the matter.
'Children, look into those eyes, listen to the dear voice, notice the
feeling of even a single touch that is bestowed upon you by that
gentle hand!' exhorted the 19th-century British historian Thomas
Babington Macaulay:

> Make much of it while you yet have that most precious of all
> good gifts, a loving mother. Read the unfathomable love in those
> eyes, the kind anxiety of that tone and look, however slight your
> pain. In after life you may have friends, dear, fond friends, but
> never again will you have the inexpressible love and gentleness
> bestowed upon you, which none but mother bestows.

A loving mother and her kind anxiety . . . her unfathomable love . . .
Auberon Waugh has recalled his mother's 'unfathomable love' as

she chased him for over a mile applying nettles to his legs in an attempt to make him more athletic: he was 3 years old at the time. The original Mommie Dearest, Joan Crawford, so dubbed by her daughter Christina in the savage memoir of that name, was remembered less for her gentle touch than the 'kind anxiety' of her coat-hanger discipline, the film star's favourite instrument of correction for young Christina and her little brother. In a similar vein Nancy Reagan, as her biographer Kitty Kelley revealed, once 'smashed' her daughter Pattie 'in the face' with a hairbrush till she was black and blue.

Yet in her own eyes, Nancy was never anything less than a good mother, her stance on all the issues implied in Republican Party rhetoric of 'family values' unimpeachable. Joan Crawford, Marlene Dietrich and Bette Davis were equally outraged to learn that their offspring did not share their roseate memories of the motherhood experience.

Indeed, the greater the monster, in many cases, the greater the conviction of being a wonderful, wonderful mum – a bubble, according to psychologist and therapist Alice Miller that we have to burst, if we are to acknowledge honestly the emotional abuse an unhappy or misguided mother can commit:

> The discovery that I had been an abused child, that from the very beginning of my life I had had to adapt to the needs and feelings of my mother, with no chance whatsoever to feel any of my own, came as a great surprise to me ... In my paintings I came face to face with the terrorism exerted by my mother, at the mercy of which I had lived for so many years. For no one in my environment, not even my kind father, could ever notice or question the child abuse committed under the cloak of child-rearing.

Banished Knowledge – in the poignant title of this book, Miller expresses her sense of the absolute prohibition that prevents a child from confronting how far short of the impossible maternal ideal its mother may fall. For women are not angels, even at their best. At worst, some of the casual, even trivial acts of cruelty that mothers are capable of defy belief. As a sensitive, nervous child, insomniac by the age of 8, Mia Farrow invented an imaginary friend called Mildred to keep her company through the white nights when sleep would not come. On one family cruise Mia's mother, the actress

Maureen O'Sullivan, briskly announced that she had thrown Mildred overboard. Mildred had drowned. So long, Mildred!

The monster mother – how ready are we to acknowledge that behind the cliché of the 'angel mother' can lurk the devil in disguise? When Bill Wyman took a shine to her daughter, London celebrity-seeker Patsy Smith unhesitatingly encouraged the 13-year-old Mandy to work her passage to the good life offered by the wrinkly rocker and heartless Stone. When Wyman finally tied the knot six years later, Smith showed up on Mandy's honeymoon. When the marriage collapsed after one week of cohabitation, Smith celebrated Mandy's divorce by getting engaged to Bill's son, a move which will make Mandy's ex-husband her step-grandfather. And she has confided every detail of her daughter's married life to her good friends at *Hello!* magazine every step of the way.

But a mother does not have to be a monster on the Patsy scale to succeed in hurting her children. Every human being must be able to recall at least one act of coldness, neglect, or blistering insensitivity at the hands of a mother who was otherwise as loving as any child has the right to expect. Most of these acts were trivial by adult standards, routinely performed and easily forgotten. But it does not take many of them to turn 'mummy' into 'monster'.

The monster mother has as many forms as she has ways of making her children feel bad. But not all her children. 'Every mother of more than one child has a secret favourite, so secret that she may go her whole life through and never admit to herself which one it was,' said the American writer Gail Godwin. If only most mothers were so discreet. One of the most painful moments of growing-up comes when a child realizes that a brother or a sister enjoys more than its share of the mother's love.

Especially a brother. Throughout history girls have had to live with the knowledge that every society yet known places a higher value on a boy child than on a girl, and that a mother is thereby encouraged to take less pleasure in a daughter than in a son. And this is before any personal or Oedipal considerations come into play. Which they so often do, as the world's daughters will attest, and most of its sons. 'There is an enduring tenderness in the love of a mother to a son that transcends all the other affections of the heart,' wrote the nineteenth-century American man of letters Washington Irving:

It is neither to be chilled by selfishness, nor daunted by danger, nor weakened by worthlessness, nor stifled by ingratitude. She will sacrifice every comfort to his convenience, she will surrender every pleasure to his enjoyment, she will glory in his fame and exult in his prosperity and if all the world cast him off, she will be all the world to him.

'My mother was the making of me,' said Thomas Edison. 'She was so true and so sure of me I felt I had someone to live for, someone I must not disappoint.' Such uncritical adulation may not in fact be in any child's best interests. But it can hardly be in anyone's best interest that it is generally extended to less than half of the world's young. For how many women can ever say the same?

The writer Laurie Lee has given a sensuous evocation of the special smother-love reserved exclusively for boys:

I was still young enough then to be sleeping with my mother, which to me seemed life's whole purpose. Alone at that time of all the family I was her chosen dream companion, chosen from all for her extra love, so it seemed to me ... They were deep and jealous, those wordless nights as we curled and muttered together, like a secret I held through the waking day which set me above the others. It was for me alone that the night came down, for me the prince of her darkness, when only I would know the huge helplessness of her sleep, her dead face, and her blind bare arms. At dawn when she rose and stumbled into the kitchen even then I was not wholly deserted but rolled into the valley her sleep had left, lay deep in its smell of lavender, deep on my face to sleep again in the nest she had made my own.

Even today the girls of a family will find themselves helping with the evening meal and then having to wash up, while their brothers are set free to do their homework, or simply to go out. 'You can't expect boys to take the same interest,' was one Midlands 15-year-old girl's explanation, baffled that the question was even asked. How many mothers ever stop to ask themselves if this is good mothering?

From experience, very few. Yet a son can expect all it takes. A 1991 Lancaster University survey of Britain's top entrepreneurs found that over 70 per cent attributed their success entirely to their mothers: they 'provided the grain of sand around which these men have built their pearl', according to the researcher Reg Jennings. A classic example is that of the designer George Davis, founder of the retail chain Next, whose mother boasted that she never smacked him, never nagged or criticized him, always gave him whatever he asked for and was always there when he came home from school. Davis sums it up: 'She idolises me – and she would kill anybody who harms me. It used to be embarrassing when I was younger.'

'Younger' for Davis meant behaviour which included average-to-poor school marks, dropping out of university, coming home drunk, and going through a difficult divorce from the mother of his three children. But nothing could shake his mother's adulation:

> Whether he likes it or not, I adore George. I worship him. If he committed murder, I would shield him. I can't change. Even my granddaughters reproach me. 'Nana,' they say, 'he's not God.' I have a daughter whom I also love, but there's always been a special bond between George and myself . . .

'*I have a daughter whom I also love . . .*' Can anything equal the exquisite coldness, the dismissiveness of that? What price daughters when a woman can bear a son?

What price daughters anyway? Barbra Streisand, actress, singer, film-maker and *femme extraordinaire*, broke down and wept on the nationwide US TV show *Sixty Minutes* as she recalled her mother's routine coldness and contempt:

> She never said to me, 'You're smart, you're pretty, you could do what you want'. I would say to my mother, 'Why don't you ever give me any compliments?' She would say, 'I don't want you to get a swelled head.'

Marje Proops, doyenne of agony aunts after a lifetime's service at the *Daily Mirror*, had served her apprenticeship to the agony trade at home, where her mother always introduced her as 'the plain one'. This casual brutality, however, pales into nothingness against the studied inhumanity of the child-hating British upper classes. Auberon Waugh's mother, when not on nettle patrol, was said to be happier with her cows than with her children. To the English, country matters, often more than kith and kin. Women sharing a nosebag in the Shires will make a three-day event of parading the photographs of

a new colt or filly foal. Yet any enquiry about the baby is answered
with a cold: 'The sprog? He's with nanny, of course, in the nursery.
Where do you think he is?'

Where indeed? But even by these standards, the Duchess of Beaufort, dowager of a house dating back to John of Gaunt and mother
of the biographer Lady Anne Somerset, is in a class of her own:

> Anne was such an ugly baby that everyone called her 'Monster'.
> Even when pretty, she liked being called 'Monster' Somerset.
> Then she got married to Matthew and became 'Monster Carr',
> but it didn't sound quite as good, so she's dropped it. Since
> Anne and Harry had such a marvellous nanny, my husband and
> I didn't have to bother bringing them up. And they certainly
> preferred Nanny to me. In some ways I wish I'd spent more
> time with them, but I wouldn't change anything. I liked being
> able to tell Nanny, 'Well darling, I'm busy with a nice game of
> patience, so off you go with them' . . . The nanny brought them
> down beautifully dressed, and they stayed with one from five to
> six in the evenings and at weekends. They really lived upstairs
> . . . All the children automatically went away to board when
> they were nine. Anne went off to become a weekly boarder and
> she hated it. I remember driving her there once, and she started
> getting all breathy and she bellowed and cried and the car shook
> . . . I wasn't particularly upset at losing her . . .

• • •

> Sometimes I ask myself whether it will ever be possible for
> us to grasp the extent of the loneliness and desertion to which
> we were exposed as children.
>
> Alice Miller, *The Drama of Being a Child* (1987)

• • •

In effect, the brutally narcissistic mother whose all-consuming self-
involvement allows no room for her child in the sealed circle of her
life and love, is little more than a child herself. 'What these mothers
had once failed to find in their own mothers, they were able to find
in their children,' writes Alice Miller: 'someone at their disposal who
can be controlled, is completely centred on them, will never desert
them, and offers full attention and admiration.'

But woe betide the real child when the child-mother cannot cope. The egregious Elizabeth Smart, author of *By Grand Central Station I Sat Down and Wept*, castigated by the critic John Carey as a 'Rebel Without a Clue', had four children by the minor poet and philanderer of the 1930s, George Barker, without the slightest idea of how she was going to provide for any of them. 'This morning I hit [the baby] Christopher in the face with my fist, because of George's letter, because of the landlord's bills,' she records in her journal for 1944. But even then her strongest feeling was for herself: 'It is unfair. I am crying with guilt and humiliation.' For Alice Miller, such child-like self-absorption on the part of the mother cannot help but damage her child. And it can be avoided: 'It is up to us as adults, depending on how we treat our new-born infants, either to turn them into future monsters or to allow them to grow up into feeling, and hence responsible, human beings.'

Others argue that 'children are resilient'. Certainly it is amazing what some children can absorb without complaint: their capacity to adapt to what they find is truly awesome. 'Monster' Somerset looks back with what even sounds like affection on the derelictions of the dowager: 'My funniest memory of her is when she didn't arrive to pick me up from school. They made some discreet calls and finally tracked her down to Lord's. She'd clean forgotten about me and had nipped in to watch a spot of cricket. She's like that sometimes.'

Other children take a bleaker view. Another reluctant conscript to the ranks of motherhood was the British social work pioneer Sally Trench. 'I didn't plan my sons,' she announced. 'My husband was a Polish Roman Catholic who had me pregnant the moment we married. If we'd stayed together I daresay I'd be on my 22nd by now.' Trench was also one of the women like Mrs Davis, mother of the godhead George, who hasn't much time for her own sex: 'I'm generally not good with girls because I can't knit or sew, so I was delighted when my first child was a boy and prayed for my second to be one, too.'

But motherhood clashed with Trench's real mission in life, the charity Project Spark, which she set up to deal with difficult and disruptive children. Trench herself sums it up with offhand clarity: 'I was on duty 24 hours a day and the boys had to be fitted into my work routine . . . I was tougher with my own children than with the Spark kids, because I knew they would accept it.' But not, she admits, without protest: 'They would have terrible moods when nothing could console them and they shut themselves in their room. I couldn't even put my arm round them.' '*My mother put her work before her children,*' says her younger son Nik. '*I didn't think it then, but I do now.*'

To make an emotional orphan of her child, a mother need not be cold, neglectful or violent. All it takes is the inability to feel for her child, as a child, and to put those needs first. The British novelist Lee Langley recalls a mother separated from her husband and alone in India at the close of the Raj, a woman who sought the classic consolation for her loneliness without any awareness that she was thus abandoning her daughter to fear, grief and loneliness too:

> When she was drinking, she loomed over the house with a menacing, almost threatening expression. She seemed to fill the whole horizon, and it was a baleful presence. When she was sober she was lovely and I ached for that, but I so rarely had a chance of experiencing it that in the end I came to the conclusion that I actually hated her, and when I was eight I began counting the time until I could leave her.

Particularly vivid in Langley's memory is the time when 'the money was up' and her mother promised her 'a proper Christmas', something they had never managed before: a doll, a cake, a turkey, a tree, and coloured baubles all of spun glass. Full of promises, Mother set off shopping. As the afternoon wore away, so did Langley's hopes:

> It was quite dark when a rickshaw pulled up and she was helped out of it by the rickshaw man. She staggered in, and her face was covered with blood and her stockings were all torn and ripped and there was blood running down her legs ... It was terribly sad actually because she had done all the shopping, and then she thought, Oh I've done so well, I'll have a drink ... So there she was, bleeding and distraught, and I was thinking, I'm going to be done out of my Christmas again ...

Langley's childhood ended at the age of 8, when she realized that she had to leave her mother as soon as she could. But in every real sense, her mother had already departed, if she had ever been there at all.

Being there ...

This activity or quality, something that the mothers of the past seemed to manage without even thinking about it, in the full contemporary sense of the phrase is proving the hardest thing to do. The central female character in Nora Ephron's film *This Is My Life* observes that if children have to choose between their mother being happy out of town and suicidal in the next room, they'll take suicidal. 'As far as kids are concerned there is only being there and not being there,' comments Ephron. 'We can't delude ourselves that it's better for them if we work. *Everything that's good for you is bad news for your kids.*'

Yet the basics are quite simple, if only we could accept them. We have never acknowledged the total, almost impossible demands that mothering makes, demands quite at variance with women's freedom, autonomy, individuality, economic independence and almost everything else women have learned to hope for in the last 25 years. It is rarely acknowledged either, that the 'good mother' aspect of the wifely role is also inherently in conflict with that of wife as lover: many women are horrified to discover in the wake of pregnancy that the body which has been given over to child-bearing will never belong in the same way to them again.

Nor are the effects of childbirth only physical. The qualities required to make a woman a warm and passionate lover include the ability to abandon herself to sensation without consideration of time, modesty, or external constraints. She needs to be able to answer a man's desires and her own at midnight or dawn, stay in bed till noon, obey the pleasure principle as the first imperative of life. Yet good mothering requires the very opposite of this, the capacity to subordinate personal and selfish desires, to put the child first, and to find fulfilment through the satisfaction of that small other, and not of the self: all this good mothering most sternly and unremittingly demands. Similarly the 'good wife' role demands that a woman takes pleasure in the care of her man, her home and her family, not in her own erotic voyage of exploration and delight. These demands, often made on a young mother who has yet to become her own woman, and a young wife only just getting to know her husband, can and often do lead to an occlusion of a woman's sexuality, temporary or permanent.

And all this is without consideration of the feelings of the man, who may have severe problems of his own at finding the breasts and body that were his playground suddenly usurped by a tiny but ferocious competitor. No wonder then that even a wanted child can often cause its mother to regret its very existence. 'Look at post-natal depression', says psychotherapist Adam Jukes, head of the London Men's Centre. 'Women who don't want their children are designated as depressive, when the truth is, they didn't want children. What they're really suffering from is the failure to live up to the massive cultural expectations of motherhood, not anything hormonal or innate. And that won't necessarily change. *Most men experience parenting as a duty, and my guess is that women do too.*' At its worst, this feeling may translate into violent action. In 1993, Maxine Davis of Leicestershire, unable to cope with the crying of her five-month-old daughter, threw her into flood waters near her home, where the baby drowned. She told police, 'I feel so relieved. I just tossed her into the river and all my troubles went with her.'

Not all women are cut out for motherhood: in some cases, the woman's biology denies it, in others it might have been a blessing if it had. Yet as long as we cling to an ideology that privileges mother-hood over every other female activity, we shall continue to see unemployed teenagers making the only adult choice open to them, and young wives inexorably propelled into maternity whatever their inner reservations or fears.

Is this fair to a child? 'I know I'll have to stop working soon, I'm nearly 30,' women say, or, 'We thought we'd go in for a baby next year, now we've got the car, got the house, got the fitted kitchen/ dishwasher/microwave/fridge-freezer, it's time.'

The time to have a baby is when that new life is calling so strongly to be born that nothing in the world can silence it.

As long as women go on having children simply because they have uteruses, as long as they are encouraged to do so as their right, duty and supreme function, and as long as they are then cast adrift to float uneasily betweeen 'expert' authority, their own imperfect mem-ories and experience, and today's laissez-faire, then too many chil-dren will not get the mothering they deserve. And only the fully committed mother, fully supported in every way, can be the 'good enough' mother for the children we all deserve.

There are signs that it is becoming easier for women to make the unconventional choice and openly decide that motherhood is not for them, since a generation of post-Sixties women led the way. 'It was a deliberate decision, I never had any desire to have them,' said Shere Hite, author of *The Hite Report on Female Sexuality* (1976). 'I just didn't see how I could have a career and do all that.' More recently Carol Decker, lead singer with the pop group T'Pau and now a successful solo artist, announced that she would never have a child. 'I don't have a maternal bone in my body,' she says. 'I know my biological clock is ticking away, but I'm not prepared to bring a child into the world just in case I regret not having one later.' *Every child a wanted child.* If only more young women were able to say the same.

This is not to degrade or denigrate motherhood by placing it on a par with any other 'career choice'. On the contrary, *the degradation both of mothers and of the children they produce is implicit in the assumption that every woman can do it, every woman should do it, and all they need are their 'natural maternal instincts' along with regular doses of 'expert' advice.* Surely we can now admit that for motherhood as for life, each individual needs choice, empowerment and control. How much of each does a woman really have?

No one will attempt to deny the importance of the mother in the formation of the healthy and happy individual. Only by fostering the right of every woman to make a clear and informed choice can we hope to have children who will come into the world to the most loving welcome and the best of care. Yet despite her universal, we might say archetypal, importance at the centre of the child's world, the mother is not the only star of the dawn story. Even in Greek mythology, no female makes a baby by herself. Every child must have a father. What of him?

• • •

> Children begin by loving their parents; after a time, they judge them; rarely, if ever, do they forgive them.

Oscar Wilde, *A Woman of No Importance* (1893)

• • •

CHAPTER 3

Father Almighty

If poverty is the mother of crime, stupidity is its father.

Jean de la Bruyère, *Les Caractères de
Théophraste* (1688)

It's all that any reasonable child can expect if the dad is
present at the conception.

Joe Orton, *Entertaining Mr Sloane* (1964)

SHE BROKE THE bread into fragments, writes Victor Hugo in *Les
Misérables*, and gave them to her children, who ate with avidity.

'She has kept none for herself,' grumbled the Sergeant.

'Because she is not hungry,' said a soldier.

'Because she is a mother,' said the Sergeant.

We take it for granted that to become a mother, a woman will
learn almost overnight to set aside her own needs and desires, and
be able to put her offspring first. How does a man become a good
father, one who can keep his children on the rails and yet teach them
to fly? What does he have to give up? 'If he has been your baby, or
you've been his,' says London marriage guidance counsellor Judy
Simonides, 'both of you are in for a cruel awakening when the real
thing comes along.'

But the new mother can expect a very different experience from
the new father, Judy advises mothers-to-be. 'When the baby arrives,
you have been given someone new to love, someone to whom you
will be the most wonderful person in the whole world. In contrast,
he has to live with the fact that he will never be number one in
anyone's life again.'

He also has to understand that until he can accept this, he will
never be a real father, but will remain for ever his partner's eldest
child, competing with the others for her attention, Judy contends.
Any man may have difficulty in dealing with these feelings of being
dispossessed, a displacement, psychologists suggest, which inevitably echoes the first expulsion of boys from the paradise of infancy,

when they were driven out of what A. E. Housman called 'the land of lost content', cut off from their mothers as the price of being men. *But until he has at least contemplated this and his own ability to cope with it, he cannot be the father every child deserves.*

This is not easy, even for professionals in the field. 'I can remember what a blow it was for me when my wife became pregnant,' says psychotherapist Adam Jukes, 'and the panic it induced. It can feel like a life sentence, rather than a gift. It's a real crisis – it signifies the end of your own childhood, the end of the fantasy that you're still 18 and waiting for Miss Right, that you're still living in a temporary place till the Princess walks round the corner.'

And most men get little help with this struggle, or even acknowledgement of what they are going through. Like new motherhood, new fatherhood is similarly surrounded by a conspiracy of denial. 'You get all the slaps on the shoulder and rounds of drinks in the pub,' says Martin, whose first child was born a year ago. 'But no one ever tells you what it's really going to be like.'

In all the euphoria, men say, any bad feelings will be strictly taboo, and understanding will be rare. When a baby is on the way, outsiders show sympathy for the mother, and ask after her. There will also usually be concern for any existing children, and open discussion of whether or not they may feel jealous of the new arrival. Yet who ever extends this consideration to the soon-to-be-usurped father, especially to the man expecting his first child?

'They're all over your wife, she's the only one who counts,' Martin recalls. 'It's as if once you've done your bit, you don't exist any more.' Yet the feelings of an adult male are likely to be every bit as powerful as those of a 2- or 4-year-old: feelings of intense pride mixed with a powerful sense of loss, awe and delight clouded by fear and uncertainty and even dread, a volatile chemical compound for the untried reactor of any young male ego to contain. 'It's a source of enormous conflict for men,' says Adam Jukes. 'They can feel utterly abandoned, jealous of the child, and envious of the woman's capacity to feel maternalism. Among those I work with, it's one of the main triggers to battering, it can even precipitate a life-threatening attack.'

And inevitably every father is struggling with this at the time when the woman who used to be his and his alone is totally absorbed in the new arrival, and quite unable to give him the undivided emotional concentration that he enjoyed before. Irma Kurtz sums it up: motherhood, she writes, is 'the one true, great, successful romance'. Often this redirection of attention is experienced by the new father as a withdrawal of love in the simplest, most hurtful way. Researchers at the University of Minnesota, Minneapolis, recently established that three months after childbirth, over 40 per cent of women still did not welcome sex, because of pain or discomfort during intercourse and difficulty reaching orgasm.

Since many women withdraw from sexual service in advance of the birth as well, this can mean a considerable period of enforced celibacy for the male partner. 'I will admit I used being pregnant to sign off sex with David,' says Susan: 'I can't explain it but it just didn't feel right any more.' Her friend Jane agrees. 'From the moment I knew I was pregnant, I wanted to keep my body for the baby, not for him. I know all the books tell you to keep your sex life going right up until the last minute, but I thought that was just propaganda for the men. I never took any notice of it.'

Peter, an accountant, describes his wife as 'off the road and jacked up in the workshop', sexually unavailable to him for over eighteen months before, during and after the birth of their first child. 'No, of course I wasn't happy to go along with it! But it was Hobson's choice, I had to put up with it. And from the cracks I was picking up from the other blokes down at the rugby club, I knew I wasn't the only one. It happens to us all.'

And it happens unannounced and unsupported, for Peter would no more have dreamed of turning to his rugby cronies for comfort than they would have seen fit to whisper a few helpful words of support into his ear in advance. Nor will the birth of the baby automatically restore to a man the lover he has lost. Even after childbirth, the Minnesota study found, many women do not return to 'pre-pregnancy levels of sexual experience'. Instead they establish 'new sexual baselines in keeping with their additional responsibilities'.

Which usually means that the child, or the mother's need to service it, must come before her husband's sexual satisfaction. Indeed it is the mark of her shifting priorities that what used to be *their* sex life can now become *his* appetite alone. The woman who has had less than five hours' sleep a night for months on end, and who is already gritting her teeth against the 2 AM call, is hardly likely to welcome her husband's advances with yelps of joy and open arms and legs. 'But I'm only asking for *ten minutes!*' one desperate husband pleaded with a wife who had made this excuse, the mother of their six-month-old baby. 'But it wasn't that,' his partner told me. 'It's the giving out, more giving out, when you feel you're being eaten alive already.'

All this is something a man is never prepared for, and it can present the competition between himself and his child in the starkest possible way. It is hardly surprising, then, that some men look elsewhere for the attention they feel they lack, to restore the supremacy they know they have lost. Scott Fitzgerald remarked that a woman was never so susceptible to an infidelity as immediately after the arrival of her first child. The same would seem to be even more true of men. 'The time around the birth of a baby is an especially vulnerable one for men embarking on affairs,' says Judy. 'The new father feels that he must restore his ego somehow.'

Most women will remember being relentlessly harassed at least once in their lives by the husbands of pregnant friends. Most sufferers from the little-boy-big-dick syndrome, however, do not visit on their wives the humiliation suffered by Kelly McGillis, star of *Top Gun* and *The Accused*. Five days after the actress had given birth to her second daughter, her husband, yacht-broker Fred Tillman, was discovered lurking in a shrubbery, pretending to be a gardener and offering $50 to a passing prostitute for on-the-spot sex. Except that the lady passing was only pretending to be a prostitute, and a swift twirl revealed her to be a member of the Florida Vice Squad in disguise. McGillis herself had no speaking part in this drama. Her role seems to have been confined to the off-stage silent scream.

• • •

> How much longer will we go on putting up with a situation
> where men pay us back what they owe to mother?
>
> Christiane Olivier, *Jocasta's Children* (1989)

• • •

Hopefully by the time the two little McGillises reach the age of awareness, their father's offence will lie deep under the sands of time, buried by a lifetime of shaping up to what a good father ought to be.

Yet what is that? Historically, the question was never asked, and never had to be. Father was the head of the household, the undisputed king of the family domain, and the god in their living machine to the members of the lesser creation who were his charge and his responsibility. Men from the poet Milton to the Puritan divine Cotton Mather took it for granted that theirs was the right, theirs the duty to order and shape the lives, minds, hearts and souls of their children, while the mother's role was limited to providing for all lowlier, physical needs. The importance of the father's dominance, vigorously proclaimed from the earliest written texts down to the 20th century, was founded on the age-old belief in the innate inferiority of both women and children to men, as the gender historian Professor Michael Kimmel explains:

> Men were thought to have superior reason, which made them less likely than women to be misled by the 'passions' and 'affections' to which both sexes were subject. Children were viewed as inherently sinful, ruled by powerful impulses as yet ungoverned by intellect. Because of women's weakness of reason and inherent vulnerability to inordinate affections, only men could provide the vigorous supervision needed by children. Fathers had to restrain their children's sinful urges and encourage the development of sound reason.

Thus there was no question of where the power within the family should reside, as this mid-nineteenth century poetic homily from America makes clear:

> The father gives his kind command,
> The mother joins, approves,
> The children all attentive stand,
> Then each obedient moves.

The Token of Friendship, or, Home,
the Centre of Affections (1844)

Within this framework, which endured through most of human history until very recently, the father was the undisputed pivot of the family. He was the moral arbiter and decision-maker, chairman of the board and company treasurer, dispenser of rewards and black marks, both punisher and protector. To sustain his task, the father was equipped with a phenomenal battery of legal and social sanctions, most of them deriving directly from those of the paterfamilias of Ancient Rome, who enjoyed the power of life and death over his children from the moment of their birth. As authorities from Livy to Valerius Maximus make clear, on the father's word alone was a baby kept alive, sold into slavery, or abandoned to starve to death.

The same was true even of adult males as long as the father was still alive. As late as the conspiracy of Catiline (63 BC), one of the conspirators was put to death without trial, simply on the command of his father.

The power of the father has been remarkably resistant to challenge or the process of change. Even in the modern period, the 18th-century philosopher and prophet of 'the social contract' Jean Jacques Rousseau was able to consign all his five illegitimate children to foundling hospitals, despite his protestations about the innocence of childhood. Strong vestiges of that power linger even today. In a 1980 case that exposed the reluctance of the law in Britain to challenge these ancient patriarchal rights, Muthana Muhsen, a Yemeni father resident in this country, sold his two daughters aged 14 and 15, both British citizens, into enforced marriage in the Yemen and virtual slavery.

When their mother sought their return, the British government refused to intervene on the grounds that the matter lay 'outside its jurisdiction'. The Foreign Office, which had known about the abduction and rape of the two young women from the very first, did nothing, insisting that they were Yemeni nationals by marriage and hence outside British protection. For *eight years* the two sisters were forced to labour in the fields and to cohabit with 'husbands' they had been bound to without their knowledge or consent. Only a public outcry and the intervention of a local MP eventually brought any attention to their plight.

Even then the young women were forced to choose between regaining their freedom, and abandoning the children they had borne in the intervening time. The elder, 23-year-old Zana, returned to Britain, but Nadia, one year younger, remained. 'It was not easy to give up my son, but as a boy he will have his freedom in the Yemen,' Zana said. 'But Nadia was told that her daughter Tina would be married when she reached the age of nine. She could not leave her behind to do that.' Back in Britain, when Zana sought to press charges against her father, the Director of Public Prosecutions refused to handle the case, claiming that there was 'insufficient evidence'. Only when Zana obtained legal aid over ten years later was she able to take the action that all the official bodies had failed to instigate. For who, even today, as many asked at the time, will readily claim the 'jurisdiction' to risk a raw challenge to the oldest jurisdiction of all, what H. G. Wells called 'the law of the Old Male', the *patria potestas* of the Romans, patriarchal power?

•••

I just wanted it admitted that my father had done wrong.

Zana Muhsen, on hearing that she had won her civil
action against her father in 1991

•••

The Muhsen case was a retroactive battle against antiquated concepts
of the possession and control of children that most men, in the industrialized West at least, never consciously entertain. Yet now? Where
does the Father stand?

Never before has it been so difficult to know. 'What are fathers
really for?' was the anguished demand of the British writer Sean
French:

> Our notion of fatherhood is often just a word for all the things
> that are important in an environment in which children are
> growing up – stability and relative prosperity, for one . . . When
> we say that children need a father figure we often mean that
> they should be protected from harm, taught the difference
> between right and wrong, given an education, given fun, love,
> and confidence in themselves.

All of which, others might feel, is just as much the concern of the
mother, grandparents or teachers of the child, and totally unspecific
to the role of the father. And many fathers, as French observes, may
pass the 'stability and prosperity' test with flying colours as constant
husbands and reliable breadwinners, and yet be cruelly deficient in
other ways: 'There are those boys who are sent away at seven to
prep school and never again meet their parents except during holidays. And there are plenty of two-parent families where the father
works such long hours that his children never see him except at
weekends, and perhaps not even then.'

Absentee fathers are now coming in for the kind of condemnation
previously reserved for 'working mums', the heavily attacked
mothers of yesterday's 'latchkey kids'. Yet to any generation before
ours, today's litany of reproach, *you weren't there for me*, would
have been well-nigh incomprehensible. Consider the judge's
grave indictment of Woody Allen's inadequacies as a father
when he granted custody of the children to Allen's estranged

partner, Mia Farrow. How many men could listen to this without a twinge?

> He did not bathe his children. He did not dress them, except from time to time, and then only to help them put on their socks and jackets . . . He does not know the name of Moses's teachers or about his academic performance. He does not know the name of his children's dentist. He does not know the names of his children's friends . . .

The judge could have been talking about my father. And there are thousands like him, men who would have been deeply uncomfortable with the idea that they should engage more closely in the lives or the physical care of their children, especially girls, and yet who would have been insulted by the idea that they were not good parents. Until very recently, no more was expected of a father than a distant benevolence and a monthly pay cheque.

And things haven't changed so much, says psychotherapist Adam Jukes. 'If they're honest, most men still think, "the children are yours, keep them out of my hair!" They want a wife and chidren at home, but they don't want to take any responsibility except the financial. Men talk about how they love to come home and play with their kids, but really they never spend more than 3 or 4 hours a week with them. Looking after children is a brain-damaging activity. Shared parenting is a severe blow to male narcissism because they have to put the children first, and most men don't want that.'

What of the much-trumpeted 'new men'? 'I'll tell you when I see one,' a girlfriend caustically remarked. In most households, even if she is working full-time, the mother still totally services the children's lives, washing, cleaning, making packed lunches, remembering birthdays, dates and key commitments like the dentist on the 27th, dinner money on Monday, sports kit on Thursday and Venture Scouts on Friday night. This work is very rarely undertaken by any father, however devoted he may be. As Adam Jukes points out, any re-definition of the burden of child care between men and women must involve a complete remodelling of the world of work, and that is something we are unlikely to see.

It also means the male of every family, the individual who has traditionally been 'the cared for', learning how to care. The simple machinery of child care – the need for perpetual vigilance, the ability to pay constant attention to the child and to anticipate every danger – make demands that even the newest of 'new men' may find beyond their scope. In two recent cases in Britain, 2-year-old Victoria Brewerton drowned after falling into a garden pond while her father worked on fences nearby, and 11-month-old Matthew Hastie was strangled when he slipped down in his high chair after his father forgot to fasten the strap between the baby's legs. Other less tragic incidents include fathers injuring children by involving them in adult sports or DIY, activities simply beyond a young child's scope to enjoy or even to negotiate without risk. The vital shift to a child-centred perspective seems one that men can find especially hard to make.

And what exactly is the force of today's 'being there', even if men were able to achieve it? A father's presence in the family is of very limited value unless he is prepared to engage with it in an adult, non-competitive way. 'My father came back from the war when I was 8, and my brother was 10,' recalls David, a London lawyer:

> And from the moment he moved back in, it was as if he expected my mother to make up for everything he'd been through in the last six years. He didn't give a shit about us. While he was away, we'd all been one happy family, all on the same level. Now he had to be first the whole time, at every meal he had to have the first helping and the last gobful, he had to be pampered like the big baby he was. He'd been an RSM in the army, running a regiment. Now he treated us like dirt and made my mother do everything for him except wipe his arse!

As soon as he could, David cut off all relations with his father: 'I'll never forgive him and I'll never forget, he blighted our family life.' The bitterness that remains is not reserved for his father alone: 'He's a selfish old bastard, and he always will be. I blame my mother for giving in to him. But I don't suppose she had much choice in those days.'

• • •

> You do not do, you do not do
> Any more, black shoe . . .
> Daddy, I have had to kill you . . .
> Daddy, Daddy, you bastard, I'm through.

Sylvia Plath, 'Daddy'

• • •

'Those days' are not so far away from us, even now: even the best of today's fathers is not so distant from the time when the demands of the paterfamilias invariably dominated those of the children. And the supreme selfishness of the old-style patriarch almost beggars belief. Auberon Waugh, the distinguished editor of the *Literary Review*, has recalled the thrill of the arrival of the first bananas in Britain at the end of the Second World War, when a beneficent government decreed one for every child. Waugh and his two younger sisters, who had never seen a banana in their lives, eagerly awaited their first taste of the fabled fruit. But when their bananas appeared, all three were served up to his father Evelyn, who promptly loaded the plate with cream and sugar and before his children's eyes, gorged the lot.

The modern mother may be less ready than the cow-loving Mrs Waugh to defer to 't'Mester', 'y'fahtha', or simply 'the Man'. But today's fathers are often no less determined to remain the king of the castle, fighting off any challenge from below, particularly if it comes from a son. Even the traditional fatherly activities, as the ex-convict John McVicar has acknowledged, can rapidly be turned into a competition, a game of one-upmanship in which the father displays his own prowess, feeding his ego at the cost of his son's. 'We had titanic battles on the tennis court and chess board,' McVicar has written of his struggles with his son in the bleak and moving memoir, *Like Father*. 'But the only time he really indicted me for the past was over sport':

> He reminded me of a football game we played over the park when he was a toddler. The winner was the first to reach ten goals. He said, 'Sometimes I would be winning by eight or nine goals to one, and I really used to think I was going to win. I wanted to win more than anything in the world, but you never let me. *Not once.*'

McVicar agrees: 'I plead guilty to that charge too. No mitigation.' How many other fathers would have to say the same? How many mothers would have to admit that they have witnessed this behaviour in their men? Is winning so important? Can it even be called 'winning' to defeat a child of 4? And why do women so rarely intervene to put a stop to this damaging nonsense?

McVicar's boy grew up to progress from credit-card thievery to serious fraud, 'robbing banks with a pen'. By the time McVicar wrote this his son, now a man in his twenties, was on the run from charges of armed robbery and the abduction of a 14-year-old girl for unlawful sexual intercourse. With hindsight, McVicar makes an unforgiving self-assessment of his failure to 'be there' for his son from the earliest days: 'He was already skilled at hiding his inner turmoil, but even if he hadn't been, I was too busy indulging myself to have helped him uncover and master it.'

However late in the day, at last McVicar is now on his son's case, and by extension, his own. Yet as he openly admits, for this child at least, the attempt to be a better father has come too late. The power of any father's example is always likely to be stronger than words of good advice, a truism summed up in the grimly fatalistic proverb, 'like father, like son'. Do the erring, selfish, self-absorbed fathers not see this, or do they not care what they do, even when the evidence is before their eyes? For decades the film star Oliver Reed has been celebrated for his 'hell-raising' antics (news-burble for 'violent drunken brawls'). Yet the pages of admiring press coverage take on another colour in the light of a report like this recent item from the *Daily Telegraph*: 'Mark Reed, 30, son of the actor Oliver Reed, was sent for trial yesterday charged with causing grievous bodily harm to a man in a pub in Raynes Park, south-west London.' In all his 'roistering', did the lovely 'Ollie' ever stop to think that he might be damaging his son's life and prospects as well as his own?

And who knows what the young Reed or the young McVicar think? Part of the problem for children in recognizing the truth of weak, foolish, selfish or deceitful fathers lies in the reluctance of adult society to do the same. Film director John Farrow, father of the more famous Mia, was a hard-drinking sex addict whose idea of a joke was to consign drunken guests to a wrecked car he kept on his estate, so that when they came round they would believe they had almost killed themselves in a terrible crash.

A confirmed Catholic, Farrow also indoctrinated Mia so forcibly with a terror of sin and death that when she first saw a nun at the age of 4, the black flapping figure sent the little girl into hysterics. Farrow disliked his children so much that they had to live in a separate wing of his house. Yet he was widely admired as a good Catholic husband and father, the author of several scholarly religious books.

For his services to the faith, this whited sepulchre was named a Knight of the Holy Sepulchre by Pope Pius XI.

● ● ●

> The principal determinant of modern neurosis is the personality of the father, which is always lacking in some way or another, whether absent or humiliated, divided or sham.

Jacques Lacan

● ● ●

Growing up to learn the reality of a father like Farrow must have involved a peculiar kind of suffering. But many fathers seem prone to pretensions that their offspring have to live to strip away, often at considerable cost. Perhaps the greatest gift a father can grant his children is permission to see through him, if he will only climb down from his pedestal and pass up the temptation to play God. Yet again and again some fathers seem compelled to impose themselves like a jealous God on their children, applying unrealistic standards of prowess or achievement to boys, arresting or disregarding the development of girls, driven only by the conviction that they are unquestionably in the right, free to go or to stay as they choose, seemingly careless of any consequences to their child.

And this carelessness seems in many cases to shade with remarkable swiftness into something far worse, from the child's point of view at least. The father of the British industrialist John Harvey Jones regarded his only son as a hopeless 'rabbit', and tried to teach him to swim by throwing him in the deep end of a swimming pool. The daughter of the world-famous children's writer Roald Dahl left school at 15 and 'just messed about' because Dahl was 'afraid of academic women and advised [her] to learn to cook and to look good'. Her father subsequently stood up at her wedding and informed the assembled guests, 'You would assume that having done so many things, Tessa did none of them well. *You would be right.*'

What notion of fatherhood lies behind actions such as these? Is it ignorance, clumsiness, maladroit humour, or can we call it cruelty to its face? For time and again, fathers seem to have a gift for the crushing word or gesture whose painful impact remains with the child all its life. The South African writer and anti-apartheid activist Ronald Segal saw his daughter in a school play and told the stagestruck girl: 'Well, Miriam, you will never be an actress.' Today he admits 'it must have been a great wound', 'one of those remarks that sears its way in': Miriam was 11 at the time. Yet Segal has no sense of overstepping a father's role. She'd be 'the first to agree' now, he protests, and anyway, he was right. 'It wasn't said cruelly or thoughtlessly, just to stop a total delusion.'

Does fatherhood itself bring with it the automatic assumption of the right to dictate the child's reality, the right to be right, whatever a man may do? Many fathers are remembered for this kind of insensitivity, often on a monumental scale. The American writer Letty Cottin Pogrebin recalls the aftermath of the death of her mother with a stumbling bewilderment whose pain shines through even today:

> My father gives away my mother's things ... Unmindful that I might someday have a home of my own and wish to own concrete mementoes of my mother's life, my father lets the relatives pick through her closets and drawers like scavengers at a flea market. He lets them load their arms and pack their cars and take away her history.

And not only her mother's history. Her own was soon to be up for grabs, as Pogrebin found. She returned from her first semester at college to find that her father had sold their house and most of its furniture, rented a one-bedroom apartment with his new wife, and relegated his daughter to a daybed in the hall. She didn't need a whole bedroom just for college vacations, did she? Did she even need any room in his new life at all? Pogrebin didn't know. She was 'confused and betrayed':

> At first I excused my father's behaviour, blaming his maleness for his mindless insensitivities, blaming his new wife for everything else. Gradually it became clear to me that 'his behaviour' was who he was.

Your behaviour is who you are ...

This simple nostrum ought to be carved on tablets of stone inscribed in letters of fire, and handed to every new father before he makes any input into the rearing of his child. Translated, this means, *a child is not an adult – make allowances*. The television producer William Miller recalls how as a boy he 'desperately wanted to impress' his father, theatre director and polymath Jonathan Miller:

But whenever I showed him a biology project, instead of him saying 'Brilliant', he'd say 'Yes, *yes*, and you must read so-and-so about the swim bladder'. He was so thrilled by my interest he just wanted to expand my knowledge. But it just made me aware of what I hadn't achieved. So eventually I stopped showing him my work. It was my fault. I kept wanting his praise.

So praise them, always praise them, the second commandment ought to run. What is this conviction so many fathers have that they must apply their own external, adult standards of criticism to their children's first stumbling attempts in life, rather than meeting the child on its own terms? A conviction, moreover, that they feel justified in acting on with small consideration for the feelings of the child? Any child's self-esteem is built brick by brick with encouragement and approval, and the lack of these can be permanently damaging. Discouragement or disapproval can remain with the child for life, however ill-deserved they may be. Molly remembers going joyfully to her father at the age of 13 with her end-of-term grades showing nine As and a B. 'What happened with the B?' he demanded.

The greatest weight of the self-regarding, self-satisfied and brutally demanding father is likely to fall not on a daughter, however, but on a son. It is extraordinary how many men from Prince Charles to Oliver Stone have to live with the knowledge that their fathers do not value them, and will be driven to put them down whatever they do. Aides to Prince Philip describe occasions when the duke would reduce Charles to tears with the force of his 'tongue lashing', even as a grown man. Oliver Stone undertook to film the story of The Doors, his wife Elizabeth says, because he identified with the lead singer Jim Morrison in his lifelong struggle against his bullying father, an admiral. Stone's own father, a World War II veteran, consistently belittled Stone's traumatic army service, calling the Vietnam war 'nothing more than a skirmish'. Stone at least came home alive: the son of Errol Flynn, driven by the sleepless fury of a much greater shade, sought his passport to heroism in the jungles of Cambodia and died at the hands of the Khmer Rouge.

Daughters, too, can spend their lives chasing the approval of a father who did not love enough. In the long downward spiral of her life, Sarah Churchill never ceased to see herself as 'a father-girl', though Winston Churchill himself denounced her as 'a mule' and 'a bitch' whenever she crossed him. Through a series of doomed marriages to older men, through a humiliating public battle with alcohol and the failure of everything she tried from acting to war work, her father remained 'the only man who really counted in her life,' recalled her friend the actress Judy Campbell. 'Nothing would induce me to live my life again,' Sarah said as she lay dying. 'But I don't mind going, because I know Papa is waiting.'

Papa is waiting . . .

A man does not have to be as famous as Churchill to cast a long shadow over his children's lives. Men and women of 30, 50, 60 can still be seen engaged in struggles which at their root are simply a desire to win and hold the approval of 'the old man'. Why is it so hard for men to learn the secret of unconditional love? The love that learns to love the happiness of the child more than its own, and to take its happiness from that?

Just as mothers must learn the extent of their power, and only opt for motherhood if they can grow into that, so fathers must learn to tread the opposite route. The power of the father is so pervasive that his first step must be to devolve it. To do this, he has to see himself as a responsible adult, not as a competitor to the young newcomer, his partner's senior child, the neediest person of those entitled to lay claim to her love.

Today's father must grow down even as he learns to grow up. He must understand what lies ahead and make a conscious election for paternity, just as his partner too should have exercised the right to choose maternity for herself. He must then unlearn the lessons of his own boyhood, and stop fighting, competing and jostling for attention. He must substitute pride in the person and personality of his child for pride of achievement, and accept that there is more to his lifelong task of fatherhood than kicking a ball around with his sons.

For in parenting, as in so many aspects of life, power is the key. Both parents possess willy-nilly an enormous power over the little helpless creatures given into their charge. They also bring to their roles a backlog of hopes, expectations and fears from their own past histories, all primed like time-bombs to go off at key points of their children's lives: the entrance to school, the onset of puberty, the slow agony of adolescence. Each parent carries his or her own loading, his or her own flashpoint or point of no return. What happens when these two so different people, one mother and one father, come together to make one great big happy family? Do they – and how do they – make the children we deserve?

•••

I'll be profoundly wise, liberal and understanding. I'd be surprised if I was a less-than-perfect father.

Woody Allen on the birth of his son Satchel

Murder, like madness, seems to run in families.

George Henry Lewes

•••

II

THE HOLY FAMILY

Families tend to have very romantic ideas about themselves.

Arminta Wallace, 'The Family That Frays Together . . .'

CHAPTER 4

Happy Families

Parents are permitted to destroy their children's lives with
impunity. Although this destruction is for the most part
repeated in the next generation, it is far from being
forbidden. All that is forbidden is to call it a scandal.

Alice Miller, Banished Knowledge (1991)

There are only two families in the world, the Haves and
the Have-Nots.

Miguel de Cervantes, Don Quixote (1615)

HAPPY FAMILIES – what is this game we all feel compelled to
play? Tombstone memorials of parents from antiquity onwards
depict matched rows of dutiful children on their knees in grateful
prayer, eyes raised adoringly to the heavens as if still seeking the
blessing of the great parental shade. A millennium and more later
we are still saddled with the myth of the 'perfect' family, and the
drive to create it seems to be stronger than ever.

As is the image of family perfection which confronts us from every
billboard, TV advertisement or sit-com. Somewhere, if only in the
great attic of the eternal adman's consciousness, there is a veritable
universe of smiling moms and cheerful, manly dads happily romping
with legions of lovable moppets, cute little girls and sturdy little men.
Under the tyranny of this myth, we are rapidly approaching the stage
where a family is as much a demonstration of a successful lifestyle
as a house, occupation or income.

For the aspiring professional couple in particular, 'the children they
deserve' seem to be taken as an automatic entitlement of progress in
life, like expensive foreign holidays or a larger car. As commodities
which both reward and proclaim the parental status, the so-called
'designer children' are approached in the same coldly acquisitive
spirit as other consumer durables, ordered up in accordance with
clear preconceptions of how they ought to be. What price the idea
of the family as a healthy but imperfect structure, whose function is

not to look great but to provide a secure inner reality, a firm base and solid foundation for the growth of a well-adjusted child? How much attention can even be given to the child, when the parents' vision of the family is of an external reality, a unit focused outwards to attract the maximum of admiring looks?

•••

I can trace my ancestry back to a protoplasmal primordial atomic globule. Consequently my family pride is something inconceivable.

W. S. Gilbert, *The Mikado* (1885)

•••

Nowhere is the desire to create the perfect family more evident than in the efforts of those who fail. Throughout human history adoption has been the classic remedy for childlessness, with more than one well-documented case of female surrogacy thrown in: Sarah, the barren wife of Abraham, urged the patriarch to father a child on her maidservant Hagar, in order to build a family she could call her own. Single mothers in recent years have been castigated for failing to turn in their babies for adoption, as if adoption always offers a better start in life for the unplanned child. In reality, what we are learning of the adoption procedures of the past has contributed to the supreme confusion of the present, where a rash of current cases on both sides of the Atlantic shows our legislators, care workers, and parents both biological and adoptive, struggling to make sense of what is happening, and to establish good modern precedents and practices for the way ahead.

For the errors of the past are legion, and their consequences are with us still. Most of them sprang from the blatant disregard of any rights or needs of the child in favour of the policies or preconvictions of the adult world. When native Australian Beverley Moore fell pregnant in 1963, she was 14, and the baby's father was too. To Beverley this was not so strange: 'Aboriginals, they been having babies for thousands of years, and women, they've been surviving.' Her white social worker did not see it that way. Beverley's son Russell, one of the last casualties of the Australian government's policy of forced assimilation of Aboriginal children into the dominant white culture, was taken away from his mother by the ironically-named Aboriginal Welfare Board at three days old. She did not see him again for 25 years.

Russell was adopted by a Protestant minister and his wife, and renamed James Hudson Savage after a 19th-century missionary. Witnesses later testified to a harsh and punitive upbringing which left the little boy terrified of his adoptive father, and a childhood growing up in the hostile surroundings of the American South, after the family unwittingly moved from Australia to an area dominated by the Ku Klux Klan. Even without this personal and racial persecution, however, it is doubtful if Russell would have been happy. More than 90 per cent of these 'assimilation adoptions' were later found to have broken down, 'leaving', as one observer reports, 'a sad flotsam of Aboriginal children in psychiatric institutions and penal establishments.'

Russell/James proved to be no exception to the general rule. Wayward from 11, by his early teens he had graduated to alcohol abuse and violent aggression. At 15 he received his first conviction for assault when he and two friends tried to rape and murder a woman in a car park. On his release, he attempted to rape his adoptive sister. After a near-fatal chase in a stolen car, he found himself back in prison, where officials reported that 'his attitude is one of despair, and he seems to have given up on himself.' On his final release he went on a two-day bender of crack and alcohol, and ended up in a blind alley where he raped and killed a local businesswoman for the $80 she had in her purse.

Beverley Moore, who had subsequently married Russell's father, saw her son for the first time for 25 years on trial for his life. Sentenced to death, Russell was reprieved on appeal when the US Supreme Court accepted the defence submission that he was suffering from a schizoid personality disorder as a result of his traumatic past. But he will never be a free man, says his lawyer George Turner: 'He'll die in prison, and he'll die young.' In the meantime, Russell writes to his mother and new-found family from the solitary confinement where he spends his days:

> I wish I could have found all of you before any of this happened
> ... I need to know how you and the rest of the family feel
> about me. Am I still your son?

Russell's adoptive parents, who had children of their own, seem to have been motivated to take him by religious ardour, or social duty, or both. Others have had an equally obscure motivation, which may not always be deeply questioned. What, for instance, has compelled Mia Farrow to assemble a collection of orphans from around the globe whose race, history and culture have given them almost nothing in common except her drive to make them hers?

Mia herself has consciously accepted that her child-collecting is some kind of reparation to herself for the abuse of her past. 'My real childhood is my children's childhood,' she says. She clearly believes in giving herself a good many chances of an action replay. Married to André Previn, she gave birth to three children, and adopted three more from Vietnam. After the split with Previn, she adopted Moses Amadeus, a Korean boy with cerebral palsy, and Dylan, a newborn girl from Texas. Her relationship with Woody Allen produced another son, Satchel.

Yet clearly Farrow does not subscribe to the school of thought that families need fathers. Even as the relationship with Woody was collapsing in a cloud of pain and acrimony, even after she had sent him the famous Valentine representing their children on meat skewers with a knife through her own heart, she hoovered up two more children, an Afro-American crack baby and a blind Vietnamese girl of 10. In a final proprietary gesture, all the more surprising in view of her own childhood terror of her father's religion, she had all of them baptized as Catholics.

What lies behind this? Does any woman need 11 children? Does any child need to be part of such a battered caravanserai, a fatherless tribe of off-the-peg rejects trailing through life in Mia's wake? Can we call this in any sense 'a family'? Or is it simply the compulsion of what child psychologists call a 'gatherer', one who needs, in the derisive phrase of Woody Allen's supporters, 'fresh babies' on a regular basis, like a 20th-century female Bluebeard?

Either way the whole process stems from the idea that a would-be parent has the right to choose a child and make it theirs, long before the child is able to have any say in the matter. And in a world where children have long since ceased to be regarded as a gift of God, their status as pure chattels has been oddly confirmed rather than diminished by this loss of sanctity. This point was forcibly established in a 1987 case that rocked America to its roots, when lawyer Joel Steinberg and his common-law wife Hedda Nussbaum were indicted for the murder of their adopted daughter Lisa.

Behind the horror of the sustained battering that led to the 6-year-old's dreadful death, lay another tragedy that attracted far less attention, the ease with which these two dangerously dysfunctional individuals had been able to find not one but two children to adopt. For years before the adoptions, Steinberg had been a batterer of psychopathic proportions, and had already reduced Nussbaum to 'mush', as she was described at the trial. His criminal law practice was all but criminal itself, Nussbaum's one-time employment as a publishing editor had long been ancient history, and both were regular users of cocaine.

Yet still they felt that children were a necessary complement to their lives, an entitlement they should not do without. In the absence of any offspring of their own, they would simply have to get them another way. Although Steinberg's practice had included arranging many private adoptions, neither Lisa nor the baby boy they procured after her to complete their perfect family had ever been adopted legally. 'It would be more accurate to call them stolen children rather than adoptees,' commented the writer Joyce Johnson.

• • •

Neither of these people is fit to raise a canary.

New York taxi driver during the Farrow–Allen
custody hearing

• • •

These cases, extreme though they are, encapsulate some of the recurring themes of adoption: the problem of the rights of the child, the impulse of some adopters to take on all the orphans of the world, the urge of others to have no more than 'the perfect family', two children, boy first, as in all the adverts. And this is before any of the immense legal or procedural difficulties associated with adopting come into play.

It would be comforting to report that international adoption laws and procedures have been tightened up in the wake of the Steinberg case. But it would not be true. Professionals on both sides of the Atlantic are still struggling with the huge, almost intractable problem of any system which has to cope with the insatiable hunger of the childless, set against the simple shortage of suitable children to adopt. From an all-time peak of 89,200 legal US adoptions in 1970, reports the US National Council for Adoption, the figure has dwindled every year until now, when for every available healthy white child born, there are more than 50 families longing to give it a home, a position echoed in all the industrialized countries of the world.

In such circumstances, abuses cannot but flourish, above all in the market economy of modern capitalism. One childless American couple, Rose and Ed Garguilo of Connecticut, after years of trying unsuccessfully to have a child of their own, were delighted to hear in 1992 through their lawyer of a baby soon to be born to a young woman who had decided not to keep the child. Visiting Angela Andrews and receiving her assurance that she would be pleased to let them have her baby, they were eager to contribute to Angela's living and medical expenses, showing their commitment as good parents to the care of 'their' baby before it was even born.

Sadly, so were nine other childless couples, equally desperate for a child. At Andrews's trial for fraud, theft, illegal placement of a child and other charges, it emerged that she had bilked all these unfortunates to the tune of over $50,000 against the birth of a baby that she had no intention of parting with anyway. 'Adoption is not a dirty word,' said Richard Schwind, the prosecutor in the case. 'But it has been set way back by Andrews.'

At least the Andrews baby had no notion of all its other 'parents' lining up to lay claim to it. The same could not be said of 2-year-old Jessica deBoer. Born to an unmarried Iowa factory worker in 1991, Jessica had been given to the childless deBoers at birth, after a pre-natal agreement that she could legally be theirs. Within days, however, the birth mother had changed her mind. Aided by the child's father, she filed legal process for the return of her child less than a month after the birth.

Wisely or not, the deBoers decided to fight, attacking the mother Cara Clausen and her boyfriend Dan Schmidt as feckless and unfit parents, and claiming that Jessica would have a better chance in life with them. Their claims were comprehensively dismissed by the presiding judge: 'Neither Iowa law nor US law,' he wrote, 'authorizes unrelated persons to retain custody of a child whose natural parents have not been found to be unfit, simply because they may be better able to provide for her future and her education.'

American public opinion was outraged. 'With flagrant disregard for the best interests of the child,' wrote one correspondent to *Time* magazine, 'the confused court has sanctified blood and cast aside the ties that really bind families together. In doing so the court has sent the alarming message that genes reign supreme, over love, nurturing, permanence and stability. Apparently home is no longer where the heart is, but where the sperm come from.'

Others however observe that US adoption law, like that of every other country in the world, almost invariably gives priority to the claims of the birth parents, and see the deBoers as selfishly trying to pervert the whole issue of 'the child's best interests' for their own personal gain and pride of possession. In seeking to alleviate their own pain of childlessness, it is argued, they have inflicted the traumatic pain of separation on the child they claimed to love, and who must now leave the only home she has ever known to pass into the care of strangers. In such a debate, no one can win, and the child can only lose. It is to be hoped that the little girl who became Annie Lee Clausen Schmidt halfway through 1993 will grow up to forget that Jessica deBoer ever existed.

Yet even without such abuse of processes or people, there are inherent problems in adoption which were rarely, if ever, fully confronted in the past. Those were the days when social workers used to match babies to adoptive parents so closely that the child could be passed off as the new parents' own. 'When we adopted Michael 25 years ago,' Janet Simkins, a Manchester teacher, recalls, 'the woman from the adoption society took our height, colouring, education and everything into account, and later told us proudly that Michael's parents and ourselves were virtually interchangeable.' Photographs today show a tall young man who actually seems to resemble both Janet and her husband, so close is the match.

This 'as-if-they-were-your-own' practice died a swift death with the rising post-Sixties shortage of children for adoption, and the harsh realization that availability now was substantially to be among those children who were never going to grow up into tall, healthy, highly intelligent or able-bodied adults. Yet exactly as with the desperate drive to keep birth-damaged children alive, so the couple driven frantic by the unsatisfied urge to build a family may often be led into saying 'yes' to any child the social workers may offer, without thinking through all the implications of the case.

Children with 'learning disabilities' or 'special needs' – how often do child-hungry parents translate that into 'will be lucky to attain a reading age of 7 and has no hope of progress beyond fifth grade', or 'will always be difficult, aggressive and severely disturbed?' Those who do, of course, and who understand the challenge that lies ahead, can find such a child infinitely rewarding. But it takes a special couple with a special kind of love and the clear knowledge that whatever they will create from this child and others like her or him, it will not be 'the perfect family'.

And it may prove considerably worse. Pamela and Stuart, childless and willing to adopt or foster in order to have a child of their own, were offered Timmy by their local authority when he was found under a hedge after a family of travellers had passed through. At an estimated age of 5, he was mute, incontinent and completely passive, having apparently been treated as a baby all his short life, yet deprived of all stimulus and play. 'He only needs bringing out,' the social workers assured Pamela.

Ten years later, she has indeed brought him out, having taught him to speak, take care of himself, and function in society. But his intelligence has never recovered from those early years of crushing deprivation and, unable to read or write properly, he will always remain in need of remedial help to manage the simplest things in life, like filling in forms. When he leaves school, he will be unlikely to get a job, and at 15 has already started to get angry at his notable lack of success with girls. As a result of these frustrations, he has also become increasingly aggressive with Stuart, and frequently attacks Pamela, too, for having 'taken him away' from his 'real' parents.

Britain now has seen the filing of its first 'adoption divorce', when a couple who adopted an abused boy in childhood are seeking to return him to the care of the local authority from which he came. The level of the damage the boy had suffered was, they say, kept from them, and it was in any case beyond their capacity to repair. The ten-year struggle to cope with the boy's escalating violence has cost them their family, friends, and even their house, which they had to sell to pay for help and care for him.

The case has started a flood of correspondence throughout the country from couples in the same situation. Their advice divides roughly half and half between 'get out as soon as you can' and 'never give up'. Either way, it was generally agreed that the case would fail, as in due course it did: a legal adoption cannot be legally reversed.

Not that it matters to Pamela and Stuart. Their son is planning his own solution to the problem. Soon, he promises, he will be out of their hair, 'on the road', looking for his real mum and dad.

•••

Whom thy soul seizes as their kin, they are thy kin. Whom
thy soul seizes not as thy kin, they are not thy kin.

Rabindranath Tagore

'Who was your mother?'
'Never had none!' said the child with another grin.
'Never had any mother? What do you mean? Where were
you born?'
'Never was born!' persisted Topsy.
'Do you know who made you?'
'Nobody, as I knows on,' said the child with a short laugh.
'I 'spect I just growed.'

Harriet Beecher Stowe, Uncle Tom's Cabin (1852)

•••

The unparented Topsy in Harriet Beecher Stowe's famous anti-
slavery novel, like Dickens's equally celebrated Oliver Twist, stands
as a paradigm for the eternal emotional orphan that any may become
who are deprived of the knowledge of their parentage. For the consequences of adoption may go on and on. What seems like a finite
solution at the time to the desire to create a family, may simply be
the creating of a Pandora's box of troubles primed to burst open in
the next generation.

And burst open it usually will. For with or without the special
problems of those who have been damaged or abused, looking for
'the missing part of yourself', as one adoptee poignantly described
it, is a preoccupation with many who grow up in ignorance of their
biological kin. This hunger in the child, an ironic echo of the hunger
that drove the adoptive parents to seek a child in the first place, may
arise at any time: in adolescence, or when contemplating marriage,
on the death of an adoptive parent or the arrival of a first child. And
there is no predicting how it will turn out. The only certainty is that
there is no turning back the clock.

Jane, adopted at birth, spent ten years between the ages of 15 and
25 looking for her mother. When they finally met, says Jane, 'we fell
into each other's arms in tears, and it was as if we'd never been
apart.' Birth fathers, on the whole, tend to be less ready than mothers
to acknowledge the past: one biological father in the Midlands, living

less than twenty miles from an adult daughter desperate to meet him, if only once, has had his wife call her up to order her to stay away.

Coming back into the life of a natural parent who has thought you gone for ever is fraught with the peril that attends any journey into the unknown. Ann, born and living in England, tracked her mother down to an address in America, and wrote at once to ask when she could come. 'I'd saved enough money for the plane', Ann recalls, 'so I just packed my case and waited':

> I was over the moon, I never doubted she'd want to see me as much as I was longing for her. She *never replied*. I had to write three more times before she even bothered to acknowledge my existence – and even then it was just one line to say that it was all in the past for her now, that she was very happily married, and would I not pester her any more.

Adoption counsellors are at pains to stress that the stories that adoptees may discover can often make them wish that they had remained in ignorance. 'You always imagine that your mother really wanted you, that she really loved you and simply couldn't keep you because of money or something,' says Greg:

> I found out instead that my mother's family had plenty of money, and she was no poor little waif who couldn't stand up for herself. In fact she was a scholar at a college in Cambridge, and she decided to give me away because I would have ruined her university career, she'd have had to leave. So she pretended to have glandular fever, took a few months off, dumped me and calmly went back to her studies. My father didn't abandon her either, like I'd always assumed, they were going to get married all along, and afterwards they did. Now there's a whole happy family I ought to have been part of, *and never will be*.

Perhaps anticipating that they may encounter, like Ann and Greg, a lot more than they are prepared to take on board, the majority of adoptees do not take steps to trace their birth parents. Many do not even appear to think of it, says Dr Alexina McWhinnie, who has made a special study of adopted adults for the University of Dundee. Only a minority, she records, suffer the sensation of being torn between two sets of parents: 'They are quite clear that their mummies and daddies are the people who brought them up. Adoptive parents are regarded as the "real" parents.' Those who feel this confidence in their adoptive parents, she concludes, are also quite clear about their own identity, and do not feel 'second class'.

Indeed the cause of any emotional difficulties for adopted children, predictably enough, is the same as that in any biological family: lies, deception or manipulation on the part of the adults. 'I told Sarah that she was adopted from the very beginning,' says Fiona. 'I used to make up little stories about how Mummy and Daddy went to this beautiful place where there were thousands of beautiful children, and we chose the one who was the most beautiful of them all. That was always her favourite bedtime story.' In the same vein, Rachel used to cuddle her adopted son Richard to sleep with a little rhyme a woman friend taught her on the day she brought Richard home:

> Not flesh of my flesh, nor bone of my bone,
> But still in all possible ways my own.
> Never forget for a single minute,
> You grew not under my heart, but in it.

When this open and loving procedure, designed to make the child feel not rejected but chosen, is not followed, however, children can suffer considerably from any secrecy or evasion over their adoption. Above all they can feel denied in their deep need to question where they come from, and to be given the raw materials to make sense of their own existence. Yet at the same time, Dr McWhinnie has established, adopted children strongly disliked repeated overt reference to their situation by outside agencies such as schools, and resented constant insistence on their status and its implications. 'It is like planting a tree,' says Dr McWhinnie, 'and then digging it up all the time to see if it has taken.'

For a child is not a commodity, a chattel, or a blank slate, it is a sensitive, sentient adult-in-formation. Adoption is not the simple solution for childlessness that it was seen as in the past, and should be undertaken with the focus on the chosen child, not to fill a hole in the life of the parents. As with mothering for women, we need to get away from the idea that having a family is an inalienable right and duty for every couple, the only justification for their existence. Teachers, friends, relations, social work agencies, adoptive families and biological families, ignore this at their own peril, and even more their children's.

•••

May you be the mother of a hundred sons.

Hindu compliment to a bride

•••

'The perfect family, two children, boy first' – when biological parenting is possible, how have we allowed this adman's fantasy to come to represent the most desired of family forms in the West? And how do we respond to the severe reduction if not destruction of female children in cultures where a quiverful of sons is prized above any number of despised daughters?

Every child a wanted child . . . *Planned* parenthood is one thing, *controlled* reproduction quite another. With the rapid proliferation of new birth technologies, there are serious dangers ahead. Now techniques devised to save human life or to improve its quality are being perverted to uses for which they were never designed. Now the frustrated mother of girls can have an amniocentesis to enable her and her husband to destroy any pregnancy save that of the longed-for son. 'Every child a wanted child' does not mean that a child may be thought of as a 'must-have' item to be ordered up according to a fixed choice, or simply cancelled when unwanted, like something ordered from a catalogue.

Families should be organic, individual, and *different*. To desire otherwise is a perfect example of consumerism gone mad. That is the only fitting description for the dreadful 'trade in gender' currently establishing itself in America, Britain, Canada, Oman, Pakistan, India, Jordan, Malaysia and Singapore, all the countries where Dr Ron Ericsson and his ilk have set up shop. Ericsson himself, a reproductive scientist turned entrepreneur from Wyoming, USA, sports a blue baseball cap emblazoned with the slogan THE SPERM FIRM. His multi-million-dollar business offers 'the gift of sex selection', the right to determine the sex of an unborn child.

It's simple, says Dr Ron. Separate out the male sperm from the female sperm, let them fight it out among themselves, and all you're left with are 'gold medal winners'. At a success rate of 80 to 85 per cent for those wanting boys, the method is far more reliable for producing male babies than female: success in ensuring the weaker sex for the parents hoping for a girl comes in at a mere 67 to 70 per cent. But that's all right surely, doctor, since most people are going to want boys? 'I don't care what the critics say,' Ericsson replies. 'I know the tabloids are going to tear me apart, but I don't care. Every mention means another baby and more business for me.'

Defenders of the 'choose the sex of your baby' school, including Ericsson, insist that their work adds to the level of human happiness and promotes a positive gain for society by reducing the number of babies a couple will have in the effort to 'try for' the sex they want: 'The real problem comes when they've had four boys and are desperate for a little girl to go shopping with mummy.'

Other observers tell a very different tale. Anjolie Kapardia is a counsellor formerly working with Indian families in Britain, now established in New Delhi. 'You want addresses, you want names? There are twenty, a hundred clinics here that exist only to abort foetuses which prove to be a girl.' Her sombre view is confirmed by Dr Gautem Appa, a lecturer at the London School of Economics: 'There are villages in India where you can't get clean water, but you can get amniocentesis.' On current figures, Dr Appa says, already in India there are 7 per cent more boys being born than girls, through the deliberate use of selective post-amniocentesis abortions, or subsequent female infanticide.

Britain and America may not resort to the age-old 'birthing box' of Asia, the box of dead ashes kept ready to suffocate female babies at the end of the delivery bed, where the unwanted girl takes a swift nose-dive to oblivion before she can draw her first breath. But from the adman to the dustman, no honest observer of the Anglo-Saxon scene can doubt that the birth of a son is as important here as it is anywhere else. 'Of course they'll all want boys, it won't be simply the Asian women,' said a senior British gynaecologist. 'My God,' said a woman friend to the the journalist Libby Purves when she covered this story, *'they're trying to wipe us out!'*

Some support for this statement came in an ensuing *British Medical Journal* review, when a study of the first results of sex selection clinics operating in America, Asia and Europe showed that of the first 251 couples treated, 236 had chosen boys, while only 15 opted for girls. In a move that horrified British public opinion, the governing council of the British Medical Association supported the clinics, recommending that parents should have the right to choose the sex of their child: 'We should come down on the side of patient choice and autonomy,' said the chairman of the council, Dr Jeremy Lee-Potter.

'Patient choice' in this context is a cynical perversion of the concept, others say. 'I'd bet a hundred quid that most clients will be distraught Muslim or Asian women desperate to produce a son,' observed Professor Robert Winston, infertility consultant at Hammersmith Hospital. This infamous recommendation of support was subsequently overturned at a general meeting of the BMA, where doctors were vociferous in their opposition. Only sound medical reasons, it was agreed, such as the clear risk of a child being born with a sex-related genetic defect like muscular dystrophy or haemophilia, should ever constitute a reason for sex selection. At the next general meeting of the British Medical Association, Dr Lee-Potter failed to win re-election to his post.

But this issue is not one for the medical profession in isolation. Nor are Asian and Muslim families alone in their overwhelming preference for a boy child over a girl. 'My own hopes are that the sex choice dilemma will set in motion a debate on just why boys are generally considered the more favoured sex,' writes the British commentator Liz Hodgkinson. 'In no present society anywhere in the world are girls actually preferred. *Why not?*':

> On the whole girls are prettier, brighter, less trouble and quicker learners than boys. They are less violent, less likely to get into fights, take drugs, rape, and commit crimes. But many men still consider it is more 'masculine' to produce a son, and the idea that women who produce sons are somehow more valuable has not disappeared . . . But because [parents] can have the sex of their choice, does this mean they will automatically have the child of their choice? No way has yet been found to guarantee a nice personality or high intelligence.

With or without sex selection, Hodgkinson concludes, 'the perfect, TV-ad family will continue to elude us . . . We can only hope that sex selection does not lead to yet more parents being disappointed in their children.'

• • •

It's the ultimate in consumer choice.

Dr Ron Ericsson

What is it, a boy or a child, I wonder?

William Shakespeare, *The Winter's Tale*

• • •

In the making of the family, we all assume we can, and we thus assume we must. We think of children now as a right, not a privilege: not given, but ordered, like a pizza 'to go', a Big Mac or a take-away chicken chop suey. And in the grip of the vision of the designer lifestyle, we all want families that are designed, not haphazard, each child spaced and placed till the family as a whole resembles nothing so much as an exquisite piece of table-scaping for a particularly smart dinner party.

How far this is from the reality of most people's lives, only they know. But 'they' never get to set the standards and establish the criteria. If they did, perhaps they would be able to get through to the powers that be, that the old idea of the family, let alone the ad-fantasy designer version of hard-working Dad and home-loving Mom with two perfect children, is now as antiquated as gas lighting, hansom cabs and organ grinders in the London streets.

For families now may come in any shapes and sizes and changing combinations. They may be with or without fathers, as single women or abandoned wives go it alone. Without mothers, too: single parents now number more and more males, as today's divorced or widowed men make the effort to bring up their children by themselves, some-thing almost unheard of before the 1960s. A couple who have only one child may now consider that a family, whereas to others it will only feel like a family when it is big enough to play football five a side. The only certainty about the modern family in the industrialized world is that with fewer than 25 per cent of families now conforming to the pre-1960s model of family organization, it is less and less likely to consist of a breadwinning father, an economically inactive mother, and two children.

And whatever the nostalgia of our politicians and opinion-makers, we cannot go back. New family systems call for new challenges and solutions, not a reversion to the thinking of former times. Yet how do we build a family today that will be happy in the ordinary, average, completely unremarkable way of the past we seem to remember from our own childhoods, a family that will keep its children on the rails, off the streets, and out of all our hair? How do we avoid creating a family of 'have-nots', children who never know the simple feeling of security and content which is our best defence against the acts of aggression and destruction that more and more seem to assail us from those without this base? Many parents today have lost the confidence that this is now possible in today's increasingly corrupt

world. What are parents for? There is only one answer – they are
for their children. How in a 'good' family can we bring this about?

•••

Is this asking too much? Under some circumstances it is
much too much, a great burden, while under others it is a joy
and an enrichment. It all depends on what the parents
themselves experienced in the past, and what they have to
give.

Alice Miller, *Banished Knowledge* (1990)

•••

CHAPTER 5

Enough Is Good Enough

*We were poor but we refused to be pitiable, and although
we were Black, we felt precious . . . we refused to be losers.*

Florynce Kennedy, *Color Me Flo*

O NCE UPON a time, the world knew how to rear its children. The
world and his wife agreed on how to produce the children they
deserved. Parents were deemed to be in the right unless they went
spectacularly wrong, so much so that even the dreadful Mrs Joe
Gargery, the mother-substitute who regularly terrorizes and torments
the young Pip in Charles Dickens's *Great Expectations*, could be
depicted as winning approbation all round for her skill in bringing
up the boy 'by hand'.

Now child psychologists patiently guide mothers and fathers
through the mechanics of handling their children in an intensive
therapy programme known as the Parent-Child Game, today's
answer to the problems of bringing up the young in an era that has
less faith in the laying on of hands. Devised by teams of American
psychologists in the 1970s, this technique has now been successfully
employed worldwide as a means of imposing discipline without tears,
and re-establishing the control of parents whose offspring are
seriously out-of-hand. Based on the commonsense premise that
when repeated correction and instruction have failed to make
a child behave, then something different must be tried, it argues
that this will usually be the opposite of what parents are doing
already.

For faced with a naughty child, most parents will naturally tell
him (the so-called 'non-compliant' children are far more likely to be
boys than girls) to stop it. If that does not work, they will tell him
again, more angrily every time. They will then become so exhausted
with constant threatening, criticizing and scolding, that when the
child is good they simply fail to respond. The naughty child is therefore getting all the attention that children naturally want when he is
behaving badly, and receiving no reinforcement or reward for being

quiet and well-behaved. Without realizing it, therefore, the parents are actually training the child to behave badly.

To combat this, parents and child play together in a special unit of a children's clinic or hospital where an unseen child psychologist supervises the interaction through a two-way mirror, talking into a microphone that allows him or her to speak directly into an earpiece worn by the adult. In a standard programme, the instruction consists of a simple series of 'Dos' and 'Don'ts': *do* tell the child when he is behaving well, *do* enter into his game and ignore minor bits of bad behaviour, *don't* keep on hectoring and haranguing when it is clear that this is not working. 'Some of the parents when they start here are doing more than 100 of our "Don'ts" in a 10-minute session,' says Sue Jenner, principal clinical psychologist at the Children's Department of the Maudsley Hospital in London. 'By the end they are often down to half a dozen.'

Studies in child centres in Oregon and Georgia where the Parent-Child Game was developed have shown that 66 per cent of the child participants show normal or near-normal behaviour when followed up four to eight years later. Even with what psychologists assess as 'end-of-the-line' children whose difficulties do not come to light until they are severe enough to attract the attention of the police or social workers, 'around 30 per cent will improve significantly,' says Dr Stephen Wolkind, the Maudsley's consultant child psychiatrist. As well they might, Sue Jenner suggests, once their parents receive the help they need. 'The central message is terribly simple,' she says. 'Show love in a way that is meaningful for the child. Do you know the one thing that parents find most difficult about the game? Having me praise them through the earpiece. No one has ever told them they are any good before.'

Yet, however successful they may be, such 're-learning' programmes will only ever be available to the most wayward, violent or dangerous of today's children, simply through the scarcity of resources and personnel. And how have they become necessary? 'I think we've lost it, in fact I think we lost it when these mothers and fathers were children,' says economist Howard Steiner. 'Otherwise they'd have a better idea of how to do it, and we wouldn't be in the mess we are now.'

If we have lost it, how do we get it back? What are the elements of good parenting, of an upbringing that will deliver us and our children from the seven devils that seem to lurk inside every alienated, unhappy, aggressive child? Psychologists are anxious to stress the concept of 'good enough' parenting: the concept of the 'perfect' mom and dad in itself can make parents feel anxious, inadequate, and resentful. 'Do the best you can, and then accept that that's as good as it gets,' is the advice of family therapist Tom Snowden. 'Don't live with your failures, but don't try to bury them either, just resolve to do better next time.'

But no one can be even 'good enough' when they simply don't have enough. Undoubtedly one key factor in the rise of problem families and their worse-than-problem children has been the longest, deepest and most savage recession that the modern world has ever seen. Along with their parents, studies show that children everywhere grew poorer all through the 1980s, with a measurable effect on their health, well-being, education and opportunities for employment. In a decade that has seen increasing numbers of women and children begging on the streets and subways of all the major cities, many children have been out of sight and out of mind in conditions so appalling that time now seems to be running backwards for them to the miseries of the Industrial Revolution. Then as now, a hard core of criminal children occupied an inordinate amount of public attention while the vast majority went over-worked and under-educated into a premature adulthood and an impaired life. This is John, a thief of 14, known to the police of one inner city as 'the Rat Boy' for his skill in evading police by hiding in drainage and heating systems. This is Jane, 12, unable to go to school in her run-down town because she has to look after her younger siblings while her mother works. When the cash won't go round, Jane must go 'lifting' if the family is to eat.

What price the high-minded concepts of a caring society now? There is no human problem that is not made easier by money. There is no human misery that is not made worse by poverty. Poor children are inherently more likely to become either criminal or the victims of crime than their better-off counterparts in the middle and upper classes, or at the least prone to absorb anti-social values in which they lose both the will to be part of an active, healthy society and the belief that it could even come about.

More detailed studies, such as that recently carried out by the US Center for the Study of Social Policy, suggest that family incomes in poorer families continued to fall *even when parents worked longer hours*. As parents worked more and earned less, this reduced the time that they could spend with their children even to keep the youngest off the streets. 'Families typically have less time to devote to the supervision, education and care of their children than they did two decades ago,' says Judith H. Weitz, co-ordinator of the Center, a non-profit organization in Washington DC. 'These families are both time and money short.'

Lack of supervision is only one manifestation of the damage that may occur in a family where money is tight. The effects of the recession in Britain have meant a rise in domestic violence, said a senior police officer in a British television documentary of 1993. Discounting the suggestion that the recent sharp rise in attacks on women and children in the home is due to an increase in reporting, Andrew May, Assistant Chief Constable of South Wales, asserted that 'pressures within family life are now far greater. That must exacerbate the problem.'

And 'the problem' will not simply go away. Nor will children simply 'grow out of it' or 'get over it', in the facile commonplace assumption that the passage of time overcomes every childhood difficulty from growing pains to sexual abuse. Children growing up in violent homes learn to look on violence as the norm. With the loss of their traditional role as the breadwinner and undisputed head of the family, more and more men are likely to resort to violence of some sort to restore their sense of self, or to vent their anger and frustration. In an age that is never again likely to see full employment, where millions are out of work and those still employed are working harder than ever, what is being done to address, or even to acknowledge, the adverse long-term effects of all this?

• • •

> Resolve not to be poor. Whatever you have, spend less.
> Poverty is a great enemy to human happiness; it certainly
> destroys liberty, it makes some virtues impracticable, and
> others extremely difficult.
>
> Dr Johnson

• • •

Yet not all poor families become violent, or deviant, or both. The American civil rights activist and lawyer Florynce Kennedy has left a chirpy account of her Black family's 'refusal to be pitiful':

We never felt like losers. We were the exact opposite of the Marilyn Monroe syndrome, the beautiful golden goddess who because of her bad childhood and sense of worthlessness was never able to feel like a goddess. We were little black pickaninnies, but because of the way we were treated by our family, we felt very favored. I remember how at Christmas time Zella [Flo's mother] would call all the creditors and tell them she wouldn't be able to pay them because she had to buy something for her kids. She always made it clear to us and to everybody else that we were something special and to be indulged. Her feeling was, 'I want these children to know we care about them, that we give them the best we have . . .'

In support of this, Robin Skynner, former Chairman of the Institute of Family Therapy and co-author with John Cleese of *Families and How to Survive Them* (1983), has identified seven key characteristics of the 'basically healthy family', none of which has anything to do with money:

- An essentially positive approach to life and other people, often manifested as a high level of humour, fun and enjoyment.

- A strong commitment and sense of involvement, and an unusual degree of closeness and intimacy.

- A capacity for individual members to be independent, separate and happy on their own.

- Efficient communication between family members with open, frank and clear conversations about everything.

- Firm control of family activity by the parents, after consultation with all involved, and as far as possible the accommodation of all points of view.

- An equal-power coalition between a mother and father who can resolve issues easily and amicably.

- An ability to cope with change and loss, even including the death of loved ones.

'It's true, it's all true,' says Rosemary of this list, looking back on 'a childhood so trouble-free I never knew it wasn't the same for everybody until I got old enough to notice:

When I think of my mother [who died when Rosemary was 15] I always remember her smiling or laughing, offering somebody a bite to eat or a cup of tea. My father was hospitable too, and they always got on well together, I never heard them row. It's a terrible cliché I know, but they never exchanged a cross word. I know now that there must have been more to it than that, and I think she put up with a lot more than I would ever have, my father's invariable Sunday lunchtimes down the pub, for instance. She also died pretty young, she was only 53, she was ill for a long time, and she kept all that to herself, so I know she must have bottled a lot up. But whatever it cost her, it was great for us kids. We really did grow up in an atmosphere of peace and harmony, and that stays with you for life.

Peace and harmony – these domestic ideals seem almost as old-fashioned in today's emotional climate as the horse and cart. 'Not in front of the children' sounds as absurd and antiquated now as its companion dictum, 'Children should be seen and not heard.'

Yet there was some method in this old-world madness after all. Verbal violence can be terrifying to young children until they become so degraded by it that it becomes the norm. How many couples today make a conscious attempt not to argue, shout or get angry with each other when their children are around? Some would indeed argue that allowing their children to witness conflict in a relationship is 'more honest' and 'truthful', and 'a better preparation for life.' In the wake of some unholy alliance of D. H. Lawrence and Sigmund Freud, in a deep modern-day confusion of the urge to be honest with the refusal to be repressed, the 19th-century virtues of consideration, respect, fortitude and restraint within a partnership have given way to our late 20th-century approval of behaviour which often seems the exact opposite.

Lawrence himself brawled viciously and often with his equally volatile wife Frieda, and firmly believed that violent mental and physical struggles were the destiny of love's true warriors and the mark of the exceptional relationship. '*They are chosen, ah, they are fated for the fight!*' he wrote ecstatically of the ideal lovers in the poem 'Look! We Have Come Through!' What Frieda and he 'came through' was in fact no romantic ideal but rather the dragged-out depravity of another brutally abusive relationship: Katherine Mansfield and John Middleton Murry record seeing Lawrence slapping

Frieda's face, pulling down her long hair to tear it out in handfuls, and punching her breasts, while she did her best to beat him in return.

Lawrence's conviction that 'real' love was only expressed through strife has left uncounted numbers of damaged couples trailing in its wake. Equally harmful was his strenuous promotion of the idea that individuals were justified in abandoning marriage and family ties in pursuit of romantic love and personal fulfilment. This self-serving philosophy, with its inherent disregard of the welfare of any children involved, has proved extraordinarily powerful in the generations since his death. It has been used to justify every marriage split, fuelling the rocketing rate of divorce in modern times, and has served to reinforce the narcissistic antics of matrimonial wreckers and bolters from Ernest Hemingway to the Princess of Wales.

How did this sordid sado-masochistic 'Lawrentian' entanglement between the miner's son and the Prussian officer's daughter ever become elevated to one of history's grand passions? Even more, how have we allowed the idea to get abroad that a strong and healthy emotional relationship is distinguished by the ability to row and brawl, to 'get it all out in the open', to 'clear the air'? Few will disagree with the right of consenting adults to do what they please in private. But when these habits are thoughtlessly translated out of coupledom and into family life, children can suffer, as Gail recalls:

> Rob and I had often thrown things at each other when we were courting, I certainly felt it proved the strength of our feeling, and also it could even be really rather fun. I remember one time I threw a tin of Ovaltine at him and the lid came off halfway across the kitchen and we found ourselves in a flying cloud of sticky little brown crispy bits, and laughed so much that we ended up in bed. But after Daisy was born, he annoyed me once and I threw a glass of milk over him. She was less than one, she couldn't even talk, but she started to scream and scream and she just wouldn't stop. I never did it again!'

Babies are born highly sensitive to external stimulus and will react badly to any sudden loud noise or disturbance of their personal universe. Explosions of anger and either verbal or physical violence in a family can be terrifying to a child, as psychotherapist John

Bradshaw explains: 'When Mom and Dad, step-parent or whoever the caretaker [*sic*], are most out of control, they are the most threatening to the child's survival. The child's survival alarm registers these behaviors the most deeply.' For that reason, then, acts of anger or violence will constitute a lesson they are unlikely to forget. From there it will be only a matter of time before they begin to put into practice what they have learned, in one way or another.

And inevitably, the parents who have trouble managing each other and their own emotions are likely to have difficulty exerting any control over their children. It is often a paradox to outsiders that the parents who shout the loudest, strike out at the least provocation, hit the hardest and threaten the worst penalties are those who have the least real authority within their families. Their children seem to learn at an early age that even vicious blows and cruel punishments may simply be shrugged off.

The reason for this is 'confused disciplining', according to the British Crime Survey of 1991. 'In such families, the atmosphere can be punitive, aggressive and hostile, yet at the same time permissive,' says Dr Eric Taylor of the British Institute of Psychiatry. Family therapists agree. 'The child soon learns that it is being punished for annoying the parent, rather than for doing something that is wrong in itself,' says Wendy Wilkinson, who works in the Family Service Unit of an Inner London borough council. 'And the irritant itself will vary according to the parents' mood, the time of day, or how much they've had to drink. So the child can't even learn how to avoid the same trouble next time.'

Not surprisingly, families and environments in which chronic inconsistency prevailed were far more likely to produce children who were unstable, insecure, deviant or criminal. Yet in all the debate on handling and controlling children, one key fact is often lost from view: *that children want to please.* They are not born in a state of aggravation, flexing their tiny muscles until they can grow big enough to anger and distress their parents. When they do, they may not even know what has provoked a parent's fury. Jessica ruefully recalls the time when all the children at her son's primary school were asked to tell the teacher what was the worst thing a person could possibly do. 'Eating crisps in bed,' her 8-year-old son replied with conviction, dismissing any other suggestions involving the lesser crimes of murder, theft or cruelty.

'In fact I had caught him eating crisps in bed and completely flown off the handle and howled and screamed as if he had committed a murder!' Jessica recalls:

> The truth was that I'd just had to make up three beds on my own for visitors arriving the next day, it was late at night, and my first thought was 'Oh God, I just can't change another bed tonight!' In fact it wasn't necessary at all, because he hadn't really made a mess, so my frenzy had no real connection with what he was doing. When I found out about it, of course I could straighten it out. But it made me wonder how many other times I'd got his wires crossed like that.

'Not to worry too much, this is something we all do,' says family therapist Tom Snowden. 'But what I think we should learn from it is that when you are angry, tense, or even raising your voice to the child, *is not the right moment to be instilling moral values*. These come out best in general discussion, in an unheated atmosphere, when the child has time to ponder on them generally and to absorb what is said without feeling that all your criticisms have to be applied directly to itself. And this can only come with time. Good time, unpressured time, and as much of it as you can manage.'

• • •

> Injurious time now with a robber's haste
> Crams his rich thievery up, he knows not how.

William Shakespeare, *Troilus and Cressida* (c.1601)

• • •

Time – this is the form of love that seems to be the most precious of all, and yet inevitably the most difficult to provide. Of all the changes that he has seen in family structures since his work began, the guru of 20th-century child care Dr Benjamin Spock sees the greatest problems as springing from the undue emphasis that parents in Western societies now place on their work: 'Our society is excessively competitive and materialistic, and there's a feeling that income and the prestige of a job are the highest priorities, while the family is taken for granted.' Yet a family cannot be taken for granted any more than a partner should be, and parenthood, like marriage, has to be worked at if it is not to deteriorate as it has done in recent years. Fathers and mothers must take equal responsibility for this state of affairs, Spock says, strongly criticizing the macho-male corporate business style that keeps men away from their families for long stretches at a time, as well as the zeal with which women have now joined the workforce: 'Many women have now taken on the narrow and often mistaken values of men,' he says. 'Women have joined the rat race.'

Not always by choice, any more than their men, as we have seen. But where parents are lucky enough to have financial room for manoeuvre, recent research suggests that their children, if given the choice, would infinitely prefer more time with their parents to any rise in their standard of living that the increased income can provide. There is simply no substitute for parental time and attention, according to the first systematic study of happiness in childhood carried out at Eastern Michigan University in the USA. Even before starting on her research, psychologist Dr Alida Westman suspected that children were not as thrilled by the outlay of cash as parents usually thought: 'When I asked children what made them happy, they usually replied in terms of social activities, such as making a snowman with Dad,' she says.

Splashing out for expensive presents at Christmas, then, as a way of making up for absence or neglect for the rest of the year, is no compensation, it seems. Indeed Dr Westman's research suggests that they are a complete waste of money. For while presents certainly loomed large on every child's list of what gave them pleasure, those which gave the greatest happiness were usually the simplest of all, such as bats and balls.

And forget Nintendo or Tiny Tears. The latest electronic wizardry or micro-gadgetry seemed only to impress parents – for whose delight, one may guess, they were bought in the first place. Dr Westman agrees. 'The most technological toys available were not mentioned – for example dolls that talked or urinated. My latest research among toddlers shows that wooden spoons and pots and pans are much more popular than expensive toys.'

The same determination to spend money in lieu of time, and the same misdirected overkill, may also be applied to a child's activities as it grows older. Parental care and attention can come to mean the constant provision of a programme of activities that would put paid to an over-energetic adult. 'The ambitious or competitive middle-class parent in particular is liable to feel that the child's life is not complete without a whole slew of out-of-school acitivities,' says Tom Snowden:

> I worked with one family where the 12-year-old daughter was so bad at French that the parents insisted she took up German as well, in a spare hour or so she had after her piano lesson on a Wednesday night. Of course education is important, but this kind of cramming is the antithesis of that. A child needs just as much time for self-initiated play, developing their own interests and hobbies, or simply sitting around. What we call 'day-dreaming' is in fact the vital process of assimilating life and all that is going on around.

Once again, it seems, the problem stems from seeking to impose adult-determined rhythms on our children instead of allowing them to develop and follow their own. A child simply sitting by itself and thinking, points out the writer Deborah Jackson, is likely to be rousted out and cheerfully dragooned into 'joining in' whatever activity is going on at the time. Yet 'all children need time to sit and stare':

> Researchers have found that the brightest children are those who have been allowed to stare without interruption, and this may be the time when mental concepts are roughed in ... we think nothing of disturbing our children's time, which – in the long span of life – ought to be the one thing they have on their side.

•••

There's no such thing as quality time.

Norah Ephron

•••

Part of the problem, Jackson suggests, lies in the Eighties' invention of the concept of 'Quality Time', the hour or so at the end of the day when the parent aims at an intense, positive interaction with the child in the interval between arriving home from work, and the child's bedtime. Yet surely, given the nature of the young child's biological clock, the very notion was always the wrong way round. Children are larks, not owls, undoubtedly at their very best first thing in the morning, bouncing around bright-eyed and bushy-tailed as their parents struggle up from the primeval sludge of adult sleep.

And there's the rub. It is asking too much for the average over-worked and over-stressed parent, who may not yet have made up all the sleep lost in the child's babyhood, to rise with the dawn chorus too. So if working parents are to make a special effort to be with their children at all, 'Quality Time' has to come in the evening when the adults return from work. Yet this is undoubtedly the worst time of all for tired children who ought to be simply winding down to a gentle, easy sleep. If they have been in the company of another carer all day long, the simple appearance of Mummy or Daddy with their exciting aura of the outside world and the change they bring in the tempo and texture of the child's day, can be an untimely stimulus, defeating sleep for much longer than the prescribed hour.

'Quality Time', with its promise of closer or deeper attention than the child has received during the rest of the day, can also become a break in the routine which the child will want to drag out by refusing to go to bed, no matter how exhausted it is. Adults too will be tired by this time, stressed or drained by the events of a working day, and rarely capable of responding freshly and creatively to the rearing of a young child in which, as Einstein remarked, 'imagination is more important than knowledge.'

As is spontaneity. The mind of a child moves rapidly from moment to moment: a 3-year-old cannot save for the parents' pre-determined hour of 'Quality Time' all the unforced questions and observations that in themselves can constitute the 'quality' side of parenting, and lift the whole process from a chore to a joy. From the request 'How does a baby get in there?' to the dreamy demand, 'Why didn't God turn the moon all the way on tonight?', these are the moments of intimate trust and truth on which later mature communication can be built.

This is not to say that mothers should not go out to work, or that carers are unable to deal with these inquiries every bit as well as the biological parent, if not better. Most of the mothers who like me left their children in nurseries and nursery schools while they were work-ing were only too grateful for the skilled attention and added stimulus they received there, giving them a happy start in life which continued throughout their educational careers. But when I picked them up I could never convince myself that they were like VCRs that could be programmed to fit into their parents' adult schedule just because their father and I had time to share. I also quickly found, as every parent does, that the quality of the time spent with children increases in direct proportion to the amount of it.

And there is not so much time after all – only a few years in which as parents we can make our mark, getting it more or less right, or getting it wrong. It is one of the most harmful effects of the late recession that it is so difficult now for any parent to drop out of the workforce as so many mothers formerly did, and spend time with the children before it is too late. For it is now becoming increasingly clear that disturbance in children may begin a good deal earlier than is generally thought. Every nursery now will have experience of a compulsive rocker, head-banger or perpetual masturbator, the child who is unable to stop its distressing or antisocial behaviour however often it is rebuked. Very young children may become difficult or recalcitrant, violently aggressive or severely depressed, with serious consequences for their mental or emotional health later on. 'If we are going to affect behaviour,' says Dr Fiona Caldicott, 'from three to six years is the intervention time.'

Too often the source of the distress will go unnoticed, and the distress itself will therefore not be healed. Something happened to the writer Samuel Beckett as he was growing up, a crucial injury to his sense of himself as a positive, worthwhile individual which left him with the lifelong sense of futility and desolation that marked all his work. Yet whatever the incident, it happened before Beckett could even remember it. By the time his conscious memory began, any joy he might have taken in life was crushed beyond repair. 'One could say I had a happy childhood,' he later observed, 'but I showed little talent for being happy. My parents did all they could to make a child happy, but I often felt very lonely.' The overwhelming sense of defeat and lack of control the playwright experienced from childhood onwards is summed up in the key phrase from *Krapp's Last Tape*, 'can't go on, must go on'.

Beckett was at least fortunate in being able to develop through his writing the patterns of distraction, consolation and creation that gave structure and meaning to his long and lonely life. Those less able to re-work or to recreate buried or painful raw experience must tread a harder path. Dr Fiona Caldicott sums it up:

There is a progression from unco-operative behaviour in pre-school children whose parents have difficulty managing them, to antisocial and aggressive behaviour, including delinquent acts, in older children. In a small minority, this extends to serious violence and major criminality in adult life.

How then do we best manage our children from their earliest days? The first and most simple requirement, it seems, is simply to *pay attention*. In a terrible panic with my first baby, I well remember confessing to an elderly acquaintance my dread that I didn't know enough to be able to look after a child.

'Don't worry,' said the old lady, 'you don't need to know anything, she'll teach you.' Then she paused and squinted at me, head on one side. 'If you let her, that is.'

From that point on I tried to let my daughter tell me whatever she wanted, thought and felt. I found that simply asking her 'do you want to play with this?' or 'have any more to eat?' or 'go to see so-and-so?' avoided about 90 per cent of the battles that friends seem to find unavoidable with their children. Even when these battles commenced, when a friend's 2-year-old girl or 4-year-old boy was raging with anger and seemed out of control, I would always feel that it was worth asking the child, 'Can you tell me what is going on, what the problem is?'

Parents often have the fear of 'spoiling' a child by indulging its whims or 'allowing it to rule the roost'. Certainly we have all seen infant tyrants who seem to terrorize their parents with captious, unreasonable demands backed up with violent temper tantrums every time they fail to get their own way. One friend's 4-year-old son who refused to talk except in words of his own making, had a habit of suddenly screaming 'Roh! Roh! Roh!' in a high, thin, glass-shatttering wail until orange juice was hastily provided. Another 3-year-old girl would never go to sleep unless in her parents' bed, and if she happened to wake while her mother or father was carrying her back to her own, would scream so persistently they had to take her back to their bed and start the whole thing again.

But this is not the behaviour of children who have been considered, heard, and *acknowledged*. Rather is it the increasingly frantic activity of a child who is pushing ever more desperately against the parents' refusal to see that it is only a child, and firmly treat it like one.

First-time parents in particular are prone to the deep fear that if they cross their newborn child in any way, they may be thwarting its psychological development and damaging it for life.

On the contrary, says health visitor Charlotte Wilson, it is far more harmful to the child to realize that it is living in a universe *without* a strong system of supportive controls. And to feel in addition to this that it has actually succeeded in usurping the parental role can make the child even more anxious and confused: 'A child doesn't want to feel in control of his parents. He finds power bewildering.'

So, of course, do parents, which is why we can often exercise it erratically, inconsistently, inappropriately, or not at all. There is also the ongoing problem of trying to balance the needs of a young child against an adult routine that has become infinitely more complex than the lives our parents led. Toting young infants on and off intercontinental planes, in and out of restaurants or late-night parties, will suit only a few: regular meals, a steady routine and early bedtimes, boring as they may be, seem to benefit the majority of the growing young. But our first, last and best clue must always be the individual child. If we can pay enough attention, we can learn to distinguish what the child needs as against what we think we need for or from the child.

Such attention cannot be paid without a heavy personal commitment, and that, it seems, we are all too reluctant to make. A major nationwide survey of British family patterns 'Family Lifestyles 1993', conducted by the market research organization Mintel, showed a disheartening gap between what British parents say, and what they do. Under questioning, 80 per cent of parents virtuously proclaimed 'an exceptionally high degree of interest' in their children, and declared that their children would be the last to suffer from any hardship, financial or otherwise, that afflicted the family. But of the same parents, 88 per cent said that they considered it more important to spend time together than to do anything with their children. A staggering 20 per cent declared that they took no enjoyment in spending any leisure time with their children at all.

Still less, it seems, are we ready to put in the work that paying full attention requires. Psychotherapist Scott Peck identifies five ways of responding to a child's attempts to talk to us in his 'new psychology of love, traditional values and spiritual growth', *The Road Less Travelled* (1983). We can:

- Forbid the child to speak – 'believe it or not, there are families in which the children are virtually not allowed to talk'.

- Permit the chatter, but simply not listen to it, 'then your child is not interacting with you but is literally talking to thin air or to him- or herself'.

- Pretend to listen while proceeding with your own train of thought, 'appearing to give the child your attention and occasionally making "uh huh" or "that's nice" noises at more or less inappropriate times'.

- Selective listening, 'a particularly alert form of pretend listening, wherein parents may prick up their ears if the child seems to be saying something of importance, hoping to separate the wheat from the chaff with a minumum of effort'.

- True listening, 'giving your full and complete attention, weighing each word and understanding each sentence'.

These five ways of listening, as Peck drily observes, 'come in ascending order of difficulty, with the fifth, true listening, requiring from the parents a quantum leap of energy compared with the other less effortful ways.' But considering that parents will spend many precious hours and hard-earned pounds at Christmas on the latest, the costliest, the most fantastic of consumer goods, can we honestly say that in the far more vital question of moulding their character and forming their self-esteem, anything less than the best will really do?

Not that paying attention necessarily means hanging on a 6-year-old's every word, as Peck is at pains to stress. Another tried and true way of making a child feel present in your attention is to play with her or him. From the earliest days of life, children can play: it is no contradiction to say that play is their work. Through play they learn almost everything they need to know, at the time when they need to know it. Research from the 1980s onward has shown that children who are played with develop what psychologists call the 'theory of mind' *up to a year earlier* than those devoid of this stimulus.

This 'theory of mind', the awareness that other people have different minds, thoughts and reactions from the child's own, is quite crucial to child development at every level, emotional, social and intellectual. 'Pretend play' like Hide and Seek helps children to realize that they are separate from others, and that each person has his or her own reality. Before the age of 2, children playing this game are likely to put their hands over their eyes and say 'Hiding!', thinking that because they cannot see anything, no one else can see either, and above all that no one can see them. After about the age of 2, however, they grasp that there are two sets of vision, theirs and others', and that they have to conceal themselves away from the eyes of onlookers to be truly unseen.

In all types of play, though, it is important to listen to the children concerned, to feel for them, to join in when it is appropriate, and supervise closely when it is not. Above all, they must be allowed to choose, to make their own decisions from the earliest age, and to control their own small world. For the truly happy families allow their members to co-exist peacefully each at their own level, to be, and to feel, both at one with the group and a separate and self-standing individual. Such families confer what Alice Miller has defined as 'a healthy self-feeling', the certainty that the feelings and wishes one is experiencing are part of one's self:

> This certainty is not something one can gain upon reflection; it is there like one's own pulse, which one does not notice as long as it is functioning normally. This automatic, natural contact with his own emotions and wishes gives an individual strength and *self-esteem*.

No one seriously disputes that the foundations for such 'strength and self-esteem' are laid in the family. The empowering force that it remains for most of us is tellingly indicated by the fact that in the face of any distress, most of us wish to turn back to that warmth and security, while in the eye of any success or achievement, we still wish to lay our triumph at our parents' feet for their approval, just as we did the first well-smudged finger-painting from playschool, wobbly hand-made ceramic, or overcooked product of the cookery class.

By the same token, most of our life wounds come from the same place.

The child is father to the moan . . .

What happens when the family's force for good is transmuted into a force for pain and destruction? How does it come about that those who should protect us, our ever-loving parents, are the very ones who, in the poet Blake's vision of love perverted into eternal torment, make a child's Heaven into one endless, unutterable Hell?

•••

Love seeketh only self to please,
To bind another to its delight,
Joys in another's loss of ease,
And builds a Hell in Heaven's despite.

William Blake, 'The Clod and the Pebble'

•••

CHAPTER 6

Love and Non-Love

People who neglect their children in the grossest ways
more often than not will consider themselves the most
loving of parents . . . love and non-love, as good and evil,
are objective and not purely subjective phenomena.

M. Scott Peck, *The Road Less Travelled* (1983)

All happy families resemble one another. Each unhappy
family is unhappy in its own way.

Leo Tolstoy, *Anna Karenina* (1878)

W HY DO SO MANY PARENTS make their children unhappy,
when they have almost certainly started out with entirely the opposite
intentions? How can the love almost automatically given to a tiny
baby curdle into the non-love which breaks out as family tension,
conflict, cruelty and neglect?

At some level, all wrongs to children must spring from our inability
to remember what it was to be a child. Most of us will find it difficult
to handle a child in the way it deserves if we were ourselves subjected to the kind of treatment that denies a child's needs and rights,
blunting our sense as parents of what young people rightly can or
should receive. All childhoods are unhappy, whether we know it or
not, said Dostoevsky: if this is true, it must mean that most of those
responsible for children's happiness, their parents, were unhappy in
childhood too, whether they knew it or not. And since most will not
wish to acknowledge this, they will not want any demonstration of
their child's unhappiness to resurrect the pain of their own.

Such parents may indeed punish the child all the more severely,
the more she or he reminds them of their own long-buried past. 'I
had been abused as a child,' Alice Miller writes, 'because my parents
had undergone similar experiences in their childhood, and had
learned to regard that abuse as being for their own good. *Because
they were not allowed to feel and thus understand what had*

happened to them in the past, they were unable to recognise the abuse, and so passed it on without a trace of guilty feeling.'

This denial of awareness and the resulting lack of feeling hold the answer to the question that is invariably raised when some extreme example of child cruelty or neglect comes to light, *how could they do it?* In a random selection of cases reported or prosecuted during the preparation of this book, how could 'they' leave an 8-year-old girl completely alone locked in an empty house for ten days: beat a 10-year-old boy every Sunday night of his life whether he had done anything or not: shut a 12-year-old out of his house all night: tell a 14-year-old that she'll never amount to anything because she's just shit, *shit*, SHIT!

They can because they do not know any better. Nor have their own experiences of the past ever taught them to expect anything better, if indeed they expect much at all. As professionals in the field are at pains to stress, most ill-treatment of children is not deliberate, not a conscious act of cruelty designed to cause pain: 'The distortion of personality by random, innocent circumstance is much more common than real wickedness,' says the barrister and crime writer Frances Hegarty, who writes as Frances Fyfield.

In real life, then, the highly-coloured 'cruel father' or 'wicked step-mother' who have dominated the explanation of such events from the days of folk tales down to the tabloid accounts of the present day are rarely found among those who make children unhappy, whether in the perfect drawing-rooms of the coldly rich or the cramped tenements of the decaying towns and cities of the world. There the occurrence of deprivation and neglect, insensitivity and brutality are no pantomime-style special events, but regular features of daily life, unnoticed because unfelt.

Many offences against children are indeed almost invisible, unseen because unquestioned, even passed off as the actions of good parents. Jonathan bitterly resented the fact that his father had prevented him from going to university, keeping him at home under his thumb to work in the family business. As an adult he now makes great play of the fact that his own son Tim is at college, openly inviting praise for his own more liberal stance in contrast with his father's old-style bullying.

But in Jonathan's insistence that Tim could only read a subject of his choice, in the deliberate withholding of money to keep the young man on the tightest possible rein, above all in the unquestioning assumption that Tim too will join the family business as soon as he leaves college because 'he'll bloody well owe it to us by then!', Jonathan shows that he has learned only too well the lessons of patriarchal control. Latterly he has begun to resent Tim's lack of affection for him, and gloweringly looks forward to the time when Tim will feel the weight of 'coming into the business': it will be the making of him, he declares, for after all, 'the old man knew what he was doing: it made a man of me.'

What kind of man? is the question no one asks. A heavy smoker, alcoholic, and a compulsive womanizer, Jonathan has shown that he can only manage his life one gasp, one gulp, one grope at a time. But those who do not learn from the past are always condemned to repeat its mistakes. The parents who refuse the task of confronting, examining and reassessing their own history and how their parents handled them, yet continue to insist that every offence against them, every cruelty visited upon them was 'for their own good', will always stay locked inside that still small circle of their own peculiar hell.

• • •

The concept of cycles is crucial, because cycles are not only difficult to break, they are addictive. The most primitive part of our brain, the reptilian, contains our most primitive strategy for safety and survival – repetition . . . We cling grimly to a familiar pattern, even when it's clearly not working.

Arminta Wallace, 'The Family That Frays Together . . .'

• • •

One of the healthiest signs of today's parenting can be seen in the fact that some adults are at last beginning to break the cycles of repetition by speaking out about the life wounds that their own upbringing has inflicted upon them. 'We are admitting that there is an issue here,' says psychotherapist Robin Skynner, co-author with John Cleese of *Families and How to Survive Them*. 'We no longer think that we have to pretend to be perfect.' Bette Midler has shared the pain of a childhood darkened by emotional and financial poverty, by the bitterness of her mother and the coldness of her father, 'a real withholding kind of guy: I don't remember a single time he ever gave her a kiss.'

People think of 'Bette Midler' now, she says, as 'bold, brazen, bright and bawdy, take no prisoners, noise, noise noise.' But who is she really?

I'm the waif sitting in the corner, the shrivelled-up little waif, the little worm in the corner. You can't imagine what it's like to live inside me with these emotions constantly beating at the gate. I look at other people and I think they must be dead. I am definitely not dead, but I wish some of this stuff would lie down for a while.

'The Divine Miss M' is struggling hard with 'this stuff', not only in her relationship with her daughter Sophie, 'the strongest, closest love I've ever had', but in her work: she described her outré persona as 'the Queen of Camp' as 'everything you were afraid your little girl would grow up to be – and your little boy!' Nor is it any coincidence that she chose to produce and star in a new remake of *Stella Dallas*, the 1925 film portrait of a woman who believes she is not good enough to mother her own daughter, and so gives her up.

Bette Midler's range of abilities, like that of Samuel Beckett, allows her at least the possibility of a creative reworking of her childhood. This remedy for a poverty-stricken and hungry youth was not available to the reared-in-deprivation Jackie Kennedy Onassis, for whom the word 'shopaholic' was invented, or to the mentally barefoot Imelda Marcos, caught for ever transfixed in the headlights of history by the hideous and telling grandiosity of her 2,700 pairs of shoes.

•••

> Abandonment includes the following: neglect of
> developmental dependency needs: abuse of any kind:
> enmeshment into the covert or overt needs of the parents or
> any family system needs.
>
> John Bradshaw, *Healing the Shame*
> *That Binds You* (1988)

•••

For it is crucial to recognize that *from the moment we come together as male and female to make a family, what we create is not simply a unit, but a system*, a series of connections to our own past and to that of our parents, which together can form a more powerful and deadening imperative than we can ever imagine in advance. In its most benign form, this manifested itself in my mother-in-law's firm pronouncement on my first pregnancy that a boy was undoubtedly on the way, because 'Mileses have sons'. She had had two boys, as had her other daughter-in-law, so that was that.

But my family ran to girls. When my daughter arrived, around the time of my sister's first daughter and my other sister's second, mother-in-law was delighted, but deeply disconcerted too. And for the remainder of her life there was always a certain self-consciousness in her relation to her granddaughter that was simply absent from her dealings with 'the boys', including my own son.

Mother-in-law lived and died in sweet ignorance of family systems theory, and without harming a fly. The damage comes when any family system takes over the lives of its children, denying their autonomy and predestining them to repeat the sufferings of the past, or to echo them by creating new patterns of their own. This is particularly visible in the high-profile lives of stars like Judy Garland and Liza Minnelli, where the child seems almost pre-programmed to live out her mother's triumphs and disasters and to make the same mistakes. But it may afflict any family, high or low. When suburban secretary Wanda Holloway felt that her 13-year-old daughter Shanna was not achieving the high-school success and popularity that were her due, she did not react like any other downhome US mom. Instead she hired a hit-man to search out her daughter's chief rival and her mother, and to kill them both.

On trial for attempted murder in Houston, Texas, a tight-lipped Wanda gave no indication of why it was so important to her that Shanna should become cheerleader of her class, even at the cost of human life. Nor did the defence reveal any childhood hurts or slights that might lie behind this extraordinary move, still less the family expectations that had made Wanda so homicidally certain that her daughter and hers alone had to be the leader of the band. But the depth of the wound is evident from the response. The tragedy is that so many women must have identified with the desperate Wanda, not with the young victim or her mother, if only in their hearts.

Most children do not find that their parents will literally kill in order to ensure that they live up to what the family expects. But too many children at every level still suffer a routine denial of their rights of self-determination and a systematic invasion of their personal boundaries in the name of a family tradition that no one can question, and none reject. Nancy Cooper comes from 'a dynasty of medics', and from her earliest days was made to feel ashamed of reading novels and poetry, and gaining poor grades in scientific subjects. She worked hard enough to win a place at Cambridge to read medicine, even to gain entry to the high-prestige formerly all-male college where her grandfather, father and brothers had studied, rather than to the women's college attended by her mother. But it was no good, she says:

> I just couldn't do it. There came a point where I was working like a slave and it still wasn't good enough, I just couldn't do it. I can't describe the misery and hopelessness, I think I must have had some kind of nervous breakdown. At any rate, I dropped out after three years without getting a degree. That meant I had blown my chance of higher education, so of course after all these brilliant doctors, I was instantly branded as the family imbecile, a real failure. I've never really amounted to much since then. That was my chance, and I wasn't up to it.

It was my fault . . .
I wasn't good enough . . .
Again and again this refrain surfaces in the lament of those who have failed to live up to a family system. Even when the sufferer develops a little more insight into the part played by others after years of analysis or self-analysis, the sense is still strong that somehow they themselves were really to blame all along. Beverley Davison, daughter of a leading British conductor, was a child prodigy at 3, and a virtuoso violinist among the handful of exceptionally gifted young musicians chosen to attend the Yehudi Menuhin School at 9. At 25, after an unsuccessful struggle against a growing stage fright which would literally paralyse her before every performance, she 'got on the telephone, and cancelled a year's work in 20 minutes'. But only her sister would acknowledge her distress: 'The rest of the family would not mention it at all because they thought I was crazy. I had broken the mould,' she says.

A family more inclined to judge itself rather than its offspring might have wondered at its own part in making Beverley so 'crazy' that her 'slim, elegant' body ballooned up to 22 stone through bouts of overeating. Beverley herself attributes her problem to 'being a good little girl' who at the same time was denied a normal childhood. Even then, however, she takes the blame on herself: 'I had this need to win my parents' approval . . . my problem was not the violin but what I had been doing on it.' Not a word against the family, the system that had made her what she is.

Yet how fair is it – how realistic, even – to blame parents for what they do not know they do? In families with any kind of a 'problem child', therapists commonly find that the individual is only part of a wider system of dysfunction, which has to be addressed before there can be any hope of change. In the families of alcoholics, for instance, it is commonplace now to discover that many either come from families with a similar history, or have partners or children who are alcoholic or suffering from other addictions, or both.

'My parents were the original Sixties hop-heads, they did everything that moved, grew or flew on the face of the earth,' says Melody. 'For me it was just a natural progression.' A natural progression into an alcoholism and heroin addiction that, at 30, she is still trying to overcome. Could Melody or the millions like her ever say to their parents, *you could have taught me so much – how come you taught me this?*

• • •

> They fuck you up, your mum and dad,
> They may not mean to, but they do.
> They fill you with the faults they had,
> And add some extra, just for you.
>
> Philip Larkin, 'This Be the Verse'

• • •

Man hands on misery to man, broods Philip Larkin, himself the son of a man who kept a statue of Hitler on his mantelpiece and thought the Führer had some pretty good ideas about life; *it deepens like a coastal shelf* . . .

Some parents, it is true, are able to see when the family system does not suit a particular child, and make the necessary changes. Cambridge-educated merchant banker and novelist Janet Cohen speaks with great honesty of the pain involved in taking this step:

Our problem with Henry, our elder son who is now 19, was that we were trying to force him to do something he just didn't want to do. He was 16 and we wanted him to get good A-levels and go to university. He wanted to be a horse-rider and take part in three-day events, and wasn't interested in further education at all. We spent the most appalling two years trying to push him down the route we expected him to follow. It was a non-stop battle beween us and him — awful and futile. We should have recognized a true vocation, for he certainly has one . . . *the trouble was that no one in the family had done anything like it before* [italics inserted].

But for every parent who eventually comes to see that the system may not suit the individual, there are countless numbers who will stick to the predetermined script even to the point of family estrangement and breakdown. Such parents cannot come to see where they are going wrong, because they do not see at all. They do not listen and they do not look. When they hear, they do not believe. When they believe, they will usually disagree, reserving the right to be always right while the child is in the wrong. Mohtilal Patel, a wealthy London industrialist, repeatedly insisted that his son must accept an arranged marriage, as Patel himself had 40 years before. But Chandra Patel had been born and brought up in Britain, and he argued furiously that he had the right to make his own decision.

Finally Chandra told his father that the choice had been made: he was in love with a fellow-student at London University and they were planning to marry as soon as they graduated. At this Mohtilal hastened on his plans, choosing a girl from among his contacts in India and arranging to have her flown to England without delay. At the time he was supposed to be meeting his bride-to-be at the airport, Chandra Patel lay down on a petrol-soaked bed beneath a photograph of his girlfriend, and set fire to himself, dying in the flames.

• • •

The way I see the world, we are all constantly at risk from the people we love most. They, after all, are the only people who can do us serious damage, a damage that lasts for ever.

Jennifer Johnston

• • •

Is it possible to state too often that *we must listen to our children*, pay attention to them before it is too late? No parent will find this easy to do, still less to live by, while we are ourselves struggling simply to stay afloat or fighting to make something of ourselves, to build a career or carve out a living, to make our mark. This in fact constitutes one of the most common forms of neglect, the determination on the part of the parents to follow their own dream, to get to the end of their own personal, private rainbow, no matter what the cost. Film actress Glenn Close had a wonderful childhood, she says, roaming free with her brothers and sisters on her parents' 250-acre farm in Connecticut. It was just a shame that it had to end when she was 7.

That was the point at which her parents, as working lay members of a semi-religious sect, moved to the Belgian Congo, then in the throes of its bloody struggle for independence. With the establishment of the Republic of Zaire, Close's father stayed on to work for President Mobutu, overseeing the establishment of medical installations all over the country, only to have his life's work overthrown as soon as he left. He sacrificed his children to his broken dream, Close feels now, sending them away to boarding schools and so amputating their childhood. Glenn Close is among many who now say, 'I suffered from being separated from my parents.'

Looking back, it is astonishing to recall the confidence, the callousness even, with which young children were formerly 'sent away' to school, simply dispatched like packages, removed from circulation. While Enid Blyton diverted children all over the world with her never-ending sagas of the Famous Five and their friends having fun, her own two daughters were firmly packed off to languish at a girls' boarding school in the Midlands. While they were there, the level of interest that the famous children's author showed in her offspring led the staff to call them 'the blighted Enids'.

At least they were in their own country. The film-maker Don Boyd was sent from his home in Kenya to the rugged Scots public school of Loretto by his father, for no better reason, Boyd remembers, than that 'they played rugby, he was obsessed with the sport, he wanted me to play rugby for Scotland.' As the 9-year-old Boyd was being driven to the plane, his mother began to cry, imploring her husband not to let the boy go. Worse was to come:

I remember getting on to the Bristol Britannia turbo-prop plane at Nairobi airport, and looking out of the window, and seeing my mother literally running down the airstrip towards the plane in floods of tears. It looked as if she was screaming, 'Don't go, don't go.' That was an absolutely ghastly moment because I knew I wasn't going to see her for over a year, and I was very close to her. And that event ruined our family. I am certain that in sending me to boarding school when we were a close-knit family and pretty happy, it caused the splitting of the family, and my mother became an alcoholic, and my parents divorced 10 years later ... And that affected me at school, but it wasn't because of the school, it was because of my parents.

It was because of my parents ...

So much of a child's life is 'because of my parents' that it remains a runnning sore how rarely parents seem to take this into account. Frances Hegarty has spoken of a doctor father so supremely self-involved that he was capable of driving right past her on an open country road without seeing her at all: 'He taught me never to rely on anyone,' she says. Visiting days at her convent boarding school 'began with such high hopes and always ended with a fight', until she realized that her parents 'could never be trusted to give advice': 'my childhood ended at 10'.

Another victim of middle-class neglect, the actor and comedian Robin Williams, seems never to have had a childhood at all. Wearing a blazer and carrying a little briefcase everywhere he went, he grew up as a lonely mini-adult in a 30-room mansion in Detroit: 'I played with myself and that's the only joke about it.'

Williams's father, a Ford Motors executive, was, in the classic litany of today's complaint against absentee fathers, too busy with his work to pay much attention to his son. When the mother is absent too, even if she works alongside the father in the family business, the child is doubly orphaned. The chef Anton Mosimann recalls a childhood of what sounds like crippling solitude:

I was an only child, and I was very lonely when I was growing up. I got up in the morning, and cooked myself breakfast, then I went to school by myself.

Mosimann's father, a restaurateur, was 'married to his business', and his mother, as the child discovered, was married to both.

But loneliness was not the only peril besetting the neglected child. When he was 10 years old and alone at home one night, the house was entered by a burglar currently terrorizing the neighbourhood, who as the child knew, had already killed two of the local towns-people in their homes. Hiding under the bed, Mosimann saw the intruder come into his room and stand within a foot or two of him, before ransacking the bedroom and the rest of the house. The boy was still under the bed, paralysed with terror, when his parents came home, several hours later.

The killer was caught, but that was not the end of the story for Mosimann:

> I never had a good night's sleep afterwards. I used to wake about 2 or 3 in the morning worried that the burglar would come back and kill me ... When I read about burglaries or murders in the newspaper I still get goosebumps. I still have nightmares: hearing his footsteps on the stairs, breathlessly watching those wet shoes and being afraid something awful would happen to me ... Even now, in those dreams, I pray that he will not look under the bed ... The terror is as acute now as it was for that 10-year-old boy. I have never talked about it since.

• • •

> Laugh, and the world laughs with you,
> Weep, and you weep alone ...

> Ella Wheeler Wilcox, 'The Way of the World'

• • •

Home alone ...

A flurry of recent real-life cases on both sides of the Atlantic have cast a questioning light on the irresponsible, even dangerous trivialization of the issue in the 1991 film starring Macauley Culkin. The dam-breakers of public opinion on this issue were Chicagoans Sharon and David Schoo, who pushed off for a little winter sun at Christmastime 1992, leaving their daughters Nicole, aged 9, and Diane, 4, at home alone with a list of instructions about food, bathing and bedtime. On their return, the Schoos briefly became the most hated couple in Christendom, a hatred increased rather than diminished in May 1993 when they were sentenced to what *Time* magazine described as 'the mild judicial spanking' of community service and 30 days of house arrest as a taste of their own 'home alone' medicine.

The Schoos' was a bizarre and blatant act of neglect revealing an almost pathological coldness. But there has to be a deeper explanation of the almost hysterical frenzy their action aroused across the world, a frantic loathing of the sort previously reserved, in America at least, for Commies, fags, and draft-dodgers. Certainly the Schoo case tapped into all the hidden US angst about the Brett Easton Ellis, *Less Than Zero* generation, the over-pampered kids who may have their own TVs and VCRs, their own computers, analysts and cars, who can have anything they want except get ten minutes of their parents' time.

But at a simpler level, the truth is that many parents do not have the best time in the company of their own children. This fact is cheerfully acknowledged by travel companies and tour operators who build into their holiday packages special arrangements to take the happy holidaymakers' children off their hands on any trip from the moment of touchdown. In France, as in the US, children are sent off to *colonies de vacances* as early as five years of age. They may then be packed off without their parents every summer for the next twenty years, and no one finds this strange.

For the less privileged, 'home alone' has always been an all-the-year-round reality, not an annual holiday treat. Many children alone in the past did not even have a home to be alone in: little Jo the crossing-sweeper in Charles Dickens's *Bleak House* was typical of the thousands who, like the armies of the motherless still roaming cities from Rio de Janeiro to Bogotá, have no home but the streets. In Britain today, millions of working women may not want to leave their children alone, but have no choice: for today's 7 million British schoolchildren, there are fewer than 300 after-school schemes to take care of the under-14s who have working mothers. As a result, a fifth of all school-age children are now left alone throughout the school holidays, and a sixth go home every night to an empty house. World-wide, where they did not exist already, 'home alones' have proliferated rapidly in tandem with the recession. This situation is unlikely to change as long as women continue to be co-opted into the labour force as a cheaper, more tractable alternative to men.

Yet still the child left at home alone will be able to distinguish between the mother valiantly struggling to make ends meet, and the self-absorbed narcissist whose attitude to his or her child seems to be 'out of sight, out of mind'. The British mother who hit the head-lines in the summer of 1993 when it was revealed that she had left her 11-year-old daughter to fend for herself while she holidayed with her boyfriend in Spain, similarly defended herself from any charges of not caring for her child. It was all a stunt, she said, on the part of the   girl:

> Gemma is a very talented little actress, and she has pulled this off. I am not a wicked mother, in fact she is a wicked daughter. I have had au pairs and nannies – everything for that child.

Everything, in fact, except the attention the child clearly craved. Despite a hue and cry for her arrest, and a court hearing which resulted in her daughter being made a ward of court and taken into care, Yasmin Gibson refused to curtail her trip:

> I will come back on the date of my return ticket, in about another couple of weeks. Gemma is not coming here, and from what I hear she is happy and has people to play with. She has got to an age where she is being awkward and playing me up. She is a real madam and has a big ego. She makes up all sorts of stories and even pretended to have a broken foot once. Gemma is looking for attention. But I still love her very much.

What are we to make of the last two sentences: *Gemma is looking for attention*, but in spite of that, the mother seems to suggest, *I still love her very much*? It is the incontrovertible mark of the narcissistic parent to interpret a child's cry for attention not as a need in the child, but as a reproach to her or himself. The woman writing as 'Helen Braid' in a recent controversial account of throwing her 15-year-old son Tom out of her house and her life, blames everything on the feelings her son expressed from the moment she left his father. 'He was angry from the moment I drove away,' she says. 'He turned his face against the change with a cold, passive determination.'

This monster of implacability was 3 years old at the time. Three years later Tom's mother had had another son by the man who had replaced his father in Helen's life. Again Tom was blamed for his response: 'The hostile silence he's always adopted towards us is actually very aggressive,' Helen says. As things deteriorated, Tom took refuge more and more in silence. After another set-to, Helen told her son, 'I'm sick of you, sick of your miserable face. Jim and I would be happy if it wasn't for you. Why don't you go and live with your father and leave us alone?'

That, Helen admits, was saying the unsayable, doing the unforgivable, in the war against her son. Tom left at once, and never came back. Now 18, he has put even more distance between himself and his mother, leaving England to live and work abroad. But Helen is unrepentant. 'To salvage the family – my husband and other son – he had to go. The three of us were at the end of our tether. If he had stayed, it would have split the marriage. So there was really no alternative.' And it was the right decision, Helen feels, for Tom's own good too: 'I think he needed to go, to find himself. Perhaps in future he will look back and see it as the right decision.'

• • •

> Can we blame a woman who did not know any better?
> Today I would say that we not only can but must blame such
> a parent, so that we can bring to light what happens to
> children hour by hour, and also enable the unhappy mothers
> to become aware of what was inflicted on them in their
> childhood.
>
> Alice Miller, Banished Knowledge (1990)

• • •

In what sense can the word 'right' be employed of Helen's decision here? How did the existence of a second family come to obliterate all the rights of a previous son? Helen clearly has such a strong feeling of being in the right that even her child's suffering is converted into her own pain: 'I felt so alone,' she complains.

This unfortunate son now faces the bleak realization that becoming an adult occurs as soon as you have to take over your own parenting, because the grown-ups around are incapable of doing it for you. On this definition, there are now very many young people at large in the world who have been forced into premature adulthood before their time, thrust unwillingly from home by the simple derelictions of those whose task it should be to keep them safe there, and whose failure will stay with their young victims for the rest of their lives. Some are abandoned so early in life that they can have no memory of a warm and secure family unit. Others are condemned to endure their loneliness within a unit purporting to be a happy family: these may in fact suffer more acutely than those who can at least see their own situation clearly, and look it in the face.

For a 'family unit' usually consists of more than simply mother, father, child; and the family drama readily expands to take in more players than the three familiar from the classic Freudian triangle. 'I believe that in the best of households there lurks brutality,' says Frances Hegarty. In a profound shift of psychoanalytical thinking, researchers are now recognizing a vital dimension of child development and potential abuse within family life that has previously been almost totally overlooked.

For hostile relationships with siblings will not normally be confined to the 'rivalry' parents have learned to look for on the arrival of a new baby, but may continue for the rest of the children's lives. 'People have been too much preoccupied with parent/child relationships,' says developmental psychologist Dr Judy Dunn. 'Eighty per cent of us have siblings, and children spend more time interacting with them than with their parents.'

Some of the greatest miseries and tyrannies most of us can remember will have been inflicted by siblings rather than by those ostensibly in control of them and of us all, the nominal powerholders, the parents. At the James Bulger trial, evidence was given that one of the 10-year-old boys who tortured the 2-year-old to death had been systematically and sadistically bullied by his six older brothers in turn. Even in normal families, feelings can run dangerously high. The actress Michèle Wade, proprietor of the legendary Soho patisserie Maison Bertaux, recalls her sister's reaction to another new arrival in the family:

> When our brother was born she was very jealous of him. I remember her leaning over the cot, examining this new creature, then trying to push his eyes in. Another time she tried to set fire to him. But it was never in a malicious way.

And this was not just a flash in the pan. Life in the Wade household seems to have been full of pranks of this kind, as Michèle recollected her playtimes with her younger brothers and sisters:

> When I was about six I decided to paint them all yellow because I'd read a book about the Chinese. I found some thick, heavy, yellow emulsion and painted them from head to toe, between their legs and under their arms. They were in absolute misery and started to cry because they couldn't breathe . . . We had to buy bottles of turpentine and sit on newspaper. It went on for

about a week. Our skin was raw and we had to have our hair cut.

Her sister Tania has her own memories of the family fun: coerced into making a shepherd's pie when Tania had friends to dinner, Michèle obliged by serving it up with bits of Tania's underwear cooked in with the filling: 'When I cut into it I pulled out my bra with all this meat hanging off it. Everyone left immediately,' Tania observes cheerfully. But still, she insists, never were there such devoted sisters: 'There has never been any tension or conflict between us.'

Of all the highly-coloured, not to say hand-embellished Wade family memoirs, none can be a greater figment of wishful thinking than this. For the lifelong competition between siblings is not simply to see who gets the most yellow paint. 'Children of the same family are locked in a struggle whose roots go back to the fight for survival,' comments Tom Snowden. 'Older children see each new arrival as diminishing their own share of the available resources, and fight to preserve their dominance. Younger children see the older ones as "taking their light", so they fight to get out from under and to catch up. So each child is constantly fighting on two fronts, struggling to get their parents' attention, and also to get power over each other.'

These power games may be conducted with a bitterness and determination to inflict pain which parents do not acknowledge at all. 'I remember really horrible games of Monopoly at home,' recalls Polly, 'when the whole idea was to trash everyone else, and really humiliate you for losing':

> I was the youngest in the family, and not much good at maths even when I wasn't in a panic about adding up, so I didn't have a chance. I absolutely hated it, but I was always made to play, or my brothers would complain to mother and get me into trouble for not being a good sport. I'm sure our mother believed we were just one big happy family when we were all in the sitting-room absorbed in this game. But I can still remember the misery and humiliation of it. And I still can't stand board games or any games much, to this day.

Small wonder then that in these circumstances, feelings of rage and powerlessness can drive a child to actions beyond its years. 'I can remember going for my older sister with a knife, I really would have killed her if I could,' says Rosemary, now a university lecturer. 'And what I remember most about it is that my parents knew about this, knew how viciously we attacked each other and fought, and *did nothing about it*. My father used to say fatuous things like "little birds in their nests agree". Neither he nor my mother ever tried to get to the bottom of our conflicts and really sort things out.'

In fact it is rare, says Tom Snowden, for parents to intervene to resolve their children's conflicts. Intervention is usually triggered only when the parent becomes annoyed, and any action is designed to stop the quarrel because it is annoying the adults, not to get to the bottom of it. And unless they ask, most parents will have little idea of what is going on: the powerful taboo among children against being a 'sneak' forbids them to 'rat' on each other or 'grass each other up'. The child who does 'tell' is likely to be even more severely bullied, tormented or punished afterwards, and like the battered wife in her own home, has nowhere to run and nowhere to hide.

But even when the parents are aware of their children's conflicts, they often fail to take them seriously enough, it seems. 'There is a widespread belief that children have to learn to sort these things out for themselves, in particular to stand up for themselves, and learn how to fight,' says University of Warwick child developmental expert Dr Janet Gilmore. 'This may be fair enough in the playground among their peers, but it's a false doctrine of equality when applied to the family. You must always remember that your children can never be equal. One will always be taller, older, bigger, or cleverer than the others. When that child establishes dominance, the others can really suffer. And there's absolutely nothing they can do.'

Tell Paula about it. 'My brother was the eldest, and he never forgave Nicola and me for being girls,' she recalls:

> He made our lives a misery from the first moment I can remember. Jumping on us in the dark, making us play games where he made up the rules, establishing humiliating forfeits if we failed, it was a nightmare. He hit us all the time, he really knew how to make it hurt. We especially dreaded the nights my parents used to go out: he had us completely in his power then.

Like Rosemary, Paula tried in vain to alert her parents to what she was going through. 'But mother just used to smile indulgently and say, "Don't be silly, dear, Martin *doesn't* hate you, he *loves* you, this is his way of showing affection."' With a failed marriage, several failed relationships and a career stalled through her low self-esteem and failure to assert herself, Paula is still trying to come to terms with the impact of Martin's 'affection'.

Paula can perhaps feel thankful that at least her vicious, bullying brother stopped short of overt injury. The charity ChildLine, set up to allow children in Britain a point of telephone contact in cases of abuse, now receives 15 per cent of its calls from those suffering not from abusive adults but from the violence and hostility of the other children of their own family. The Child Protection Unit of London's Scotland Yard recorded 318 cases of sibling violence in 1991, including 2 murders and 30 cases of grievous bodily harm. These extreme cases almost certainly represent only the famous 'tip of the iceberg' so familiar to all investigators of family or abusive assaults. For every child whose emotional distress or physical suffering becomes acute enough to warrant police intervention, there must be legions of others whose cries go unheard.

What should parents do to guard against the bully in the family? Get rid of the idea that 'blood is thicker than water', and that when children fight, 'it's six of one and half a dozen of the other,' advises child care guru Dr Penelope Leach. 'There's this great desire to assume, "Yes, it's a love/hate relationship, but the love is always stronger than the hate",' she says. 'That's probably true, but you have to be alert to the possibility that it isn't. Parents have to ask themselves, "Would this behaviour be acceptable if it was school friends rather than siblings?"'

Ask yourself, then, would you allow a child who had come to play to hit your child and reduce it to tears? To tease it so mercilessly that the child ends up screaming in helpless fury? To undermine its confidence and humiliate it with cruel nicknames and constant destructive jibes? To institute sadistic games that your child always loses?

All social behaviour begins at home. Children who become anti-social, either violent or bullying, alienated or criminal, take their first steps down this path from their own homes. It is vital, then, for parents to check this behaviour from the very start: to intervene to uphold the weaker and to inhibit the stronger, in order to prevent both from learning damaging patterns of behaviour for their lives ahead.

•••

So was it when my life began . . .
The Child is Father of the Man,
And I could wish my days to be
Bound each to each by natural piety.

William Wordsworth, 'My Heart Leaps Up'

•••

Clearly the children we deserve, deserve better than to spend their
childhood in fear of others of their own kind. Children who make
themselves a source of pain and terror to other children are not born
with this ability – they learn it, just as surely as they learn to walk
and talk. Much will be gained if every parent will shoulder the responsibility for greater vigilance against antisocial behaviour among
children, becoming swifter to observe and more determined to understand and correct it. There is still much work to be done in this area
of family awareness on behalf of the world's children, by their
parents and by us all.

For the world remains in love with the myth of the happpy family,
no matter how far it departs from any recognizable reality. One of
the most heavily mythologized families in recent history has been the
Kennedy clan, where the seniors posed as model parents to a brood
of brilliant, high-achieving, loving and well-behaved kids. But along
with the 'Galahad' image of the compulsively lecherous JFK and the
tattered banner of his 'Camelot' presidency, this piece of fabrication
has failed to stand the test of time. Both Rose and Joe, writes R. W.
Johnson, 'were extremely bad parents, and the household they
created was an emotional wasteland for their compulsively driven
siblings.'

Joe, it is true, had always been known by those around him as a
louse of the first water, a vicious bully with men, a gross and vulgar
lecher with women, a thorough-going crook towards all, and a rotten
borough of corruption at the heart of American politics. Rose's halo
as the great Catholic matriarch indeed took on an extra lustre from
this: she won universal plaudits for holding her family together
despite all that her wretched husband could throw at her.

Yet what her mothering meant in practice is only slowly beginning
to emerge – month-long stretches when young Jack lay in hospital
without a single visit from his mother, school reports which showed

Jack as having a higher IQ than his elder brother Joe returned by Rose as inaccurate, so sure was she that her favourite was the best. As a mother she could not bear to kiss her children or even to touch them, except to beat them. All her sons thereafter seem to have been left with a pathological need for approval and validation so strong that a family of four sons created one who wanted to run for President, and three who did.

For the wounds of childhood last for ever, and the knowledge of growing up without a parent's unconditional love leaves a void that no later success or triumph can ever fill. No matter how well the young Kennedys did in class, Joe Senior would brush it aside with the simple demand, *why weren't you first?* When the child is made so bleakly aware that all parental love, all approval, is contingent on achievement, then the way ahead is set.

Coldness, neglect, unreason, abandonment, the use of love as a bargaining counter, all these cause a suffering that can hardly be cured. It is an enduring paradox that the families which traditionally expect the highest achievement from the individual often do so within a system and a framework which also demands the highest degree of conformity with group or family values: Winston Churchill suffered all his young life from his early failures to follow in the Churchill tradition of social dominance and worldly success, and the late great style guru Diana Vreeland built a whole life in defiance of the family disappointment that she was not a society beauty and accomplished sportswoman like her mother and all her other female relatives.

The expectations which have power to damage a child may not even be those of high performance. 'Family values' can be negative as well as positive, and like them inflicted not from malice but from the simple refusal to grant the child the right to its own untrammelled existence outside the confines of the tribal group. So the father of 4-year-old Stephen, found to be completely mute for no physical reason when he started nursery school, angrily refused the offer of speech therapy for the boy with the declaration, 'All our family, we're men of few words.' His wife agreed. 'Steve'll talk when he's ready. My husband's brother didn't talk till he was ten. And my husband doesn't want Steve turned into one of these rabbiting nancy-boys!'

From the moment we peer into the pram and demand to know whether a new baby is like its father or its mother, we are all guilty of interpreting a child in terms of its known communal past rather than of its undiscovered personal future. To allow a baby to find and develop its own innate self and true potential, we should:

- Foster individualism in every child from the very earliest age.

- Defend its right to grow up without fear of victimization by any family member.

- Spend as much time as possible helping each child to explore different explanations of the world, to ask questions and to come up with its own answers.

- Equip it to make its own choices and provide plenty of opportunities to do so.

- Question each statement along the lines of 'there's nothing like that in our family' or 'that's the way things have always been'.

- Discourage other family members or interested parties from expecting or rewarding conformity.

- Value the individual over the system.

- Maintain strict fairness and equality within the family and always intervene to see that justice is done.

- Check any emerging signs of violence or bullying and visit the strongest sanctions on any offender.

- Welcome contacts outside the family and encourage children to develop friendships with as wide a range of people as possible.

- Listen to our children, pay attention to their differences, and allow them the right of self-determination at every stage.

Yet who could be more self-determined, it might be argued, than a woman who becomes an international singing sensation, or a man who rises to be President of the United States? Many of these sufferers from parental cruelty or neglect, from Bette Midler to John F. Kennedy, have gone on to high achievement and international acclaim. Their homes produced not child killers but child stars. Even the mute Stephen was to find his tongue at school, chattering to the other children, his teacher reported, 'as if a dam has been unblocked'. Anton Mosimann, Robin Williams and many other unhappy children have grown up to add significantly to the sum of human happiness through their work, and whatever misery they endured has not been passed on as violence, mayhem, crime. We need to dig deeper, then, to find the root of children's evil. And we are so far nowhere near the depths of the evil that may be done to them.

• • •

> Family tradition,
> The strength of this land,
> Where what's right and wrong
> Is the back of your hand,
> Turns girls into women
> And a boy to a man,
> And the rights of the children
> Have nowhere to stand.
>
> k.d.lang

• • •

III

BREAKING AWAY

She's leaving home
After living alone
For so many years . . .

John Lennon and Paul McCartney,
'She's Leaving Home'

CHAPTER 7

Keeping It In The Family

We have been appallingly slow to wake up to the
prevalence and far-reaching consequences of violent
behaviour between members of a family, and especially
the violence of parents.

Adam Jukes

Every act of punishment has something unjust about it.

Tacitus

Growing up, all children need to break away from the control
of their parents if they are ever to master the secret of self-control.
Every adult needs to be free to develop a strong and healthy personal
identity, independent of family origins, beliefs or rules. Every child
deserves the support of the adult world in this, the deepest of the
heart's early desires. 'I just wanted to be somebody,' said Samuel
Goldwyn, maestro of a thousand heroic myths of self-discovery. *'I
just wanted to be myself.'* All families make this difficult. Difficult
families can make it impossible. And the techniques they employ
range from the bizarre to the frankly cruel, and even unimaginable.

Developing an identity which will be separate and distinct from that
of the surrounding group is one of the most crucial tasks that children
have to undertake, one they cannot manage without adult help and
support. It is also a key area in which they suffer some of the most
grievous wrongs within the power of adults to inflict. Insensitivity
amounting to brutality in the treatment of the young means that many
will make the transition into adulthood scarred for life. But when
psychological maltreatment is compounded by physical or sexual
abuse, the child is left with no true self that it may call its own.

For beating a child, denying it food or freedom to move, assaulting
it physically or sexually, all constitute invasions of the victim's
psychic space as much as intrusions upon its body. Any child who
is subject to the attentions of such an abuser within the family is
indeed living with the equivalent of one of the 'body-snatchers'

beloved of Hollywood horror-movie-makers, the invisible malignity that can steal away the victim's essential self, yet leave all external aspects apparently unchanged. The lost self may be only belatedly recovered, if at all. 'It has taken me 22 years to tell this story', writes a woman survivor of childhood abuse. 'It's time to scream, to believe that screams are heard.'

Yet how often does an abused child scream out, or even raise its voice? When it does, how often is it heard? Such is the myth of the happy family, such is the legal battery of the rights of parents and, for many adults, the rigid creed of non-interference in others' affairs, that very little of what parents do to their children is ever challenged. Do or don't do – the neglect of children, even amounting to virtual abandonment, will often be neither noticed nor prosecuted until the unlucky ones become victims of an accident or crime, or, like the killers of James Bulger, criminal themselves.

Yet everywhere, whether we know it or not, whether we choose to interfere or not, children are suffering while adults stand by. Or worse – the adult standing by may be the source of the suffering, the active perpetrator. So it has been throughout history – for both the physical and sexual maltreatment of children of all social classes have been with us for as long as society itself. As non-believers have pointed out, the very concept of incest in the Judaeo-Christian universe goes back to the Bible, where it is enshrined in the Old Testament account of how God made the world. For unless the offspring of Adam and Eve had had sex with each other or with their parents, there would have been no further generations of Adam's line.

Keeping it in the family . . .

In Ancient Egypt, sisters and brothers of the blood royal were married to one another in childhood in order to keep pure the Pharaonic line. Much the same thinking about the 'purity' of such breeding lay behind the enforced copulation of black slave siblings in the American South, when the slave-owner wished to produce a better 'specimen' to be sold off.

And there was worse, much worse. When the family of a condemned criminal had to die with him in Ancient Rome, the executioners first deflowered any unmarried female of the family, down to the youngest baby girl, to avoid breaking the Roman law which decreed that no virgin could be put to death. Even one who had held the highest offices of state like the great Aelius Sejanus, effective ruler of the Roman empire under the Emperor Tiberius, was unable to save his young daughters from this fate when he fell from power in AD 31. A similar procedure is said by émigrés to be used today against the families of condemned political prisoners in Iran.

Such events may seem remote to us now: the gross cruelties which make us shiver with revulsion convey also the reflex reassurance that *it's not like that any more.* Certainly in the West we do not sell our children into slavery, send them down the mines or up chimneys, farm them out to labour in factories at home or to feed far-flung colonies on the other side of the globe, hoping either to make money out of them or to get them out of our hair. But still parents have the power to do almost what they will with a child: and still a child has no right to control what happens to its body, still less to its tender young mind.

• • •

Spare the rod and spoil the child.

English proverb

• • •

Control – the very word encapsulates the modern dilemma and with it the current debate vexing parents around the world. Where does 'control' end and 'discipline' begin? How can we ensure good and obedient children without recourse to the age-old habit of inflicting pain? As with so many aspects of child-rearing, most of the former certainties about physical punishment have dissolved without any new and agreed guidelines arising to take their place. Like the role of the father itself, the figure who was for centuries both the fount and high court of discipline, the place and purpose of punishment in today's parenting is now subject to as many different definitions as there are punishments and parents. And it can be no surprise then if some choose to err on the side of age-old wisdom, and so overstep the mark.

For the discipline of the past was frequently so harsh as to be indistinguishable from cruelty. Whipping, starvation, confinement: what passed for normal chastisement in former times looks to the eye of today no less than child abuse, open and unchecked. And these punishments were often combined with one another in an intensification of their sadism or brutality: the 17th-century diarist Samuel Pepys casually records beating one of his child-maids, then locking her in the cellar, 'where she lay all night'. Faced with a welter of evidence of this sort, historians of childhood like Lloyd de Mause now suggest that there was no time in history when children were not abused, often horrifyingly, with the full approval of adult society, its parents, its teachers or its church.

For in that world, the reason for punishing children heavily, even savagely, was widely understood and as widely believed. The 17th-century Puritan Dr John Dod, subject of the scurrilous Roman Catholic sally 'Holy Mary, Mother of God/Let me not marry Johnny Dod', taught that all children were born with 'a sparkle of evil' in them, which had to be beaten out like a forest fire, lest it should 'rage over and burn down the whole house'. But parents of other persuasions had plenty of similar authorities to instruct them in the right and need for the physical chastisement of the young. And the annals of child-rearing from the dawn of time down to the present day are stuffed with examples of prolonged and vicious ill-treatment administered to children from babyhood up to marriage – numerous girls like the wretched Lady Jane Grey were birched or beaten right up to the altar to make them take the husband of their parents' choice.

Nor did these harsh methods of child-rearing die out with other savageries of former times such as the rack and thumb-screws, cock-fighting or bear-baiting. It has long been a hollow joke in child care circles that western civilizations learned to suffer first for animals before they began to notice the miseries of children, an order of priorities epitomized in Britain by the creation of the Royal Society for the Prevention of Cruelty to Animals, while the equivalent (and later) body for the protection of children is the much less prestigious National Society. Even today, throughout most of Europe, horse-whips which can no longer be used on horses may still be legally turned against children.

Today's parents may reach less readily for the old implements of physical cruelty like the switch, the birch or the tawse, but the potential for maltreatment remains as high as ever. For we have lost little of the ancient dread of Dod's 'sparkle of evil', the deep suspicion of the 'old Adam' lurking in the depths of every child. This fear lies behind the general belief that without strict, even overbearing discipline, a young person growing up will amount to nothing, or worse than nothing. To avoid this, every society has vested in parents awesome powers of ownership and control. The physical maltreatment of the young derives its authority from the immemorial and still current idea that parents own their offspring. In law a child belongs to a parent, the parent possesses the child as it possesses its car or its cat, and it has rights over the child's body that the child does not have over itself.

These rights are currently being enforced in Britain via a series of court decisions in cases which themselves show the deep level of confusion among parents and professionals alike. A 28-year-old London mother convicted of cruelty to her daughter in December 1992, only four months later was cleared of any offence. The woman, who cannot be named, admitted beating her 9-year-old daughter on her bare buttocks with a slipper, but maintained that it was a necessary punishment for stealing sweets. Pleading her innocence of cruelty both to this daughter and to a 7-year-old who had been beaten too, the mother maintained that she had suffered herself from this 'terrifying experience' of having to appear in court, and said, 'I punish them at home because I don't want them to end up in court or in care.' Clearing her of assault in April 1993, the Appeal Judge announced, 'If a parent cannot slipper a child, the whole world is going potty.'

The same argument was employed in the defence of a father who punished his sons in a similar way. Finding the two boys aged 5 and 8 damaging a chair with a knife, the 30-year-old father, who works as a security guard, admitted taking a leather belt to the backside of each child in turn and administering three strokes, outside their clothes. Acquitted, the father declared, 'I am a good father and I did not do anything wrong':

> They were naughty and I punished them the way I saw fit. I believe that parents have the right to chastise their own children without ending up in front of a court. It seems ridiculous when normal discipline is classed as abuse. It seems children have more legal rights than adults. If more parents were stricter with their children, we might not have ten-year-olds mugging grannies. I believe in discipline when it is necessary, and corporal punishment. The law in this country is too soft.

Not in this case. The father's own defence counsel admitted that 'there was severe bruising on each child', and the case only came to light because the boys' injuries were marked enough to be noticed

by a teacher at the children's school. But it undoubtedly helped the
father that the mother of his five children stood by him throughout
the trial, clutching his hand as he was acquitted. 'We love our children, but if they are naughty they deserve to get punished,' she said:

> I was never hit as a child, but I agree with what my husband
> did. Normally I am the disciplinarian in our house but my hus-
> band dealt with the two boys that day. I was pregnant, and had
> had enough of them. I would have hit them a lot harder. We
> now want to put this behind us, and get on with our lives.

'I was given the slipper and the strap all the time as a boy,' her
husband wound up; 'it never did any harm.'

'A child well beaten cries as much as a child badly beaten,' says
the Russian proverb. Of course it is not possible to say how these
boys will turn out in years to come. But the story already has much
to tell of the stresses of modern family life: an overstrained couple
coping on a security guard's notoriously low income, a mother who
cannot manage the children she already has finding herself pregnant
again and at the end of her tether, a father whose idea of good
fathering is to come down like a ton of bricks upon the damage
caused by bored and destructive children, rather than to occupy and
divert them in the first place. How often does it need to be said that
young children do not desire to annoy adults? Still less do they want
to be beaten to the point of 'severe bruising' at the age of 5, even if
the parent sincerely believes that like the proverbial rape victim, they
were 'asking for it'.

Yet there is no law in Britain to prevent parents from punishing
their children in this or any other way, 'if the correction is reasonable
and moderate'. The defence counsel who stated that the children had
suffered severe bruising also declared that the father 'did not use
unreasonable force'. And so the court decided.

By this decision, it was not simply offering legal sanction to parents
to administer physical pain to the point of visible damage. It was
also tacitly endorsing the psychological element of physical punishment which is totally denied by the rhetoric of 'a swift clip round
the ear and then it's all over'. The infliction of any pain is accompanied for the victim with a kaleidoscope of painful emotions of
fear, humiliation and distress. When the punishment includes ritual
elements of enforced nakedness, especially the exposure of the but-

tocks in the most helpless and humiliating posture of all, then the psychological anguish can be more severe than any bodily hurt. As the perpetrators of these punishments well know, however loudly they protest that 'this is hurting me more than it is hurting you'. The resulting sense of shame to the victim, suggests John Bradshaw, is *'like bleeding inside'*:

> As shaming experiences accrue and are defended against, the images created by those experiences are recorded in a person's memory bank. Because the victim has no time or support to grieve the pain of the broken mutuality [the connection with the parent in which children see themselves lovingly reflected and accepted as they are] his emotions are repressed and the grief is unresolved. The imprints remain in the memory as do the visual images of the shaming scenes. As each new shaming experience takes place, a new verbal imprint and visual image attach to the existing ones forming collages of shaming memories.

Against such collages the sufferer usually has only one line of defence, the retreat into self. So far from the troublesome children needing 'six of the best' (the best? with what perversity of sadism did beating a child's buttocks ever come to be called that?) we need instead to try to understand the mechanism by which an increase of punishment will lead to an increased internalization of the shame. This in turn leads to a lack of self-worth and a diminution of any sense of the worth of others. With repetition comes the death of feeling, the seemingly inhuman lack of response that so alarm us in the alienated young: the reflex sneer, the shallow shrug, the blank offensive stare, the colourless obscenities worn bare of meaning, *fuck you, who gives a shit* . . .

This nightmare figure of today, the disaffected, unemployed young lout or thug, is the prime trigger for renewed calls for a return to 'traditional values' or 'old-style discipline'. A century or so ago, when parental, school, and societal discipline were at their fiercest, remedies like hanging, transportation, imprisonment with hard labour, the treadmill, the birch and the cat-o'-nine-tails were available to deal with him and his ilk. Ferocious punishments followed trivial offences: pre-teenagers were hanged for stealing a handkerchief. Yet still few members of respectable society dared to travel afield unarmed, none but the desperate braved Whitechapel or Seven Dials, and London boasted the greatest criminal underclass England has ever known.

Even today most young offenders are old hands at violence: most of those caught in antisocial acts have already felt the force of the corporal punishment so frequently invoked as the solution to the problem they present. 'All these children get plenty of the "discipline" that the hangers and floggers want,' comments child care worker Wendy Wilkinson. 'I often feel like asking them if they have any idea how much violence a young football hooligan has already received by the time he is arrested, *with no effect whatsoever on his behaviour. Because no matter how often they get walloped, they are not learning anything about right and wrong.*'

Yet still the advocates of violence persist in clinging to their faith in these outmoded remedies, rather than give their minds to seeking new approaches for a new age. In the US, Dr Spock has come under fire from critics like the prominent clergyman Norman Vincent Peale, who have accused him of responsibility for creating this generation of the out-of-hand. Dr Spock, Peale said in a celebrated post-Sixties outburst, had encouraged 'permissiveness' among parents and advocated 'instant gratification' for children.

Defending himself vigorously, Spock refuted any suggestion that his work has given parents 'permission' to raise unruly and disrespectful children. 'My book had been out for 22 years before I even heard the word permissive,' he says wryly. 'And I always thought that while parents should respect their children, children should be brought up to respect their parents too.' But he cannot agree that respect is best instilled by corporal punishment:

> At first I did not know how to handle this issue because I knew something like 83 per cent of American parents think you're just spoiling a child if you don't whack him once in a while. *But the American tradition of spanking may be one cause of the fact that there is more violence in our country than in any comparable nation* [italics inserted].

Pain, inflicted deliberately, Spock contends, will always do more harm than good. Because violence breeds violence. It can be learned and studied, even majored in, and the student never learns that violence itself is bad, simply that the greatest violence always wins. The children of violence would agree. 'I used to pray to be old enough and big enough to do my dad in,' says Derek, a farm manager in Warwickshire. He looks back with distress on an early lifetime of gang behaviour, misdemeanour, and assault, 'trying to find out what to do with all the violence I had pent up inside me.' He shakes his head. 'All I could do with it was to *pass it on.*'

• • •

There is ample evidence to show that violent punishment leads to violent attitudes among children.

Peter Newell, co-ordinator of the pressure group End
Physical Punishment of Children

• • •

Between discipline and violence, where are we now? Most of today's parents deeply believe that it is wrong to hit children, and try not to do so. Yet physical abuse remains the most common form of mistreatment within the family, professionals say, and one of the most difficult to deal with. All child agencies know what an NSPCC survey of the last fifteen years demonstrated in 1993, that physical maltreatment consistently outstrips other causes of referral to social agencies, with 29 per cent of the children suffering physical injury, 18 per cent sexual abuse, and 7 per cent neglect. Nor is physical abuse always the result of a beating or some form of sudden attack. This was brought to light by a bizarre case in 1970 when a 13-year-old child stumbled into the Los Angeles County Welfare Office accompanied by her blind and helpless mother.

The girl, christened 'Genie' by the first people to help her in her escape from confinement, had spent her life locked in her bedroom alone, alternately strapped into a child's potty chair or strait-jacketed into a sleeping-bag, fed on nothing but baby food and paddled with a plank of wood when she dared so much as whimper. The architect of her little hell and the author of her misery was her father, who oversaw every detail of Genie's imprisonment, even down to the restraining harness which he sewed himself.

'Clark' was above all a father who should never have had this role and its responsibilities thrust upon him. From the very first day of his marriage he had professed an unwavering desire never to have children, beating his wife so severely in her first pregnancy that she lost the child, and insisting on a second baby being left in the garage until 'a quick pneumonia', as he later claimed, 'took it away.'

Even then, Clark might have been able to change. A son was born who, with the help of Clark's mother, grew and throve. With Genie, the small family seemed complete. But the chance opinion of a doctor that the child might be retarded, given without any diagnostic tests on one rare visit to the paediatric clinic, seems to have triggered in Clark a paranoid determination both to protect her and to hide her away from hostile eyes. So he buried her alive in his two-bedroom suburban home on LA's Golden West Avenue – 'yet another reminder of how banal the most malevolent people can be,' comments the US writer Natalie Angier.

When she was discovered following a desperate bid by her mother for freedom, Genie was semi-crippled by a lifetime of physical restriction, incontinent, unable to chew solid food, hardly even to swallow, and above all, almost totally mute. Yet with the battery of resources now at hand to help, this latter-day princess set free from the castle of the wicked ogre could be given, so it was thought, the chance of a new life. Even if physiotherapy could not do much to help the characteristic hoppity shuffling 'bunny walk' she had developed, with her hands held up in front of her like paws, she could be taught to speak, and hence to think and feel.

But the damage Genie had suffered, as her chronicler Russ Rymer reports, was beyond repair. Despite intensive training and rehabilitation, she never seriously progressed beyond her original meagre word-hoard of 'Stopit!' and 'Nomore!' The moment for speech had passed, it became clear. Genie had missed it, and it would not come again.

Many of the professionals involved with Genie's case had thought that the speech development of this complete 'natural' would prove or disprove once and for all the controversial linguistic theories of Noam Chomsky, that language is innate and that even growing up alone on a desert island, a child would speak. Both factions were to be copiously disappointed, when all experiments proved inconclusive. Her use as a guinea-pig now over, her future as an autonomous individual impossible, Genie was consigned to the institution where she now lives, a demented and withdrawn woman sliding down the years towards middle age and death.

Genie's was an exceptional case, a saga of abuse so devastating that it left the whole of America gasping with the familiar refrain '*how could they . . . ?*'

How could the parents do this? The grandparents condone it? The neighbours not notice it? The state records have no trace of it, the state agencies never pick it up? Above all, how could the father who purported to care for his family ('I love you', said the suicide note Clark left for his son when he shot himself on the morning he was due to stand trial for cruelty to Genie) make such a desolation of his only daughter's life? 'Genie was the most profoundly damaged child I have ever seen,' one of her therapists told Russ Rymer. 'Her life was a wasteland.'

But other children suffer this sort of desolation too, even if not on such an epic scale. The actor Robert Blake, child star of *The Treasure of the Sierra Madre* with Humphrey Bogart, remembers a childhood in which his earnings supported his entire family, and his reward was to be beaten for it. His parents, he says, conspired to brutalize him: his mother would invent misdemeanours so that his father could throw him into the bedroom and attack him. As in most cases of abuse, there were combinations of punishments, and variations on the theme:

> My parents locked me in a closet and left me there all day long. They made me eat on the floor like a dog. You see, they already had a son and a daughter. They didn't want me. They'd had two abortions before me, and if they'd had enough money they would have had another abortion instead of me.

Blake went on to make a name for himself as the star of the much-loved 1970s TV series *Baretta*, and also to blow away that career through behaviour he now regards as completely self-destructive. His only creation was a family which his son has described as 'like a 24-hour crisis hot-line'. Now, Blake says, he has survived: 'I'm alive and I'm here and I didn't kill myself. But would I do it differently if I lived life over again? *You bet your ass!*'

•••

> Many people do not realize the extreme damage that can be inflicted on children by adults.
>
> Lord Justice Elizabeth Butler Sloss, presiding judge at
> the Cleveland enquiry into child abuse, 1987

•••

The physical abuse of a child invades its body space, destroying its psychic integrity and sense of self. When the abuse becomes sexual, the invasion of the body is complete. The arousal of a young child's deepest sexual feelings, the penetration of its vagina, bladder or anus, constitute an occupation so profound as to be almost a colonization of the child by the outside force. Perhaps that is why sexual abuse always seems more horrific than beating, privation or confinement, even though the degree of violence inflicted or pain suffered in the course of the uninvited sexual acts may be considerably less.

Or perhaps, as Freud came to think, the child just fantasized it. As with the debate over physical abuse (is it legitimate parental correction, or unwarranted cruelty?), the acceptance of the existence and extent of sexual abuse is as hotly contested today as it was when Freud first accepted his patients' accounts of their childhood molestation, then began to have doubts. Alice Miller recalls Freud's change of heart:

> Freud originally discovered, in the treatments partially conducted under hypnosis, that all his patients, both female and male, had been abused children and recounted their histories in the language of symptoms. After reporting his discoveries in psychiatric circles, he found himself completely shunned because none of his fellow psychiatrists was prepared to share the findings with him. Freud could not bear this isolation for long. A few months later in 1897, he described his patients' reports on sexual abuse as sheer fantasies attributable to their instinctual wishes. Humanity's briefly disturbed sleep could now be resumed.

Yet the suffering persisted. Long after her untimely death in 1941 it emerged that Virginia Woolf, whose youth coincided with Freud's early years of practice, had been sexually molested all that time by her adult cousin Gerald Duckworth. Deep and even intractable depression in adult life is now recognized as one of the consequences of sexual abuse in childhood. It is tempting, then, to speculate how much this episode, rather than her famed 'artistic temperament', contributed to Woolf's later suicide. The painter Francis Bacon was another whose childhood was foreshortened by sexual violence: for some insignificant offence in boyhood, his father ordered him to be horsewhipped by one of the grooms, a man who afterwards 'broke him in' sexually too.

Yet those were the days of the legendary Victorian repression when anyone from a groom to a gentleman, as Duckworth certainly was,

had suffered some degree of interference with the natural evolution
of their desires. Today boys are spared the fearful threat of blindness
and madness proceeding from 'self-abuse', while girls are no longer
brought up in an ignorance so terrifying that headaches and hysteria
were their only refuge. But if we have created today an easier,
healthier sexuality, if individuals are more readily able to obtain
what they want without the crippling inhibition of former times,
why does the sexual abuse of children still persist? And above all,
how does it come about within families, which above all should be
the child's safest haven and shield against any such thing?

• • •

I never told anyone.

Incest survivor

• • •

In the wake of a century of re-examination, what is the story today
of sexual abuse of children within the family? In what is so often a
'victimless' crime, because the sufferers are denied the right either to
see themselves as victimized by those who claim to love them, or to
speak out afterwards, hard facts and reliable statistics are inevitably
hard to come by. Much depends on the terminology employed, and
on the perceptions of the assaulted child. What constitutes an inappropriate approach, and at what stage does it become unwelcome
or frightening? Some families are considerably more physical and
tactile than others – the familiar slap on the backside from a father
or uncle which is felt as affectionate by one young girl might be an
unwarranted assault on another.

This emerges clearly from a 1991 survey from the Child Abuse
Studies Unit of the University of North London. Studying sexual
violence, researchers found that at least 1 in 2 children had suffered
some form of sexual abuse, defined for the purposes of the project
as 'all types of intrusive behaviour'. But when the definition of 'sexual
abuse' was tightened up and limited to overt physical acts, the figure
fell to 1 in 5.

If sexual abuse can seem to come and go like this, does it happen
to any marked extent at all? Or are some of the supposed sufferers
suffering instead from a mistaken remembrance of non-existent
events – 'False Memory Syndrome', as recent reports have called it?
In March 1992, a group of American parents who claimed they were

the victims of unfounded allegations of sexual abuse set up the False Memory Syndrome Foundation in Philadelphia. Prominent among them were the parents of Roseanne Barr, the US comedienne who shocked the world with detailed allegations of her childhood sexual abuse in 1991. Within a year of its foundation, the group had assisted 3,700 other accused families, mainly in the US, but also from Britain, France, Germany, Israel, Ireland and Australia. A parallel group now established in Britain, Adult Children Accusing Parents, also reports enquiries from many different sources.

The challenge posed by 'incest survivors' is worldwide then, it seems. But Dr Stan Katz, a Los Angeles specialist in child abuse and author of *The Co-Dependency Conspiracy*, would not even dignify the accounts of some of the self-reported sufferers with this label. 'There's no better way to get on the cover of *People* magazine than to admit you're a victim,' he says:

> Roseanne Barr recently said that she remembers being molested back to the age of a year and half, which I don't buy at all. The point is that when these people make their accusations, no one will question it. There's a false sense of celebrity from being in recovery.

In opposition to Katz, therapist John Bradshaw, one of the high priests of the self-healing movement in the US, insists that some form of family dysfunction afflicts 96 per cent of the population, leaving lasting effects.

They fuck you up, your mum and dad . . .

Do they or don't they? In common with genetic and fertility treatments, with adoption, even with the nature of the family itself, child abuse is the subject today of feverish discussion, debate and re-interpretation, as the embattled and entrenched interests of various pressure groups slug it out. Meanwhile, society struggles to come to terms with another unpleasant reality that it would much rather ignore.

Yet how can it be denied? The power of a parent is so immeasurable that it seems fitter to use Scott Peck's word, *dominion*, to sum it up. As Peck sees it:

> To children – even adolescents – their parents are like gods. The way their parents do things seems the way they *should* be done.

Children are seldom able to objectively compare their parents to other parents ... Treated badly by its parents, a child will usually assume it is bad. ... Raised without love children come to see themselves as unlovable ... *Wherever there is a major deficit in parental love, the child will, in all likelihood, respond to that deficit by assuming itself to be the cause of the deficit, thereby developing an unrealistically negative self-image.*

This power ensures that the parents' lightest decision, their every whim will carry more weight in the family than any other factor. And when a parent decides to 'keep it in the family', to give or take what they want regardless of the child's needs or desires, then the child is in peril indeed.

Figures in Britain for 1991 show a 20 per cent rise in child sex abuse cases dealt with by the National Society for the Prevention of Cruelty to Children. That year also for the first time saw the figures for sex abuse outstripping offences of neglect. By the end of 1992, the total number of registrations for all categories of abuse was the greatest since the organization began keeping modern statistical records in 1973. The same picture emerges in America: the total reported number of child abuse cases in 1980, over 700,000, by the end of the decade had almost tripled to 2,025,200.

Who are the abusers? Just as women have had to learn that they are in more danger of rape from the men they know than from the proverbial stranger in the back alley, so it has become clear that those likeliest to attack young children are not the dirty old men in the cinema or the strange youths who haunt the playground, but members of the child's own family. Fathers, brothers, uncles, especially avuncular family friends of the 'Uncle Charlie' variety, may all pose a threat which the child is powerless either to anticipate or resist.

Is sexual abuse a 'men only' affair, then? To all intents and purposes yes, says therapist Adam Jukes: 'We talk about "domestic violence" or "family violence", but in the vast majority of cases, it is not "the family" but men who are violent and abusive – 85–90 per cent of all sexual abuse is inflicted by men.' In such cases, Jukes suggests, there is an unspoken reluctance to call the abuser to account, and a readiness to offer explanations and excuses which will not stand up to investigation. 'It's widely believed that abusers become perpetrators as the result of abuse,' he says. 'My own findings to date indicate that *fewer than 30 per cent* of abusers have been abused, even when using a very harsh definition of abuse':

> And there's another question that most practitioners fail to address. Why is it, if being abused is the cause of subsequently becoming a perpetrator, that the vast majority of sexual abuse is by men on little girls? If internalized abuse is followed by identification with the abuser, and if we follow the 'inter-generational cycle of violence' theory, we should expect that the next generation would be dominated by massive sexual abuse of little boys by their mothers. As far as we know, this is not the case.

• • •

It's the ultimate taboo.

Michèle Elliott, director of Kidscape

• • •

As far as we know . . .

In fact there is no reason, Alice Miller argues, why a woman should not become an abuser of children just as much as a man: 'A father who grew up in surroundings inimical to instinctual drives,' she writes, 'may first dare to look properly at a female genital, play with it and feel aroused by it, while he is bathing his small daughter.' In just the same way a mother who has 'developed a fear of the male genital' may 'gain control of her fear in relationship to her tiny son'. Miller's own practice included male patients whose mothers had regularly massaged their genitals from infancy into adolescence, usually on spurious 'health grounds', 'to treat his phimosis' (tight-ness of the foreskin). Other anecdotal evidence suggests that this activity has not been confined to the legendary ayahs and amahs of the Raj, whose skill in handling even the most recalcitrant of boy children remained a source of amazement to their employers the memsahibs.

Official statistics suggest that these women are rare, comprising less than 5 per cent of all types of sexual abuse. But the steady trickle of cases finding their way to the British charity Kidscape and to other child protection agencies, as well as those constantly being thrown up in therapy, suggests that the true figure may be considerably higher. How high, practitioners are still in the process of finding out. Cianne Longdon, a psychotherapist specializing in child abuse, has stated that 30 per cent of her private patients over the last five years, and 50 per cent of those she has seen at a local welfare centre, were abused not by men but by women (mothers, stepmothers, aunts, adult friends or carers). More than 100 recent victims of female abusers are now on the books of Kidscape, and the numbers are rising.

Women may even have a stronger reason to abuse than men, Miller suggests:

> In many societies, little girls suffer additional discrimination because they are girls. Since women, however, have control of the new-born and the infants, these erstwhile little girls can pass on to their children at the most tender age the contempt from which they once had suffered. Later, the adult man will idealise his mother, since every human being needs the feeling that he was really loved: but he will despise other women, upon whom he thus revenges himself in place of his mother. And these humiliated adult women, if they have no other means of ridding themselves of their burden, will revenge themselves upon their own children. This indeed can be done secretly and without fear of reprisals, for the child has no way of telling anyone, except perhaps in the form of a perversion or obsessional neurosis, whose language is sufficiently veiled not to betray the mother.

We should not wonder at this, Miller concludes: 'what options are there for a humiliated woman not to abuse her small child for her own needs [when] even in cultures in which a woman counts for nothing, society invests her with unlimited powers over her young child?' This is a question that the feminist movement prefers not to ask, Miller believes, hamstrung as it is by its belief that the problem is rooted exclusively in male power and the workings of patriarchy. Female abusers are always supposed to act under coercion from the male. But how do we explain the single mother who makes her daughters aged 7, 10, and 13 strip and parade before her naked every Sunday night, and then join her one by one in the bath for extensive washing of their genitals 'to be made clean for the Lord's day?' How do we excuse the unmarried woman who finds a boy-friend to deflower her daughter, 'to make sure she gets broken right'?

In both these cases known to Birmingham care workers, the woman had no male partner. Where one exists, the mother's collusion may be as much to protect herself as to protect him: one woman who had swapped beds with her 14-year-old daughter 'to get some sleep', later brushed off the child's complaint that the father had tried to have sex with her on the grounds that 'he liked to have sex in his sleep'. How could she do this? There has to be a stronger reason than simply fear of her husband to explain why any mother would repeatedly turn a blind eye to behaviour she ought to challenge: a man's unduly close or possessive attitude to a daughter, constant midnight trips to 'comfort' the child, or regular unexplained absences from the marriage bed.

Mothers will also support their menfolk in their efforts to cover up abuse once it has come to light. One family doctor contacted the Incest Survivors' Campaign in Britain for advice in connection with a child who had suffered severe vaginal lacerations: the family said she had fallen off the toilet. Mothers may even be active participants with their men: a number of incest survivors speak of being held down by a mother while a male relative carries out the sexual act. And women will almost never be challenged themselves, even when clear evidence points their way. One woman told a conference on female abusers organized by Kidscape that she was frequently treated in hospital for her childhood sexual injuries, caused by objects as diverse as rose stems and bottles, and on each occasion her mother's 'feeble excuses' were accepted without question.

For despite widespread media coverage, there is still an extraordinary reluctance to believe that women are capable of abuse: Michèle Elliott, director of Kidscape says, 'I didn't believe it myself at first.' Perhaps this is not surprising when we consider how hard it is for outsiders to accept that abuse within families occurs at all.

Or perhaps, as Helena Kennedy QC suggests, law and custom are so weighted in favour of the male, that both male abuse and female collusion are taken as something none can question, and none prevent. For even in the grossest cases, it seems, outsiders are reluctant to credit the child against the father, and even more reluctant to take action. As a Dublin criminal court heard in March 1993, a Kilkenny father had first raped and then sadistically attacked his daughter when she was 10, continuing for the next seventeen years. In that time, he had smashed her fingers with a hammer, broken her ribs with a steel bar, and broken her nose and fractured her skull with a bottle, finally blinding her in one eye by kicking her in the face with steel-capped boots. She had an abortion at 15, and was also constantly in and out of hospital with other fractures, cuts, concussion and severe bruising.

None of which was sufficient to gain any attention during the entire seventeen-year period. The mother, a victim of the father's violence herself and too terrified to report him, lied about her daughter's injuries and did her frantic best to conceal the whole thing. Only when the girl was blinded did the truth emerge. The victim had been crying for help for years. One doctor called the father in, but abandoned the case when the father walked out again. A social worker in another hospital told the girl that her injuries were 'a family matter', and refused to intervene. Five other hospitals were later forced to co-operate with police enquiries, after having treated the physical injuries, ignored any other signs, and returned the girl to her tormentor.

Better training for social workers to recognize incest and a wider spread of information all round were recommendations called for in the wake of this affair by the Dublin Rape Crisis Centre and other Irish authorities. But publicity does not in itself necessarily lead to greater public understanding, nor to the prevention of similar evils arising again. Two widely publicized cases in Britain, the Cleveland child abuse allegations and those featuring a similar but smaller-scale scandal on the remote Orkney Isles, have in fact done much to convince the general public that child abuse claims are usually false.

Not merely false, but whipped up by social workers, as newspapers and conservative groups regularly allege: one social worker grimly outlined 'all the old long-disproved myths' that the Orkney case in particular gave rise to, 'that intelligent, hard-working, "God-fearing" people do not abuse their children, that distraught parents who tearfully protest their innocence are always telling the truth, and that children fantasize about what has happened to them with the help of videos and TV.'

But isn't that abuse? demanded Christopher Brown, Director of the NSPCC in the wake of 'the Rochdale affair', an investigation into ritual sexual abuse which foundered after allegations of 'a catalogue of errors' by social workers. The least they discovered, Brown avers, was 'a group of inadequate families living on a typical Sixties housing estate gone to seed, an environment that invites problems on all levels, including the way children are brought up.' The germ of the case was a young boy who spent half the night watching hard-core horror films until his mind was distorted and his sense of reality gone: isn't that abuse?

It is a question that we are far from being able to answer in the present state of knowledge. Adult celebrities may speak out from the security of fame and fortune as Oprah Winfrey has done:

> The show which altered me and made me confront the shame and anger I'd carried with me since I was a child was one of my early ones dealing with sexual abuse. I was raped when I was nine and abused for years by members of my family and their friends. By the time I was 13 I'd run away from home and was sexually promiscuous as a direct effect of being abused . . . I broke down and couldn't stop crying. I said 'Please stop the tape' but they didn't, and I released all the pain which had built up. I realized what had happened was not my fault, and I could stop feeling guilty.

But the small and unknown child has no TV show to answer the need to speak out, no loving fans to hear and understand her cry, no power to make herself heard, no voice. If the abuse is discovered, or if it attracts media attention, the emphasis will be on the rights of the adults, including the abuser, not on the rights of the child. The child suspected of abuse will be removed from its home like a suspect itself, and the ensuing investigation will do little to reverse this impression. Feeling guilty from the abuse, and guilty for breaking up the family, the child can also suffer consequences more appropriate to the criminal than the victim. One incest survivor described exactly how the process works:

> It was my stepfather . . . He started on me when I was 9 . . . I did eventually go to the police when I was 16 because a boyfriend picked up on it and took me there. It was terrible. I was treated like a criminal, interrogated, called names, constantly forced to deny it. After eight hours they sent me home. They'd picked up my father and given him tea and sandwiches while I had to go through all that. When I think of the injustice I still feel furious. My mum was in a state of shock and all she could say was, 'Tell me it didn't happen.' So in the end I did.

Small wonder then that abuse remains, like rape, a substantially unreported crime, in which the process of detection can be as bad as the original crime. The victim will already be condemned to a lifetime of repetition of her suffering, often experiencing flashbacks, panic attacks, and deep depressions, demonstrating an inability to form stable long-term relationships, or even to hold down a job. Such children are inevitably candidates for the random, alienated violence of the streets, either as victim or aggressor. Those for whom no one cares will never ever learn to care; and those who have not been spared the worst will see no reason to spare others from pain.

In the most violent cases of children's bad behaviour, alienation and crime, police officers remark on the almost pathological coldness and detachment that young offenders can be capable of, even amid the emotional high of stealing, 'hotting' or 'bashing', be it 'queers', 'Pakis' or each other. These children are simply reflecting back the face that has been shown to them: the blank, blind stare of the protector turned predator, who will not yield from his or her own demands even to the point of killing a soul.

• • •

I still see my parents. I don't blame them any more.

Oprah Winfrey

They were my family. When they started in on me, I felt like God had died. I have to cope with it every single day. How can I forgive when I can never forget?

Incest survivor

• • •

CHAPTER 8

The Happiest Days of Your Life

The delinquents of tomorrow can be spotted as soon as
they walk through the door on their first day of school.

Professor Fred Stone, specialist in child and adolescent
behaviour, University of Glasgow

Children should be educated to live more abundantly, not
apprenticed to a life sentence of penal servitude.

George Bernard Shaw

IN THE STRUGGLE for self-determination, school is only marginally less important than family in determining a child's future course of life. What that will be, the school may be the last to know. In her schooldays Charlotte Brontë was told to put behind her any vain hope of earning her living with her pen, and settle down to becoming a good governess. Boy George, star of Culture Club, was sternly informed that he had no talent for music. The first teachers of Winston Churchill, later to win a Nobel Prize for literature, could not even teach the 7-year-old to write. Conversely, the parents of a violent boy at a Coventry comprehensive were refused a referral to an educational psychologist on the grounds that they were 'over-anxious' about his aggressive behaviour. Ten years on, he is now serving a 25-year sentence for a particularly sadistic multiple murder.

We cannot have the children we deserve without the schools they deserve, schools which like a good family provide understanding, warmth and support, and yet allow each child to find his or her own direction and true sense of self. And a good school will serve other crucial functions, too. The teacher, far more than the parent, is well placed to identify the child not adjusting to the larger group, children who are failing and falling behind, children at risk. By the same token, teachers always know the pupils who are ahead of the pack, the 'ringleaders' or 'troublemakers', as they are usually known, whether these children are simply offering a high-spirited challenge to authority, or responsible for all the school malice and mayhem on every side. Any concerted social initiative for identifying and turning back the tide of violence offered to, and by, the children of today, must begin in the schools.

Yet every school contains a kernel of violence at its core, and only experience can teach each pupil what this means. The child's first sense of it is likely to be the treatment they receive from other schoolmates, from the day that they enter the school. 'The bigs hit me, so I hits the smalls,' a boy explained to the philosopher Bertrand Russell on his first day at school; 'that's fair.'

Nor is this kind of treatment confined to what is bracingly called 'the rough and tumble' of a boys' school. Beneath the Gilbert and Sullivan fantasy of 'three little maids from school', female academies of winsome, rosy-cheeked girls giggling together in innocent bliss, lies a reality which those bedazzled into choosing single-sex education by the schools' O- and A-level results do not even glimpse. 'Girls can pick on each other with a viciousness quite beyond the average boy,' says Molly Harmsworth, a former headmistress with a lifetime in female education. 'Once a girl becomes a target, the others can create a strange atmosphere around her without saying a word.' Nor is the cruelty always psychological: American journalist Victoria McKee still remembers the rough handling she suffered from an all-female gang at the school in New York which she calls 'Hell's Kitchen'.

Like abuse within families, bullying has for so long been the dark side of all that is valued and valuable in school life that its reality has never been truly acknowledged. But each of us, if we can bear to, will remember schoolmates ruthlessly tormented for no apparent reason at all. Some will remember being tormented. And not a few will remember being the tormentors, with whatever smart that may give to their mature consciences.

In the wake of public disquiet, most recently in Britain a Home Office enquiry chaired by Lord Elton in 1989, there are signs that adult society is at last beginning to take seriously the bullying which, it is now recognized, is endemic to school life. But like abuse again, bullying is a 'victimless crime', with the victim made to feel so bad about what is happening, so responsible for it, so guilty, worthless and ashamed, that he or she will collude with the abuser in denying, covering up or lying about the offence.

And once again as with abuse, the wider world of adulthood does not want to know. The Elton enquiry found that, widespread as bullying is, it is as widely denied by both parents and teachers. And as long as there are parents and teachers who believe that 'it's all part of growing up', 'it teaches children how to look after themselves', or 'I survived it, and it made a man of me', we shall make no headway against practices which are, for those children in danger and spinning out of control, effectively apprenticeships to a full-fledged mastery of mischief, and even a training-ground for crime.

•••

> You are sent away to board at eight. I can remember crying and saying, 'No, I'm not crying.' That's the first lie, and it only gets worse.
>
> Rory Bremner, comedian

•••

Given the flood of school memoirs, fact or fiction, from Charlotte Brontë's *Jane Eyre* to George Orwell's bitter memoir 'Such, Such Were the Joys', there can be no disputing that school is a major formative influence in the lives of us all. For willy-nilly, whether the school is 'good' or 'bad', we all absorb considerably more from 'the happiest days of our lives' than the three Rs, and our schooldays shape all the rest of our adult lives. From Dotheboys Hall to St Trinians and Malory Towers, from the Nicest Girl in the School to the Owl of the Remove, libraries teem with attempts to come to terms with what we all suffered, and return it back to us with a kinder smile than it surely wore the first time around.

And not only libraries: on film Sidney Poitier eternally strides through *The Blackboard Jungle*, while the tensions of a girls' school are glimpsed through a glass darkly in Lillian Hellman's *The Children's Hour*. The excoriating satire of *If . . .*, Lindsay Anderson's passionate denunciation of public-school life with its portrayal of vicious beatings, fagging and general torment, was known to have moved more than one old boy to tears of happy nostalgia, as did another powerful attack on the same form of middle-class privation, *Another Country*. These of course are the memories of the scribbling classes. Me, I did metalwork, as thousands could say along with the comedian Paul Merton. If there has not yet been the Great Comprehensive School Play, or novel, it can only be a matter of time.

And time is what it will take. In the history of education, the British comprehensive school occupies a similar position with regard to traditional forms of schooling as the Post Office Tower does to Canterbury Cathedral. For hundreds of years, British children, mainly boys, have been sent away to boarding school in the fixed belief that they were receiving the best start in life that money could buy. Later generations, not only in Britain but anywhere else in the world cursed with Anglo-Saxon attitudes, have also fallen prey to a system fuelled by social ambition and intellectual snobbery, which cannot but undermine any expectation of a close or normal family life.

The results of the boarding school experience, at best a disregard of the child's emotional welfare, at worst a refined form of torture, can be seen on every public-school face. How it felt from the inside is described by the writer and critic Lord David Cecil:

> Going away to school for the first time is as purely a painful experience as there is in most men's lives. It is like a rehearsal of one's execution. Strung up by two or three weeks' agonised and helpless anticipation, relentlessly, inevitably, the day arrives when one is plunged into a world probably hostile and certainly unknown, without a single link to bind one to the world of one's experience.

Despite the intimate personal note of this, Lord David is in fact writing of the sufferings of the 18th-century poet William Cowper, who was sent away to school as soon as his mother died in 1737. 'It was', Lord David writes, 'a place of torment':

> Boys have never been humane: nor did the robust axioms that governed eighteenth-century education believe in protecting people from the natural discipline administered to them by their contemporaries. Cowper, shrinking, lonely, six years old [and, Lord David might have added, newly bereaved of his mother as well], was quite incapable of standing up for himself. Within a short time of his arrival he had become a mere quivering jelly of fear.

Not without reason, it seems:

> He was so abjectly terrified of his chief tormentor, an overgrown lout of fifteen, that he only recognised him by his buckled shoes; he had never dared to lift his eyes to his face. Such a system

could not go on for long even in those days; his tormentor was expelled. But Cowper's nervous system was ruined for life.

Lord David writes of 'those days', the time in which Cowper was reduced to the madness that blighted his life, as of another world. Yet by his own account, some things do not change. The prevalence and persistence of bullying is a fact of school life continuing from the days of the Greeks through to the life of today's children. It matters little whether they are attending prestigious boarding colleges or the roughest of inner-city schools, as this playground chant makes clear:

> You get it for being Jewish,
> You get it for being black,
> You get it for being chicken,
> You get it for fighting back.
> You get it for being big and fat,
> You get it for being small,
> You get it, you get it, you get it,
> For any damn thing at all.

The writer Frederick Raphael knows about getting it for being Jewish. As a British child at Charterhouse in the Forties, he had, he says, 'no sense of solidarity whatsoever with what the Jews were doing in Palestine'. But that did not matter when the news of the deaths of two British sergeants at the hands of Israeli fighters filtered back to Britain. His enraged schoolmates embarked on 'a Jew-bait', destroying Raphael's possessions, putting shit in his shoes, heating his enemies, cooling his friends. 'My nerves were somewhat affected,' he comments now with truly British understatement. 'I lost a good deal of faith in myself. I don't think I've entirely recovered it.'

Those who dismiss such persecution as 'horseplay', or who assure us that 'boys will be boys', can have little idea of the intensity of childhood suffering: Raphael is still reliving his experience 50 years later. Nor can we delude ourselves that the situation must have improved during this time, when schools can now add being brown, yellow, Sikh or Muslim to the list of things a child can 'get it' for.

Two recent cases in Britain highlight the problem of bullying with peculiar poignancy. On the night before he was due to return to the public school Pangbourne College in Berkshire, where he was a sixth-form boarder, 16-year-old Mark Maclagan took the family dog for a walk. While his parents settled down to watch *The Silence of the Lambs*, Mark walked down the garden and hanged himself. After his death, a schoolfriend told reporters that Mark 'was bullied every single day' at school, 'every minute, literally'. Mark's study had been 'trashed', his books thrown on the floor, his drawers emptied, his locker pulled over, his mattress thrown off his bed, and all his belongings dumped in a pile down the corridor.

Young Mark Maclaglan lived and died, in the supremely English phrase, 'with every advantage'. The 12-year-old Stephen Woodhall attended a Birmingham school so rough that the bullies there disdained anything as feeble as the 'trashing' of belongings: they imposed protection 'taxes', threatening to break the legs of those who would not pay. Even out of school, the children were not safe: Stephen was stopped at the shops and forced to hand over the only money he had on him, the sum of 10p. He came home and, like Mark, hanged himself.

Both families afterwards spoke of how little they understood what had been going on in their sons' lives. Both had noticed that all was not well, and both had tried to intervene: Mark's mother had spoken to his housemaster of her conviction that Mark was being 'leaned on', and Stephen's father had been up to the school to make a formal complaint of the bullying he knew that Stephen was suffering. Both parents were fobbed off by reassurances from the school that the situation was under control. 'We were told that Mark could cope,' his mother remembers, 'that he was handling it by himself'.

As indeed he was. If Mark's death achieved nothing else, it forced an enquiry into the reality of bullying at Pangbourne, which the Headmaster had claimed was 'relatively uncommon' and 'taken very seriously' by the staff. The enquiry, held in February 1993, bore him out. A close investigation led by Dr Roger Morgan, Chief Inspector of Oxfordshire's Social Services Department, found that bullying at the £10,000-a-year Pangbourne was no worse than anywhere else.

Indeed, Pangbourne's record proved to be better than that of other schools. Although 1 in 20 of its 400-plus pupils were 'seriously and frequently' bullied, the rituals, 'initiations' and punishments were said to be less harsh than elsewhere. Dr Morgan found that only 4.9 per cent of Pangbourne pupils claimed to be bullied 'often or most of the time', compared with an average of 6.1 in other schools. Nor was bullying deemed to be a problem by many of the parents: they were clear that bullying and teasing were 'a good preparation for later life'.

This is the theory that we have seen applied to family disputes: children must learn to stand up for themselves, discover what they are made of, find out how to give as good as they get. The wishful thinking behind this is a pure David and Goliath fantasy: in reality, just as in the family, some schoolchildren will always be smaller, weaker or less dominant than others.

As such, when they are picked on, they are as likely to learn the passive panic of despair as they are to grow up to fight back. Indeed, with repeated bullying, like the poet Cowper, they may never learn how to grow into themselves at all. And while they are learning the lessons of fear and humiliation, failure and defeat, so the bully is learning the power of brute force, the triumph of unreason and the sadistic thrill of tasting a terror other than his own. *The parent who intervenes to prevent a child from being bullied, will succeed in curtailing the career of an embryonic thug as well*. Every parent should understand this.

It may not be enough, however, simply to bring the problem to the attention of the school authorities. Given the recognized scale of bullying, on official figures affecting around 6 per cent of the school population in Britain, that is, almost 2 million children, most schools will have some form of complaints procedure. But its existence is far from guaranteeing any results. 'Some schools have a culture of bullying so strong that the staff are either unable or unwilling to do anything about it,' says Dr John Stoddard, a Warwickshire educational psychologist:

> In these cases, results have been obtained by a parent confronting the bully, or better still, the parent of the bully. This needs handling carefully: there's a good reason, after all, why a young child is going in for this sort of behaviour, and it may well be in direct imitation of a violent parent. But if you can keep it cool, it can be very effective.

Others would place the burden of response more firmly on the shoulders of the child. 'Talk to them, listen to them, find out why they think it is happening,' advises child developmental specialist Dr Janet

Gilmore. 'Only then can you help them develop the inner reserves to combat it.' Tim Laskey, a professional fitness consultant, disagrees. 'Many of the procedures recommended in the existing literature are about counselling children', he says. 'This paralysis-by-analysis approach is not useful, because it dwells on the problem, not the solutions.'

Solutions, as set out in Laskey's 1993 booklet *How to Beat Bullying*, include boxing, weight training and the martial arts, for girls as well as boys. 'Fisticuffs,' Laskey says, are not the object of the exercise, but the developing of strength, self-confidence and the 'clubbiness' that goes with any sporting activity and helps to promote a child's popularity.

Non-physical talents may also be exploited to raise the child's profile and its standing in the class: popular and successful children are not natural targets for bullying. 'Every individual has at least one outstanding talent, and parents should give encouragement,' Laskey suggests. And those who believe that children must learn to handle their troubles themselves might at least equip them with the wherewithal to do so: 'I make a point of telling kids what talents they can exploit, and find ways to make them believe in themselves. If you can improve a child's self-esteem, he or she is less likely to be bullied.'

If this fails, though, and the bullying persists, you have little option but to get your child out of the school, however difficult that may prove in practice, Dr Stoddard says. 'That in itself can be a way of conveying to the authorities how seriously you take this issue, that you are not prepared to leave it to chance and simply hope, like the Micawbers, that "something will turn up".' For if your child is one of the 6 per cent who is bullied 'often or most of the time', it is hardly possible to take it too seriously, Stoddard contends:

> We know that severe bullying retards the victims' educational and social development, making them fearful, unable to concentrate, and depressed. They may also develop poor memories, suffer from nightmares and bed-wetting, or fall prey to various phobias alongside their rational fears. Appetite can be affected, with a knock-on effect on sleep and growth. These children undoubtedly do less well at school than they might have done. And the after-effects will persist throughout life.

•••

> Pain can destroy. Pain is, in fact, so powerful that the very
> idea of pain can destroy . . . even the expectation of pain in
> others can destroy.
>
> Alberto Manguel,
> *News from a Foreign Country Came* (1991)

•••

If these are the lessons learned by the bullied, what of the bully? One of the first ideas grasped by the children who are moving out of control towards establishing a wayward system of their own, is that none of the rules apply to them. From the very first day in school, as Professor Fred Stone observes, some difficult children can neither absorb nor benefit from the structures of support with which other children co-operate. They have already learned to manage their lives without the warmth and security of a firm and constant base.

For others, the lack of affection and security with which they have grown up will imperil their grasp on reality and jeopardize their development in clearly distinguishable ways, says Stone:

> Unemployment, poverty, malnutrition and poor housing con-
> tribute to mental ill-health, especially where there is parental
> anxiety and depression. The weaker families tend to disintegrate,
> the children are commonly at risk emotionally, with a cluster
> presenting danger signals and outright symptoms from infancy
> onwards.

What these symptoms are, Stone suggests, every teacher can recognize: hyperactivity, inability to concentrate, indiscriminate friendliness and inappropriate affection. The problem child will also be accident-prone and clumsy, not secure in toilet training, easily distracted and liable to be isolated from his or her peers. 'That's Tommy,' says Lurleen Williams, who teaches a reception class in an inner-city area of Washington DC, indicating one of her charges. 'Look at him now, buzzing about, knocking things over – all that energy and he can't stay still one moment to look at a book or even play with the others. He annoys them, and they're too young to accept it. He simply can't be one of the gang, he doesn't know how to relate.'

Such children may become either victims or bullies, it seems: the pendulum can swing either way. Unable to adjust to school life and the interaction of the other children, they find their own level outside the system. Some will abandon the struggle as they have been abandoned, sinking into apathy and giving up the ghost so early that ever afterwards they have only the faintest memory of the person they might have been. Others are driven to rise above the morass rather than sink into it, learning to assert their need for recognition and approval, creating their own structures from the wreckage of their disappointment in the adult world. So an Oxfordshire gang of bicycle thieves recently uncovered by British police was run by a boy of 14, via a rigid paramilitary organization of 'seconds' and 'slaves', netting thousands of pounds' worth of student bikes for resale every month.

In general, though, violent, criminal or antisocial behaviour in school will start very much younger than this. 'If we are going to affect behaviour,' says Dr Fiona Caldicott, President of the Royal College of Psychiatrists, 'the time for intervention begins between 3 and 6 years old.' Child psychiatrist Robin Benians agrees. 'Difficult and disadvantaged children comprise approximately one in ten of all children in the UK. These children are not just "going through a phase". Without treatment, the disturbance of most persists through childhood, adolescence, and often throughout adult life.'

To receive the treatment they need, difficult children have to be identified before they can suffer, or inflict, any further harm or distress. Picking them up is in fact the easiest part of the exercise, teachers say. 'Of course you can spot them, you have got their number by the first playtime,' says June Ridshaw, a London infants teacher for over 30 years. 'Most of us could tell you now, Wayne will be known to the police before he's ten years of age, Kevin will be in court by the time of his thirteenth birthday and every year after that, Melanie will be pregnant or dead before the rest of them leave school':

These are the children who constantly demand the attention of the teacher or of the other children in the playground, but have no idea how to lead a game constructively when they get it. They'll be aggressive, often violent and possessive, always refusing to share. Their first response to any frustration will be to take a swing at the cause of it. Physical violence will usually be accompanied by verbal aggression too: the language some of these very young children know would make your hair curl.

June remembers clearly the first time she heard a 5-year-old swear: '"Fuck off, you!" he said. What was so sad, he could only have learned it because someone said it to him.' And like adults, even very young children learn the value of weapons when words will not do. Sticks, stones and knives are not uncommon in the growing wave of aggression which now begins in nursery school. 'There was a child of 4 who took a knife into school and threatened the other children,' says Michèle Elliott of Kidscape. 'When a parent complained, the head teacher simply kept the child off school for a couple of days before allowing him back into class. Clearly the teacher ignored a serious problem.'

But this knife incident was far from the worst of recent cases that have come to Elliott's attention: 'There was a terrible case of a 3-year-old who was attacked by two others, aged 9 and 7. They put a plastic bag over his head, set fire to it, and locked him in a wardrobe.' The child survived, but suffered facial burns severe enough to necessitate plastic surgery.

Media coverage of such incidents tends to focus on the 'evil' of the aggressors, thrown into relief by heavily emotional portrayals of the helplessness and innocence of the victim. Few reports ever ask, where does this come from? Above all, how does it begin, especially in children so young?

Kate Tyldesley is a Child Protection Officer in Cheshire. Her experience leads her to believe that problems can arise with any child who is not corrected firmly enough as soon as unpleasant or antisocial behaviour begins to emerge. 'It starts off with name-calling and taunting, but goes on to jostling, pinching and kicking their victims over prolonged periods,' she reports. And without apportioning blame, it is important to recognize what young children are capable of, and how effective they can be. 'Children of 3 and 4 years old can be very possessive about their toys and excessively egocentric. They either try to manipulate other children in their home, or try and manipulate their parents to get some sort of a pay-off. They seek attention through aggressive acts, and learn to get their own way.'

Like other professionals in the field, Tyldesley believes that if bullying in young schoolchildren can be prevented early on, there will be fewer problems as the entire group matures. For the bully soon grasps the advantages of his or her behaviour, comments Delwyn Tattum, Reader in Education at Cardiff Institute of Higher Education: 'Once they reach the stage where they realize they can exert power over other children, they know what they are doing.' Such power-play is particularly likely to thrive in the absence of leadership from above, Tattum notes: 'Very young children need a much better ratio of supervision because they should have adult models. They should also learn to accept the authority of an adult.'

For as with crime and deviance in the adult population, by far the greatest deterrent to bullying is the certainty of swift and sure detection, and even swifter and surer retribution. Traditionally this has been the justification for the administering of corporal punishment in schools, a tradition that the old world is showing some reluctance to give up. As with the parents' right to smack, the right of schools and those in authority to beat the children in their charge is currently being reasserted against challenges which may be taken as far as the European Court of Justice.

Yet if children are responsible for some of the violence in school life, a far greater proportion has usually come down from above. In many schools, the drive towards the strict repression of students with the attendant battery of controls and punishments will be built into the regime from the earliest days, reflecting their founders' darkest anxieties and fears. The educationalist Kurt Hahn was convinced that the 'weakness' of German youth was responsible for his country's humiliating defeat in World War I. From this came his determination to re-establish 'strength, order and control' through rigid systems and tough schooling.

Hahn's *pièce de résistance* was the harshly-structured regime of the international public school Gordonstoun, which on his own admission gave Prince Charles the most wretched years of his life. 'If people have heard nothing more of Gordonstoun, they have always heard about the cold showers and the morning run,' admits Charles's biographer Penny Junor. 'If the boys were not out running half-naked in midwinter they were sailing in the icy North Sea, climbing down cliff ladders and scrambling over blazing roof tops.' Despite turning into no mean action man himself in later years, Charles has expressed his reservations about the Hahn regime with masterly British understatement. 'I did not enjoy school as much as I might have,' he told Junor. 'But that was because I am happier at home than anywhere else.'

Hahn's ideas were formulated from the even more repressive and sadistic notions of the previous generation, the generation which, as Alice Miller stresses, gave birth to the leaders of the Nazi movement in Germany, all of whom had had the benefit of a firm and well-disciplined upbringing, from Hitler himself down. 'Among all the leading figures of the Third Reich I have not been able to find a single one who did not have a strict and rigid upbringing,' Miller writes. 'Shouldn't that give us a great deal of food for thought?'

Yet the faith in inflicting privation and pain in the name of education upon the young is not susceptible to rational thought. The celebrated Roman Catholic public school of Downside must have lived up to its unfortunate name for Auberon Waugh, who held the school record of 14 beatings in a single term, and seems to have spent more time bending over than standing up. His fellow-writer John Le Carré has recalled his schooldays at Sherborne as 'one long act of sadism'. A contemporary of the disc jockey John Peel at Shrewsbury remembers that 'they practically had to wake him up in the night to administer the required number of sound beatings.' What this could mean is bleakly revealed in an anonymous memoir by a former public schoolboy:

> When you are only nine years old, you do what you are told: you *dare* not tell anyone . . . Any attempt to bring this to your parents' attention merely results in the letter being torn up (having been vetted) and a severe and barbaric beating, before you have to stand (because your backside is bleeding so badly) and write to tell mum and dad what a lovely time you are having (only to have to start again, because the tears that smothered the script hardly matched the content). Isn't that a better letter, eh? . . . Well, it is , isn't it? . . . answer me, damn you, boy . . . or do you want a darned good thrashing . . . Eh?

Now a deeply lonely, unhappy and unsuccessful man, the writer often broods on what might have been. If he had not been made stupid through fear, if he had been able to gain any qualifications, if he had been able to develop the career he knew he was capable of . . . On the verge of middle age, he still dreams of some day having a place of his own, not a rented room in someone else's house. He dreams too of somehow being able to tell his father what really happened, vindicating himself from the guilt of his academic failure and the disappointment he knew he caused. He never will, though: 'He would be too hurt.'

Following the wider European and American pattern, corporal

punishment has now been banned in the state schools of Britain. But with a blithe disregard of the disdain of other nations for *le vice anglais*, British public schools have fought to the hilt to retain this perverted and sadistic process. When Jeremy Costello-Roberts was beaten at the age of 7 by his headmaster in an English public school, his mother applied to the European Commission of Human Rights. The Commission decided that the punishment breached the child's rights under the European Convention of Human Rights, and referred the case to the European Court of Justice for a final verdict.

The case was widely expected to be adjudicated in Jeremy's favour, by extension also putting a stop to beating in all British schools outside the state school system. To international surprise, in March 1993 the Court upheld the school's right to beat, and decided that the rights of Jeremy had not been infringed. This decision was echoed in May 1993, when the House of Lords voted by a majority of seven to retain the independent schools' mandate to beat at will.

The rights of the beaters are vigorously defended by those who still cling to them. Arthur Roderick bases the case for corporal punishment on the Book of Proverbs: 'Foolishness is bound in the heart of the child.' Roderick, director of the British branch of the US educational foundation Christian Education Europe, and proponent of the Advanced Christian Education scheme at the Maranatha Christian School of which he is headmaster, is also ready with the remedy: ' "But the rod of education shall drive it far from him." A few necessary, lovingly demonstrated smacks', he says, 'can spare heaps of problems later on.'

The ACE system is now taught in more than 5,000 schools in the US, and has 45 schools in Britain since its introduction here in 1980. A further 300 British children are taught according to the ACE method at home. Paul Griffith, the founding director of ChildLine, the aid line for children in danger of abuse, professes himself at a loss to see where the love comes in: 'I don't recall Christ ever beating children up,' he says. 'I thought he said "Suffer little children to come unto me." Under this system you abide by the rules or you get hurt. You are ruled by fear.'

For all the rearguard action of 'the great floggers and birchers', as the dramatist Ben Jonson dubbed the devotees of drubbing, it seems likely that this licensed abuse of children is becoming a thing of the past. But as in the family, physical abuse, even with its added element of humiliation and psychic pain, is only half the story. Leaving the protection of home, going to school, joining the Scouts or the church choir, all these expose a child to the risk of abuse that few parents anticipate and even fewer recognize. And as in the family once again, the scale and nature of this abuse goes quite unrecognized until the abusers are forced out of the darkness of concealment and into the light of day.

•••

> He told my mother I needed extra coaching in maths. The first time he had me on my own after school, he started in on me. Of course my maths got worse. So my mother paid for two sessions a week instead of one. It went on for four years.
>
> Survivor of school abuse

•••

He told my mother I needed extra coaching . . .
What a dank and dreadful crew they are, the dismal cohorts of corrupt and corrupting teachers and priests, choirmasters and scout-masters, as they trail through our headlines, week after week, year after year. HEAD JAILED FOR SEX ATTACKS, newpapers proclaim, YOUTH LEADER ON INDECENT ASSAULT CHARGE, CHRIS-TIAN BROTHER FACES QUESTIONS BY POLICE, SEX ABUSE BY PRIESTS ROCKS US CHURCH.

The fourth estate have got their number, of course: they've sung the tune so often they could do it *a capella*. Press coverage of these incidents follows a pattern as dreary and predictable as the offences themselves, reports of court proceedings which read like Victorian morality tales complete with awful warning, the story closing with a satisfying thump as the offender gets his comeuppance. 'I have to deal with you on the basis that for a decade and more, you were in the company of vulnerable young boys,' the judge will intone, passing sentence as here in 1993 on a schoolmaster monk. 'You had a pos-ition of power and influence, which you have abused [*abused the position, note, not the child*]. What you have done must result in a long sentence. You will go to prison for seven years.' Off with his head then! And three cheers all round.

Yet however full the descriptions (the accused was the son of a minister . . . educated at . . . had studied at . . . had served as . . .), these stories are all heart-sinkingly similar, and curiously devoid of explanatory power. We never learn how or why these assaults occur:

they are taken as given, not 'boys will be boys', but men will be men. Each is treated as a 'one-off', another unfortunate incident, a special case.

In reality, abusive assaults of this kind betray strong linking features which if teased out and identified, could be used to preserve the children of the future. These salient features need to be recognized, and the work of putting defensive systems in place needs to be confronted, if we are serious about protecting children from such attacks, indeed if we have any hope of giving them the future they deserve.

First, it is clear that *sexual attacks are substantially directed at those who are already exposed and therefore doubly vulnerable.* Just as the real rapist is not the classic stereotype of the stranger with the half-brick in the dark, so most child abuse comes not from the lurker in the park but from those the victims already know. The teacher or priest is in a particularly powerful position then, because the child not only knows them, but is already conditioned to obey their every word, and aware of what could happen if obedience is withheld. 'I did not understand about sex,' said one schoolboy abused by his headmaster at prep school. 'But I did know what he could do to me.'

Where the priest is also the teacher, the combination is beyond the power of the child to resist. Brother James Carragher joined a Roman Catholic boys' school in the north of England in 1969, where he systematically abused his charges until 1990. Father Michael Creagh was deputy head of the renowned Douai Abbey School when he forced himself on a 12-year-old pupil, even following the boy on a foreign holiday with his parents. The Very Reverend Patrick O'Donnell ran a Mission of Rescue for homeless boys in Chicago, till the police discovered that he rescued boys from turning tricks on the streets only to keep them even busier at home.

It is significant that the Creagh case only came to light when the boy was at home with his parents and so for the first time felt able to resist. For, hard though it may be for parents to accept, abusers can only prey successfully on the undefended child. Physically, emotionally or psychologically, the victim of sustained abuse has already been abandoned, feels abandoned, and so abandons himself or herself to whatever comes.

For abuse is not random. Abusers target their victims carefully, and attacks are most frequently made on those who are already vulnerable. Father Carragher's favourite boy had only been placed in the 'safe environment' of the Roman Catholic boarding school because he had already been sexually abused in a foster home at the age of 6. After trying unsuccessfully to run away, this boy attempted suicide by slashing his wrists and swallowing a razor blade, finally being committed to a mental hospital. Father Creagh made his first assault on his charge when the 12-year-old sought advice and counselling for anxieties he was suffering at the onset of puberty. Away from his parents, with no other defender, the boy submitted for almost a year to the priest's insistence on masturbating him, before he could escape from the clutches of his tormentor once he was home again.

The pattern of previous assault or emotional abandonment is so clear in abuse cases that it should be a matter of priority to monitor such children with extra care. Care worker George Zanucki recognized the need for giving special attention to abused children, when he set up his private school for disturbed boys in Shreveport, Louisiana, in 1981. With cases soon referred from all over the state and a turnover of half a million dollars a year, business was flourishing and things looked good.

But not for the boys. At his trial in 1990 it was revealed that Zanucki had used the confidential social and psychological reports on his charges to decide which to make the target of his next homosexual attack. 'Active, aggressive kids were out,' said the State Prosecutor. 'Those who had already suffered abuse by an authority figure or by members of their own family, they were right up Zanucki's alley. He saw them as already "broken in".' The trial involved fifteen boys whom Zanucki had sodomized over a period of almost ten years. In all that time, he received nothing but praise for his work.

• • •

> Cruelty has a human heart
> And Jealousy a human face
> Terror the human form divine
> And Secrecy the human dress.

William Blake, Songs of Experience (1794)

• • •

Why don't they complain?

Why do abused children put up with this, shocked voices demand when yet another of these cases comes to light, why don't they tell someone, report it to the authorities?

Oh, but they do. And no one wants to know. In the second key factor which links all cases of extra-family abuse, the victims have almost invariably tried to signal their distress before the discovery, and been ignored or silenced. Part of the problem is that children simply are not believed. In a distressing case in 1991, Paul Burton, a man of 24, was charged with abducting a 7-year-old child from the seaside caravan where she was sleeping and keeping her prisoner for almost three days during which she was subjected to a variety of indecent assaults.

At Burton's trial it emerged that in the weeks before the kidnap, he had made *nine previous attempts* to take away a child for this purpose. In Burton's defence, his counsel pleaded for 83 previous offences to be taken into consideration. Investigating the most recent incidents, police found that in every case where the little girls had told their parents what had happened, their stories had been dismissed as nightmares. How many other children over the years have suffered this kind of trauma, only to have their experience dismissed as fantasy by parents too deaf and blind to hear?

The difficulties are compounded when the word of a child is set against that of a respected individual, even more a powerful institution. From 1969 to 1980, repeated complaints from the boys assaulted by Father Carragher were simply crushed. One of Zanucki's pupils confessed what was happening to another teacher: the teacher brought him straight back to Zanucki who arranged to have the boy beaten up by his fellow-pupils the following day.

More frightening still, even when undeniable evidence of abuse is laid at the door of respected figures like headmasters or priests, the first reflex of the authorities is almost always to close ranks behind the abuser and cover his tracks. Case after case shows colleagues, bosses and official bodies instinctively bending the truth or deliberately lying in order to protect the offender rather than to do justice to the victim.

'Look, for them it's a can of worms,' said a senior Midlands police officer. 'It shows their system has failed, and they have no idea how far the breakdown has spread. Of course they're going to try to hush it up.' So Douai Abbey knew of the allegations concerning Father Creagh for eighteen months before the priest was exposed in a newspaper article. At no time did they call on the social services or police for any help or guidance. No independent person or outside agency was allowed to hear the claims of the boys who said that Creagh had fondled them, to counsel them or to advise them of their rights. The response of the Benedictine authorities who ran the school was simply to transfer the priest to another school, where he would still have access to boys.

This does not surprise Ray Wyre, an internationally recognized authority on sexual abuse. Wyre, who works with convicted paedophiles at his Gracewell Clinic in Birmingham, has treated a number of Catholic priests, and accuses the Douai authorities of 'criminal naïveté' in creating a wall of silence to stifle the boys who were brave enough to speak out:

> Traditionally, church authorities have dealt with these problems in secrecy. [It's] a historic process. The priest is recycled to another parish, got to renew his vows or sent into therapy.

And it does not have to be so, Wyre insists. In November 1992 he advised the Irish hierarchy of the Roman Catholic Church on new procedures for dealing with cases of abuse. 'This is the first management structure to have taken on board that some of its employees abuse children', he said. 'No other career group has done the same.'

Particularly not the child care professionals, who should above all groups set the standard for good modern practice in the protection of the child. How far the neglect of even the most basic procedures may go, is almost beyond belief. In 1991, Britain suffered what a senior Midlands police officer described as 'the biggest sex abuse case in history, probably one of the biggest in the world.' Frank Beck, a bachelor of 49 and formerly a local politician, had as head of three children's homes, instituted 'a reign of terror', a trial court heard, under the guise of 'recession therapy' for the disturbed children in his care. Beck was finally proved to have sexually and physically abused more than 200 child residents of his homes, after an eighteen-month police investigation spanning three continents.

Complaints against Beck had begun almost twenty years before his conviction, as early as 1973. But children who claimed to have been beaten, raped and buggered were completely ignored. In 1986, two junior colleagues laid an official grievance procedure against Beck, stating that he had sexually molested both of them. Beck was simply allowed to resign his position and moved to another job, supported by a reference attesting the value of his services from his superior, the Director for Social Services. Although a single man and a known homosexual, Beck was also allowed to foster two young boys and give them a home.

Beck's offences, described as 'the grossest breaches of trust imaginable', at least were matched with an exemplary sentence, when he was given five terms of life imprisonment. The steadfast refusal of most official figures and authorities to confront the reality of abuse is only matched by the apparent desire of some judges to vindicate the abusers at any cost. A 53-year-old army major, William Humphries, known as 'Uncle Bill' to the boys he preyed on, had been sodomizing boys as young as 7 for a period of fourteen years. At his trial on charges of indecency, gross indecency, attempted buggery and buggery, the judge told him, 'You have a splendid military record and I take this into account': 'Uncle Bill' had passed his career at a staff training base. At least he received a prison sentence for his crimes. In the same spirit of forgiveness, the Douai priest and groper was exculpated on the grounds that 'there had been no element of coercion in his advances, and he was suffering from pressure of work.'

Sometimes there seem no limits to what the powers-that-be will do for the men who transgress. At the trial of the 59-year-old church worker Patrick Gilbert, who pleaded guilty in June 1993 to molesting a 14-year-old boy for two years, it was revealed that he had a previous record for indecent assault as a schoolteacher. Gilbert, a former President of the Society for Promoting Christian Knowledge, was accompanied into court by the Canon of St Paul's Cathedral, and produced a character reference from the Archbishop of Canterbury. Gilbert needed all the help he could get, as the judge sternly informed him:

With an offence of this kind only a custodial sentence could be justified. Considering the seriousness of the offence, I entirely take into account your breach of the boy's trust. You have also breached the trust of his parents, who put their son in your care because they believed you were the kind of man you appeared to be.

But suddenly, at one bound, Gilbert was free. There was a 'quality

of consensuality' to the offence, the judge decided, and the accused
had had health problems besides:

> I have a medical report which tells me that your heart condition
> is such that incarceration would or might well lead to a deterio-
> ration or even risk your life.

And there's more. Gilbert, it seems, had suffered enough already, as
the judge said when allowing him to go:

> I don't for a moment close my mind to the very severe punish-
> ment that the discovery and publication of these offences have
> been to a man involved in your career of public service, and this
> makes your situation all the more tragic.

A tragedy then. For the abuser, but not for the victim, in the eyes
of the law.

• • •

> 'If the law supposes that,' said Mr Bumble, 'then the law is
> a ass – a idiot!'
>
> Charles Dickens, *Oliver Twist* (1838)

• • •

Of course the abusers will make excuses for their actions. *I asked
her if she liked it before I did anything*, they earnestly aver, or *he
never said no*. Or *I could tell he was enjoying it just as much as me*,
or *I only did it because I loved her too much*, they can be very
seductive, *these 3-year-olds*. Many abusers openly admit to looking
for children who have been abused before. *They like it really, they
want it*, abusers swear, *I could tell straight off he was provocative,
she was promiscuous, they had played the game before*.

But the authorities? The colleagues, the employers, the judges of
these men? Do they have to excuse and forgive the offender at the
expense of the victim? When the Presbyterian leader of a Milwaukee
community was detected in the act of brutally raping a 14-year-old
who had been taking religious instruction, the community prayed
for him, not for the violated young girl. This situation was echoed
in England when prayers rang out through the medieval spires and

cloisters of Gloucester for a bishop who had corrupted a teenage deacon. Where was the victim in all this?

And the stricter the community, the more vicious the backlash against the sufferer, who by revealing the shame of the abuse, has exposed them all to shame. The process by which those who have been offended against become the offenders was starkly revealed when the 17-year-old son of a rabbi was accused of abusing two young children in a strictly orthodox London Jewish family in January 1990. For reporting the case to the police, after their rabbinical court had told them it was their own fault for having a male baby-sitter in the first place, the parents were denounced within their community as *moisers* [informers], traitors to Israel and unfit to live.

From that point the family suffered a medieval witch-hunt conducted with all the benefits of modern technology. Hate mail succeeded anonymous phone calls, which were superseded by Superglue in the locks: tension eventually burst out in a riot so severe that police were forced to remove the entire family to a safe house. A ray of sanity broke through when the community rabbi publicly rebuked the rioters, condemning 'all acts of intimidation and violence that have been perpetrated against the family'. But later the same week, he joined six other rabbis in a statement rejecting all allegations of abuse, and describing the couple as 'irresponsible people who wished to degrade and deride the holy people of Israel'.

It seems almost superfluous to restate the lessons of all this. Yet however often children are abused, we do not seem to learn the basic, simple truths. We must:

- Watch all our children, pay attention to them, listen to them and hear what they say.

- Bear in mind that even the best of teachers and youth workers may fall into temptation, and that some of the worst of men adopt these professions precisely in order to do so.

- Have a care of children in care, for they are doubly at risk, listen to what all children say and act upon it, for the failure to believe or to act is a double betrayal.

- Never, never believe that a child can give 'consent' to sex with an adult, never imagine it could have desired an adult penis or fantasized about the joy of adult penetration or possession.

- Never blame it for its own sufferings, the theft of its trust, the rape of its childhood.

Children abused, children abusive, teachers abusing, priests teaching abuse: do any children simply go to school and church, get what they need, academically, socially, spiritually and emotionally and move on, unfettered and unscathed? Of course they do. But they are not the problem.

And as the problem does not begin in school, neither does it end there. Of all the formative influences on a child, another looms almost as large as school, and in some cases larger. From home, school is the first step to the outside world. How else do children learn about the adult universe? What is their major window on the world elsewhere?

• • •

> By education most have been misled;
> So they believe, because they so were bred.
> The priest continues what the nurse began,
> And so the child imposes on the man.

> John Dryden, *The Hind and the Panther* (1687)

• • •

CHAPTER 9

The Place Where Violence Grows

James Bulger? I come from a place where what you've
just witnessed happens about twenty times a day.

Arthur Miller

In a TV and media-driven age, there are few skills more
important to kids than learning how to keep their heads
in the midst of the confusing storm of powerful images
that surrounds them.

David Puttnam

No FAMILY ever intends to produce a misfit or a murderer. No
parents wish to have a child that will be deviant, a disappointment,
or a cause for despair. When it happens, parents painfully search
their consciences for some explanation of what has occurred. 'He
has been educated,' said the mother of Jon Venables, one of the two
boys who killed James Bulger. 'He has had security with loving
parents and a loving brother and sister. He has had his holidays like
everyone else. He has had Christmas presents.' In these circumstances
professionals and lay commentators alike will scour a child's home
background for clues as to how and why this particular one should
have gone off the rails: what was the size of the family? Family
position of the offender? Contribution of the father? Attitude of the
mother? And so on, down to the tiniest domestic detail.

Yet every child, no matter how young, is not merely a product of
the family's influence but a barometer of the wider society in which
we live. When we consider how to get the children we deserve, and
how to identify the factors which produce the opposite, we cannot
ignore a major theme of the millennial debate. Those of us who grew
up on Enid Blyton and Dr Seuss are grimly aware that we now live
in a world where 10-year-olds may have seen 30 acts of television
violence for every day of their lives, and 8-year-olds know more
about the Terminator than they do about God.

What part do the mass media play in the lives of children going wrong? Today's parents are the first generation to have come of age in the full-blown media era, and most of them would feel that the diet of TV and rock and roll ('jungle music'!) that so alarmed their parents and grandparents, never did them harm.

But the TV of twenty, ten or even five years ago cannot be compared with what is seen today. In addition, the massive market penetration of videos, VDUs, computer games and electronically-generated graphics has given young children access to a galaxy of images quite literally beyond their parents' imaginings. And over it all now arches the international, indeed cosmic framework of the mass media industries, the unspoken cultural coalition of film and TV, advertising, comics, pop art and pop music, all combining to create a world in which violence becomes not the problem but the solution, the staple of everyday entertainment, and as normal, to adapt the dark words of Rap Brown, as cherry pie.

• • •

> When I was a child, if I was afraid of something I would
> think of one of my cowboy heroes. I had a model. Now there's
> nothing but the cynically created figures in some studio made
> up by people who become millionaires doing it.
>
>   Arthur Miller

• • •

Nobody who is properly treated becomes a killer or even a criminal, says Alice Miller. Child abuse is a known reality when it goes on two legs, gropes with two hands, can be recognized by its 'bottle-green eyes peering from under a twitching forehead', as James Joyce vividly pictures the strange man who terrifies the boy narrator of his autobiographical short story 'An Encounter'. How do we identify and guard against the abuse which takes place unseen, which can enter houses without a sound, pass through locked doors and walls, penetrate invisibly the mind of a child and violate its innocence with all the force of a rapist?

By the time a child is 11, acording to the American Psychological Association, he or she will have watched over 100,000 acts of TV brutality, not counting real-life violence on the news whether from Bosnia, the Bronx or Brick Lane. In a random study of one month on US television, Professor Nancy Signorelli of the University of

Delaware found that violence featured in 63 per cent of prime-time network programmes, at the rate of five incidents an hour. 'We tend to look to ideal figures to tell us how to behave, very often in movies or TV,' said Arthur Miller at a 1993 London symposium on his latest play, *The Last Yankee*, 'and the violence on TV is unbelievable.'

And mainstream TV is not the only medium which may have a powerful and immediate impact upon a still-growing mind. The Bulger case soared to instant world attention because it was caught on video, the universal language of the world. It will for ever be a blight upon what we call 20th-century civilization and a reproach to us all, that in an era when technology offered unprecedented chances of opening magic casements on perilous seas and faery lands forlorn, all we could come up with was *Driller Killer* and *Huns Fucking Nuns*.

For in a world driven by commercial rather than cultural imperatives, the 'video nasty' such as these represent was an opportunity waiting to happen. The chance for the moving-image industries to pander to the lowest common denominator in human nature, to feed appetite, not taste, was too good to pass up. If the video revolution meant that viewers preferred home viewing, then films would have to follow them there. But not *Bambi* or *Snow White and the Seven Dwarves*. Hollywood's earlier attempts to recover viewers by widening the target audiences had already produced an increase in violence which pushed back the barriers of what was acceptable, and steadily desensitized the young. Now films like *Blood Thirst* and *Toxic Avenger* became increasingly violent as the film-makers sought to carve out a genre which would hook in new TV viewers, especially those at the start of their viewing lives.

So was born a huge and vital part of the global 'entertainment industry', a multi-billion-dollar business built with vicious cynicism on the drive to recover the generation lost to movie-going, and to hook in the infinitely more vulnerable sector of those too young to watch except at home. In the 1970s and on into the 80s, films trading in extremes of sadism, mutilation, violence and torture poured from small and large studios around the world: the *Demons, Demons 2,* and *Demons 3* series from Italy, the so-called 'chop-sockey' submartial-arts 'gorefests' like *Tai-Kwon-GO!* from Hong Kong. The British Board of Film Classification's annual review of 1993 makes a measured indictment of these films and their aim: 'That was violence for kicks, gross violence of a kind which blurred any sense of right and wrong by leading the viewer, reluctantly but inexorably, down the path of pleasurable evil.'

And by design, not accident, with pleasurable and evil intent: for given the structure of today's industry, almost any films can make money if they are titillatingly conceived, cheaply produced and sensationally marketed, no matter how depraved. Indeed, low-budget films are protected from scrutiny or attack by the simple fact that they rarely get reviewed, and hence rarely, if ever, come to public attention. But with the massive global marketplace of cinema, video, television and satellite transmission, they can still command a huge audience, as Paul Dempsey of *Screen International* explains:

> The classical path for a film is the cinema release, video rental six to nine months later, video sales, perhaps at the same time as a pay television screening six to nine months after this, and a viewing on terrestrial television between 24 and 36 months after the initial theatrical release. If you get your initial figures right, you should cover your costs every time.

And with these four prime opportunities to make money, most of the low-budget 'horrorfest' films will do considerably better than that. Indeed, those which omit the expenses of a cinema screening and take the straight-to-video route are usually assured of higher profits, thereby benefiting again by keeping their products out of public view. Yet not from the view of those who might be most vulnerable to the messages these films purvey. What these are, horror videos like *The Leprechaun* gloatingly relate: *If you don't have a four-leaf clover – pray your life will soon be over!* In a similar spirit *The Mutilator* boldly sets out its necrophilic wares: *By pick ... By axe ... By chainsaw ... BYE BYE!!!*

Even so, lament its defenders, the horror movie is not what it was, the glory days are gone. 'Contrary to sensational report,' moans writer John Lyttle, 'horror video has lost a lot of its guts:

> An obvious example is that viewers of the great underground grandfather of gore cinema, *Night of the Living Dead* (1968), were permitted to watch a zombie daughter eat her mother. The 1992 remake, produced by the original's director George A. Romero, deliberately dilutes the despatchments (by gun, hammer, knife, car, fire and cannibal acts) ... The worst *Carno-*

saur can provide is a glimpse of human innards devoured by a patently plastic dinosaur, and a hand severed by a laser; we do not see the slicing, only the hand falling to the floor.

Shame. Pity about the *despatchments* too. Nothing like a good despatchment . . .

The 'video nasty' is an influence on young children's minds whose impact will not be seen in full for a generation or more to come. But even in the short term, anyone who has any knowledge of films like the *Tool Box Murders* and *Blood Thirst* can have little doubt that child viewers must be getting a sensation of some sort.

And it can hardly be the same sensation as that conveyed by *Roy of the Rovers* or *Rebecca of Sunnybrook Farm*. 'To allow a young child to stay up till all hours watching video nasties,' demanded one of the social work chiefs in charge of the Rochdale case; 'isn't that abuse?' Abuse in triplicate, many would feel: by those who make it, those who buy or rent it, and those who allow young children access to it.

Who is responsible here? Where does the buck stop? Michael Fallon, former British Minister for Education, is in no doubt:

> One in twenty 4- to 6-year-olds and one in five 10–15-year-olds watch television between 10 and 11 PM. Children, sometimes very young ones, are watching totally usuitable programmes and particularly videos. The blame obviously cannot lie with schools: parents surely must take more responsibility for restricting – yes, restricting! – not only the amount of viewing that children do, but the type of viewing as well.

How likely is this? The daring emphasis with which the Minister ventured the suggestion of restricting the TV viewing of households where the video reigns supreme shows how little he understands the operations of a home where no one may be around to perform this worthy office – where a lone-parent mother may be snatching a rare night out, or where a struggling couple, desperately working overtime, are unspeakably thankful for the TV, when they think of it at all, for without the electronic babysitter their lives would collapse.

But Fallon is not alone in feeling that unrestricted access to television or video exerts a power that young children cannot be expected to control. With this in mind, inventor Howard Gold has produced a device which enables parents to ration the time any child may spend with a video. Called The Moderator, it is a black box which can be fitted to the power supply leading to the video console, simply cutting off the video when the pre-programmed time expires. The Moderator can only be programmed by a parent using a 'control key', and it also comes with electronic seals to prevent any tampering. Gold has high hopes for his product. 'Video games are compulsive', he says. One video game company, the international giant Nintendo, gave Gold's invention a diplomatic welcome: 'We hope it will encourage parents to play the games alongside their children', a spokeswoman said, 'rather than just switch them off.'

How far that is from the reality of most parents' lives, a company as successful as Nintendo in selling to the young must surely be aware. For the innocent days when children's TV could truthfully be called *Watch With Mother*, the era when there was always a parent in the house to share in childrens' games and TV viewing and to take up the slack when interest palled, vanished at least a generation before today's parents were born. Today's children rely on television not only for their entertainment but also for their most basic sources of information and hard fact. A 1992 survey by Barnardos, the British children's charity, showed that 70 per cent of children aged 11– 13 had turned to TV for all they knew about AIDS, ironically enough to the squeaky-clean Australian soap-opera *Neighbours*. Meanwhile only 10 per cent learned anything from their parents or teachers. Information derived like this, without context or content, the Barnardo survey warns, is almost useless: 'passive acceptance of media-led messages, even if positive, is unlikely to change behaviour.'

'What is so tragic here is the parents' substitution of the electronic media for any interaction with their children, in those few brief years when it really, really counts,' says Dr Janet Gilmore. 'But at least that is better than nothing. The Barnardos survey showed that some parents refused to allow researchers any access to their children to take part in the survey about AIDS, saying that the kids knew nothing: they prefer ignorance to any form of education, it seems.'

•••

We need more alternatives to the standard harsh, dark, violent and despairing fare.

Michael Medved

•••

How is a parent to know what to do? Countless studies have sought to establish a causal link between mass media violence and real life, so many indeed that researchers now give us surveys of the surveys before any new work can begin. In 1991 George Comstock, Professor of Communications at Syracuse University in New York, reviewed 190 studies carried out over a period of 30 years, and found 'a very solid relationship between viewing anti-social portrayals or violent episodes and behaving antisocially'.

But proof positive of any direct link has continued to elude even the most detailed investigation. More than 1,000 pieces of research have been commissioned on this theme in Britain and America, making it arguably the most-studied aspect of the modern mass communication industry. The research has drawn on the disciplines of physiology, psychology, psychiatry and sociology, with subjects ranging from convicted criminals to animals wired to electrodes, and no firm conclusions have yet emerged about whether or not violence portrayed on screen leads to violence in real life.

Indeed the only certainty is the widening gap between expert opinion and the gut reaction of non-professionals in the field. 'Concerns about on-screen violence are a bit misplaced,' said Dr Guy Cumberbatch of Aston University, who has undertaken extensive research into media violence all over the world. 'It strikes me that there are areas like imitation – where people claim they have acted out or imitated a film. But we are talking about one-off cases. If a dozen or so were imitating, then we might have to do something about it.'

Dr Cumberbatch concedes that 77 per cent of research studies support the view that there is a causal link between crime and media violence. 'But in most cases the research has been quite inadequate, and on close examination simply does not concur.' He has the support of other media analysts: 'Nothing can be proved empirically,' says Steve Barnett of the social and economic research establishment, the Henley Centre, 'and it comes down to a battle of prejudices on either side.' The current concern, Barnett concludes, is just 'another moral panic'.

Why then are we left with the stubborn conviction that *there must be a connection – there simply must be*?

'The level of violence is so awful, so unbelievable,' says Arthur Miller. 'I can't help believing that it's having an effect on the behaviour of people.'

But this conviction is difficult to act on, in the face of the relentless pressure of violent material in the mass media and the hype that surrounds it. 'When the film *Rambo* came out, my son was desperate to see it,' says Rosemary, a Warwickshire university lecturer and mother of Daniel, then aged 11:

> We had the most terrible scenes, he was crying and swearing he'd be the only boy in his class who hadn't seen it. I told him I didn't care, it was repellently, disgustingly violent, and that was all there was to it. Afterwards three of the other mothers told me they wished they'd followed their instincts and refused to allow their boys to go. But they were afraid of over-mothering them.

How have we arrived at a situation where mothers can be bullied into believing that they are damaging their sons if they do not yield them up to this dangerous rubbish? Where parents are afraid to act on their legitimate impulses to protect and control 10- and 11-year-olds? And never has it been more necessary. For nowhere, no matter how remote, is now out of reach of the ubiquitous transmitters and receivers, coaxial cables and satellite dishes making possible 24-hour video and TV. Every parent must therefore make a choice, and every act of resistance to the culture of violence must be then of value, no matter how personal and individual.

Clive Bourne of Bredon Hill in the English Midlands must have seen himself as an unlikely hero in these wars. But as the headmaster of a middle school in charge of pupils between 8 and 12, Bourne recently banned all pocket computer games from his school. 'Many hand-held electronic games feature attack, destruction and combat as an essential ingredient,' he wrote to parents. 'My colleagues and I question the values such games promote.'

Why was Bourne so unusual that his action received front-page coverage in Britain's national newspapers? He was saying no more than many already felt. Bourne's letter told the parents that 'considerable concern has been expressed among all staff regarding our observed rise in the aggressive behaviour of some pupils.' This claim was swiftly countered by the manufacturers of the offending toys. A spokeswoman for Nintendo, whose Game Boy along with its rival Game Gear by Sega dominates the playground market, denied that computer games bred violent behaviour. On the contrary, recent US studies showed that they enhanced the children's imagination, she said.

Well she would, wouldn't she? And she would not be lying. The powerful impact of these images, their capacity to kickstart even the most sluggish fancy, is not in dispute. But do we really want to 'enhance the imagination' of 10- and 12-year-olds with material like this, as described by journalist Luke Harding:

> ... the new Night Trap by Sega, a gruesome computer game depicting murder and torture, involves the horrific murder of five semi-naked actresses. They are killed by being drilled through the neck and mutilated by sharp electric clamps. Teenagers [*why only teenagers?*] playing the game have to try to save them by fighting off psychopathic servants and monsters. To add to the horror, Sega has used the latest virtual reality technology to make the actresses appear real, rather than cartoon characters ... Dana Plato, who played Kimberley in the American TV comedy series *Diff'rent Strokes* ... is hung upside down in a cupboard while her blood drips into a bottle ... the actresses wear skimpy shorts, low-cut nightdresses and revealing underwear ...

Just like the home life of any of the children using this programme, Sega would say: 'We don't believe that games like Night Trap will have any adverse effect on players,' a spokesman pronounced. The firm is currently planning to use state-of-the-art graphics to develop a new range of war games. More blood and guts, then. But more money in the till.

Absence, therapists say, is the most basic form of abuse. Absence of control of this kind of material creates a vacuum into which the worst of consequences may potentially flow. After the heyday of behaviourism, most parents no longer see a child as a *tabula rasa*, a blank slate on which they can write at will. One of the glories and the pains of parenthood lies in the realization that not only the Hohenzollerns have intergenerational foreheads and noses, not only the Hapsburgs can turn out 500 years of serious jaws and prehensile lower lips. It can be uncanny to see Grandma Phyllis's smile surfacing on a 7-year-old face, or middle-aged cousin Stanley's frown reappearing in the pram. It seems likely that the science of the future will have a good deal more to tell us than we now know about the genetic inheritance of each individual, and how two parents come together to make up one new life.

Yet all philosophy, all religion, all education, all morality, all structures of reward, crime and punishment are based on the observation that human beings study, learn, absorb and apply what they see around them, that they make use of what they are taught, and what they are given. If we believe that a child can learn to do well, we must accept that it can learn to do badly. In terms of TV and mass media consumption, however, the link between violent material and the behaviour of a child is unlikely to be the simple cause and effect that researchers have looked for in vain, and adult society would dearly love to have proved.

Occasionally, it is true, a causal connection can be traced between a specific act of viewing and a subsequent reaction: the release in 1991 of the gangland movie *Boyz 'n the Hood* provoked intermittent violence throughout America. The same fate followed the 1992 cult film *Juice*, about gang life in Harlem. Anecdotal evidence must be treated with care: film director Michael Winner is fond of pointing out that a rapist who claimed to have committed a sexual assault after watching Winner's violent film *Death Wish* turned out to have eight previous convictions.

All the more reason, then, for him not to have access to something as violent as *Death Wish*, one may think. But even if this rape had been his first offence, it would have been almost impossible to prove that Winner's film stimulated, encouraged or forced the rapist to do what he would not otherwise have done. For the human mind is not simply a slot machine, to swallow an idea, a suggestion or a scene and pass it along for processing into a violent act. Far more commonly, such images sink into the great quagmire of the unconscious where they work away unseen, affecting the recipient in incalculable ways, as the Cambridge philosopher Professor David Holbrook explains:

One of the problems in the discussion of the effects of violence and pornography in film and television is that many of the dynamics belong to the unconscious mind, or at least the less conscious areas of the mind. Yet at the 'common-sense' level the connections are understood. For instance, the excitement of pornography lies in our sense that we are taking from those depicted in sexual acts something they would not give voluntarily – it is thus visual rape, or a form of stealing, glamourized. Violence has a parallel appeal. It prompts what I would call false solutions, and the dynamic is that of hate ... For creative people to give themselves over to the dynamic of hate is today immensely profitable, partly because we have an industrialized culture (cf television) that is expensive to run and must use the most barbaric appeals to hold attention: and partly because at a time when people at large feel that their lives do not have much meaning the dynamic of hate seems to offer a substitute. Many today have given themselves up to the dynamic of hate to survive and it is for this reason that we have what the *Los Angeles Times* calls 'a degenerate culture'. But as the late Raymond Williams declared, 'culture teaches', and it is in this that the danger lies.

But the danger remains as yet too vaguely defined for those concerned with its consequences to have any confidence in calling for firmer controls as a remedy. Devoid of any firm proof that watching violence on TV or video leads children or others to commit violent acts, research is currently at an impasse, and parents' hands are tied. It may be, though, that those concerned with the effect of unregulated viewing are looking in the wrong direction. Perhaps the problem of TV and video lies not so much with the *content*, objectionable though that may be, as with the *form*.

Because TV is potentially dangerous in itself, whatever it is transmitting. For all its power to stimulate, its 'magic carpet' facility of whisking the viewer away to strange lands, of teaching foreign languages or exotic culinary arts, of enriching our image-bank with pictures of coral islands and ice-capped mountain chains, TV itself constitutes a form of sensory deprivation. A two-dimensional medium, it deprives the viewer of three crucial sensors when we are denied the capacity of experiencing events as we do in real life through the profound and primitive guidelines of touch, taste and smell.

The pace of TV output is another reduction of human physical control, too. Unlike the experience of reading a book or listening to recorded music, in TV viewing the bombardment of sound and image cannot be controlled. Effortlessly, hypnotically flowing out of the tube, it cannot be slowed down, reviewed or repeated. So the flickering frames usurp the viewer's autonomy of consumption and human need for control, substituting a false rhythm and the apparent comfort of a superimposed structure that is essentially hollow and delusive.

For because it is two-dimensional, TV is inherently unsatisfying, feeding our senses at only two-fifths of our normal, natural capacity. Hence its hypnotic, even narcotic power, a power that cynical producers deliberately combat with a constant increase in stimulus. This is closely connected with the rising level of violence in horror movies and 'gorefest' videos, as writer Robin Hunt explains: 'The extremes of sexuality and violence spawned were not simply a mirror on the world they reflected, but *a conscious move to fight the soporific appeal of television.*'

Especially for children, Hunt might have added, who readily drop off to sleep, above all those allowed to stay up long past any reasonable bedtime. 'Films became more sensationalist,' Hunt concludes. 'Cinematic genres were exploited and taken to their limits in order to target the young – the horror genre most of all.' Eternally titillated then, yet never sated, stimulated and simultaneously sedated, the viewer compulsively returns again and again to the source of dissatisfaction like one in the grip of a bad relationship. The higher the level of viewing, the greater the disappointment intrinsic to the very experience of it, and the stronger therefore the drive to intensify the quest.

And the senses become numbed in other ways too. The relentless market pressure of a competitive industry means an ever-escalating diet of novelty: teams of highly-trained 'experts' from computer-brilliant emotional retards to the super-smooth merchandizing thugs equipped with Harvard MBAs all toil to outdo one another in new and undreamed of sensations to tickle the jaded palate. But sensation, especially devoid of three-fifths of nature's sensory input, very soon gives way to sensationalism. And sensationalism is subject to an inexorable law of diminishing returns.

For the more extreme the stimulus, the shorter the time of response before something further still is required. Even young children become habituated, even unformed sensibilities are blunted, and with each exposure the level of sensitivity falls. As car chases had to get longer, bigger, and faster, so violence has had to struggle constantly to outdo what had gone before. Hypnotic, narcotic, now even toxic, the result must ultimately destroy all power to feel, and hence any hope of empathy with the sufferings of others.

•••

It will be worth it if in the end I manage
To blank out whatever it is that is doing the damage.
Then there will be nothing I know.
My mind will fold into itself, like fields, like snow.

Philip Larkin, 'The Winter Palace' (1978)

•••

TV violence is deprived of reality, not because it shows Tom the cat being flattened by a steamroller and then bouncing back again, but because the feelings of the viewer are being flattened. Prolonged exposure to TV means a reduction of our human grasp on life. Attempts to point the finger at Tom and Jerry then, as responsible for our current brood of alienated, unfeeling young, or at any other programmes notorious for violence, fall wide of the mark and as such are doomed to fail. Meanwhile the real villain of the piece, the TV set itself, sits quietly and innocently in every living-room corner.

And that in the end is the final, the real horror, that we have ourselves permitted the alien into the house, installing it in our kitchens, living-rooms and bedrooms. Rising violence and an associated decline in moral standards have both been attributed to film from the first moment that the first camera rolled, and with the same form of passive, narcotic, two-dimensional consumption as television, film must take its share of responsibility. But the real threat lies not so much in the cinema, which after all parents have some power to control, either physically, economically or even geographically now that more and more cinemas are being located at huge multiplexes outside town.

Still less does the danger lie in live performance, despite the defence of violence on film by the author of the novel which became the sexually explicit film *Damage*, Josephine Hart. 'The body count in a modern splatter film is nothing to that in *Hamlet* or *Lear*,' Hart told a London conference on screen violence; 'what matters is the moral content.' But this comparison between tragic masterpieces of world classical theatre and the output of the mass media cannot be supported for a moment. Sure, Euripides was violent, says the film critic and campaigner against film and TV violence, Michael Medved, *but he wasn't pumped simultaneously into millions of homes*.

Medved might have added, 'and no matter what the horrors, *you never saw them*'. The rigid rule of decorum in Greek tragedy meant that no violent action is ever seen on stage. No one shouts, no one even raises a hand except in prayer, let alone a weapon. Modern special effects, by contrast, do not blench at decapitation, disembowelling, or women giving birth to monsters. 'My concern is not with violence per se, which has been part of Western art in Sophocles, in the Bible, in Shakespeare,' says Medved, whose book *Hollywood vs America* takes the film industry to task for the rising level of violence not only in film but in society at large. 'My concern is with gratuitous and exploitative violence.'

These are the twin poles of today's horror, the invasion of the home, and the creation of special effects with all the power of a horrific reality. Even in the cinema film buffs confessed themselves nauseated by the scene in *Cape Fear* which had Robert de Niro biting a lump of live flesh out of a woman's cheek. *The Silence of the Lambs* gave Anthony Hopkins as the cannibal Hannibal Lector no less than a three-course feast. With the domestic invasion of the TV and video, given the ease with which even a one-year-old child can master the TV controls, and above all with the introduction of the supremely controllable video, there are no safeguards for the young any more.

Satellite channels in particular have spearheaded the deregulation of the airwaves. They are responsible not only for relentlessly pumping out violent films, but for a grossly cynical pattern of scheduling which clearly demonstrates a total contempt for the convention of the 'nine o'clock watershed' designed to protect the young. So the violent Schwarzenegger film *Terminator 2*, although reserved to the 'safe' hour of 10 PM, was shown immediately after the same actor's much more acceptable *Kindergarten Cop* at 8.00 as the bait to that hook. In the same spirit, *Look Who's Talking* will lead straight in to *Robocop*, and *Three Men and a Baby* into *Straw Dogs*. And these will not be the only showings. After the transmission of any Schwarzenegger film, teachers see an immediate rise in the playground traffic of bootlegged videos, as children nationwide swap illicit recordings of the darkest material, with or without their parents' knowledge or consent.

And they all have their own incalculable effect on unformed minds. Not that young children are the only ones at risk. 'Film is different,' says the actress Catherine Deneuve, 'film has its own reality':

But I am disturbed by the video revolution. The idea that someone can freeze a frame, rewind and play a scene over and over
again unleashes the possibility of sexual perversions I do not
even like to think about.

This concern is echoed by James Ferman, director of the British
Board of Film Classification, launching a campaign in 1993 to warn
parents of the dangers of allowing children access to violent or
explicit adult videos. 'The biggest problem we have is parents who
don't take the categories seriously,' he says:

> I would hate to think that any child would see *Henry, Portrait
> of a Serial Killer*. It is '18' – we have to assume that the public
> will be responsible, and '18' means '18'. If '18' means '12', then
> the system will break down. We have to say no, we can't have
> freedom for adults in this country because we can't trust adults
> to protect children.

How far can we expect adults to 'be responsible', as Ferman claims?
Not completely, must be the honest answer: certainly not 100 per
cent, the level of protection that children must deserve. 'I am often
asked by worried parents whether children are learning cruelty from
television,' writes Alice Miller:

> In my view a child who harbors no pent-up rage will show no
> interest in brutal and sadistic TV programs. However, brutal
> programs are avidly absorbed by children who have never been
> able to defend themselves against overt or subtle tormenting at
> home or who for other reasons, can never articulate their feelings
> – for example, to spare a threatened parent. So they can satisfy
> their secret longings for revenge by identifying with what they
> see on TV. These children already carry within them the seeds
> of their own destructiveness. Whether or not this destructiveness
> will erupt depends largely on whether life offers them more than
> violence: in other words, whether witnesses willing to rescue
> them cross their path. What is important to understand is that
> the child learns cruelty not by watching TV but always by suffer-
> ing and repressing.

Does TV trigger, then, even if it cannot teach, acts of violence in those who are vulnerable to its abuse? This debate, a feature of mass media production since the earliest one-reelers lit up the penny arcades, took on a new and urgent relevance after the death of James Bulger in February 1993. At the trial of the two boys accused of his killing, evidence was given that the father of one of the accused had rented more than 400 videos in the last two years, 64 of which had been of a violent or pornographic nature. One in particular, *Child's Play 3*, hired out less than a month before the murder of James, seemed to have a direct bearing on the case. Featuring an evil doll which walked and looked like a human toddler, it ended when the doll was splashed with paint and had its head beaten in on a ghost train. For reasons never established by the police, James's killers splattered him with paint before they beat him to death and left his body on a railway line.

The presiding judge, Mr Justice Morland, was not the only observer to find similarities between the video action and the details of the crime, as he revealed at the climax of the case:

> The bizarre and terrible circumstances of the killing put this case, so it could be argued, in a class by itself. It is not for me to pass judgement on the upbringing [of the two boys in the dock]. But I suspect that exposure to violent films may in part be an explanation.

There was no proof, the defence pointed out, that either of the two young killers had ever seen the horror film in question. The father indeed denied it, saying that he watched the film himself, and his son only watched cartoons. The chief investigating officer, Detective Superintendent Albert Kirby, was reluctant to draw any conclusion: 'The area of videos was one we looked very closely at, and we cannot find any specific thing which highlights that.' Other stories too could be said to offer an uncanny foreshadowing of James's dreadful death: in the Roald Dahl story 'The Swan' two bullies abduct a younger child and drag him to a railway line, where he is almost killed by a train until he flies away to safety. Like the video *Child's Play 3*, this book was available to the two young killers, through Liverpool City Library. To the police, the two boy killers were not unwitting victims of corrupting influence, but corrupt in themselves, 'wicked beyond any expectation', said a senior officer involved in the investigation, 'with a high degree of cunning and evil.' Nevertheless, the Detective Superintendent conceded, *'I would not have let a 10-year-old of mine watch the sort of videos involved in this case.'*

For at the least, as psychologists were quick to suggest in the anguished debate that gripped Britain in the wake of the trial, the influence of such material must be considered a possible underlying cause in this otherwise motiveless act of sheer malignity. 'Children of the ages of the killers are desperately trying to build their own map of reality,' argued Dr James Hemming:

> They do not only listen to what parents and teachers say, but are also alert to the language of the environment. This, in the form of some video games and other nonsense, is telling them lies about life. The result is an appalling inner confusion which can only lead to appalling consequences. Surely this case is lesson enough for us to treat the minds of children with more respect. It is not only the violence of undesirable video games that is in question, but the unreality of their message.

Cambridge psychologist Dr Janet Reibstein takes the appeal to an adult sense of responsibility further:

> Children do kill, we know, in a sudden unleashing of anger, but this is something different. It involves a level of sophistication and co-operative behaviour which doesn't go with 10-year-old behaviour. Through being brought into adult culture the children may have been exposed to videos, games, conversations where people carry out sadistic acts. The child who does not have a lot of other stimulus in life, or power, or who sees adults entertaining themselves by watching acts of shocking brutality, might see it as an effective way of gaining something.

And not only these two benighted children of Liverpool, reaching out as they did for something that can hardly be imagined as the darkness closed in. Wherever a video receiver is to be found, there this material will surely be, working its mischief on children's minds, unseen, unacknowledged and unchecked.

But not unfelt, as we are slowly being made aware. The American anti-violence campaigner Michael Medved draws attention to a 1993 survey of children in a low-crime, high-income area of Washington

DC, where teachers found their charges' written work increasingly dominated by images of mutilation and violence. 'Eyes are being pulled out, arms choped off, heads cut off,' said one. 'Usually the story ends in death.' Other motifs included violent individuals invading students' homes, feeding off the brains of the dead, stabbing a killer robot and slashing an enemy to death. Where, Medved asks, are the 'talking animals, fairy godmothers and magical journeys' of children's fantasies of former days? Gone with the wind. And these children are *8 years old*.

Of course the vast majority of such children will never grow up to mutilate, stab or kill. But it only takes a tiny proportion of the globally susceptible to copy these or any other acts of cruelty and violence to make a difference, not least to their victims. And as Medved points out, above all 'the poisoning of [these children's] imagination will still have a long-term impact on the world they inhabit, when popular culture teaches that violence is not only accepted – it is expected.'

Clearly no instant solutions will hold the key to the problems of today's young people, Medved accepts: 'The entertainment industry is correct in insisting that new efforts to restrict or tone down violent videos cannot overnight eliminate the epidemic of youth crime.' But let us at least make a start. Let us begin by agreeing that anything too violent or cruel to be watched by a child should probably not be enjoyed by its parents either: and that the dividing line for what is 'acceptable' should be drawn with the weakest and most impressionable members of our society in mind, not the strongest. 'The violence in *Reservoir Dogs* was acceptable,' argued the film critic Barry Norman, 'because it was shown to hurt. It was not something to laugh at.' How many children are capable of such fine distinctions? *Reservoir Dogs* was certified for general release, and many, many more than the adults it was intended for saw and received its message.

We can't trust adults to protect children, said a British film censor, *if children cannot be kept away from material such as this*. It must be evident now that this is true: that huge sections of the adult population are failing to protect children, even abusing them through the production and consumption of these films and images. 'I see it as an unravelling of the social fabric,' broods Arthur Miller. When the social fabric is unravelling as fast as the fabric of the family, what remains?

• • •

It is impossible but that offences will come: but woe unto
him through whom they come! It were better for him that a
millstone were hanged about his neck, and he cast into the
sea, than that he should offend one of these little ones.

St Luke, 17:1–2

• • •

IV

ORPHANS OF THE STORM

In every cry of every Man,
In every Infant's cry of fear,
In every voice, in every ban
The mind-forged manacles I hear.

William Blake, *Songs of Experience*

CHAPTER 10

When the Bough Breaks

I believe strongly that children need love and security in
a home where you have husband and wife, father and
mother and the children.

Mackay of Clashfern, Lord Chancellor

The strongest memory I have of my parents getting divorced is feeling grimly determined that it would never happen to me, because it is so violent – doubly or trebly so
when there are children – and chaotic.

Martin Amis

'DO YOU EVER REGRET getting divorced?' Kingsley Amis was
asked, years after he had left his wife, the mother of Martin and his
two other children, when Martin was 12. *'Only every day,'* he replied.

Like father, like son. Man hands on misery to man, as Kingsley
Amis's close friend Philip Larkin wrote. Despite his resolution to
remain with his wife and the mother of his two sons, despite taking
a stern line with others who fell by the wayside, Martin Amis proved
himself a chip off the old block when he too parted from his wife
in 1993 and moved in with another woman.

Although family history has a distressing tendency to repeat itself,
a solid family base is still each individual's main hope for the future.
The importance of the home life in determining a child's sense of
security is summed up by Judith Bardwick, Professor of Psychology
at the University of Michigan:

Marriage and the family are where we live our most intimate
and powerful human experiences. The family is the unit in which
we belong, from which we can expect protection from uncon-
trollable fate, in which we create infinity through our children
and in which we find a haven. The stuff the family is made of

is bloodier and more passionate than the stuff of friendship, and the costs are greater too.

John Bradshaw, the American psychotherapist and guru of a number of 'self-heal' programmes for recovery from suffering in childhood, agrees: *'Our families are where we first learn about ourselves.'* What happens, then, in families where the first lesson the child learns is that its parents cannot do the necessary work to sustain the family that they have created, cannot find enough love between them to stay together, even 'for the sake of the children'?

•••

Divorce? Never! But murder, often.

> Dame Sybil Thorndike when asked if she had ever considered
> divorce during her long marriage to Sir Lewis Casson

•••

Divorce in the old world was once regarded as such a violent departure from the way things ought to be that it required an Act of Parliament, an annulment from the Pope, or even the destruction of the Roman Catholic Church in England as in Henry VIII's divorce from Katherine of Aragon, to bring it about. Even when it became legal, it remained deeply shameful, especially for the woman. In my mother's circle, 'divorce' was such a bad word that it was never pronounced, only spelled out in whispers: 'Surely it can't be true that the Queen is going to allow Princess Margaret to have a *d-i-v-o-r-c-e?*'

At the start of her reign the Queen did not permit divorced people into the Royal Enclosure at Ascot, and even an 'innocent party', as divorcés could still be seen in those innocent days, was not received at court. Now the Queen has been forced to countenance the divorces of her sister, her daughter, and assorted royal cousins, not to mention the marriage breakdowns of two of her three sons. In the same period the US has embraced not only a divorced President Reagan, but a President Clinton whose extramarital and family history made the Reagans, even as exposed by Kitty Kelley, seem almost wholesome by comparison.

Now that divorce is accessible to all in the West, the numbers of those availing themselves of it has been startling. From 500 divorces a year among a married population of 11 million in 1900, Britain alone has seen its divorce rate increase *one-thousand-fold* in the last

90 years. In America, the home of divorce, the figures are as bleak. From a 1950 figure of 385,000 divorces, the numbers have shown an inexorable upward trend: from 708,000 in 1970 to 1,176,000 in 1990, with no sign of dropping back.

'No relationship should last longer than a fridge,' opined the model Twiggy in all the confidence of the glorious Sixties, when she parted from her then manager Justin de Villeneuve – 'and that's seven years.' The length of a modern European marriage destined to end in divorce is indeed now on average seven years. What does that mean for the children who may be born into the security of a marriage only just in time to find themselves thrust out of it?

As with television and film violence, any direct link between the unprecedented levels of western divorce and the current wave of alienated, unhappy, aggressive children is difficult to prove. Divorce itself is still a minority activity, involving between one in three and one in two of all couples in the western world. One third of divorcing couples have no children at all, while a further 14 per cent wait until the children are grown up before they sever the knot. But over half of all couples who divorce have at least one child under 16, and in a world where everything seems to be falling apart, the collapse of the primary unit of society must merit closer scrutiny.

• • •

What is divorce? Grief. It's painful.

Cliff Richard

• • •

'The varieties of cruelty that parents can inflict on their children are endless,' writes Scott Peck. Perhaps the greatest cruelty of divorce is that it is almost never acknowledged as such. *Children are resilient, they'll soon get over this*, divorcing parents assure all who will listen. *It's much better this way, we were fighting all the time, we'll all be much happier after the split, I want them to remember the good times.*

'We are all born narcissists,' Scott Peck continues, 'innately stupid about the rights and needs of others, and relatively unconscious of the organisations to which we belong ... We can and do routinely grow out of narcissism ... But such learning is not guaranteed.' Nowhere is the truth of this more evident than in the freedom with which some modern parents feel they can move out of their marriages and families as if they were simply getting off a train.

For Tom, who works in television, the whistle blew soon after his marriage to Alison, whom he had met when she was an aspiring actress of 22. Five years later, Alison had two children and was unhappily bogged down in a stalled career when Tom met another rising actress, also coincidentally 22. When Tom split from Alison to live with his new love Sally, she took over the two children and in time had her own son too. Tom told friends they were the perfect family, the one he had always wanted.

Ten years later, Tom left for another young actress of 22. It was unfortunate, but children are resilient, he said. In the ensuing short-age of money, Tom's eldest son had to leave the quiet independent school where he was on course for university, and plunge into a rough inner-city school where he sank without trace. When he resur-faced, it was as a juvenile known to the police. Meanwhile Tom's younger son developed an eye condition, unnoticed in all the upheaval, which eventually left him with less than a quarter vision in the affected eye. When last heard of, Tom's latest union, now also blessed with children, was in difficulties, and Tom was moving out. Unfortunate, he says. But children are amazing, they'll get over it.

'*It isn't true*,' says Stephanie, whose parents divorced when she was 11, 'it simply isn't *true*, you *never* get over it.' An increasing body of official opinion is now emerging to support this view: div-orce, according to the baby and child guru Dr Spock, '*always* disturbs the children to one degree or the other.' Olivia Timbs, co-author of *The Divorce Handbook*, on her own account was unprepared for the sheer weight of the evidence that divorce is 'bad for your health, bad for your purse, and particularly bad for your children,' she says: 'I have been continually surprised by the misery that divorce inflicts upon families, often more, it seems to me, than the misery of an unhappy marriage.'

For often the children have very little idea that the marriage is unhappy, until divorce occurs. 'Nobody gave it a moment's thought,' writes journalist Jo Ind of the state of her parents' marriage. 'Most of the time I was not conscious of my heart beating either.' Then the break-up began:

Divorces are messy and ugly businesses. People are not severed from each other cleanly and sharply as though cut with a knife: bones are crushed and gaping sores go septic. It is like being stabbed, and then before those wounds are healed being stabbed all over again, and those same wounds being crushed under a mallet ... My sister and I would sit crouched in a room, eyes tightly screwed up, hands over our ears, wincing 'Shut up!' as the house vibrated with the sounds of our parents destroying each other. The only way of evading the pain was to get away from home ... I used to think it would be easier to have your own divorce than to listen impotently to your parents having theirs.

Ind's account is borne out by recent research, including an in-depth study following the fortunes of 17,000 British children from 1958 to the present. The result makes stark reading for the 'they'll get over it' school of thought. This survey, carried out by Dr Kathleen Kiernan for the Family Policy Studies Centre, completely undermines the popular notion that the damage to the children of a divorce is 'only' emotional, and 'only' lasts for a short time. On the contrary, Kiernan shows that the emotional scars alone can last for a lifetime: 'It is easier to maintain a family and support network after a death than it is after a divorce,' she says.

And the damage can be far more intense than we have been led to think in other ways too. Contrary to the myth that the remarriage of a divorced partner will help to 'heal the rift' by creating a 'new family', *children do better when they remain with one divorced partner alone*. Remarriage compounds the original distress, as the children of both sides continue to wish their own parents were still together even years after the divorce. 'I never gave up,' Stephanie says, 'even when my Dad had a new baby with his girlfriend, I always called her that, I never called her his wife. It wasn't till Mum died that I finally had to accept that my family would never come right again.'

How does it go wrong? While helpful 'How To' books agonize about 'What Shall We Tell the Kids?', dealing with marriage break-up as if it were a once-and-for-all crisis, the damage goes on for years. Across the board:

- Children of stepfamilies are three times more likely to leave home before 18 than the children of homes unaffected by remarriage.

- They are less likely to continue in education, and less likely to go to university.

- As a consequence they suffer lifetime impairment of career prospects, and are more likely to face unemployment, redundancy or dismissal.

- Boys were more likely to suffer learning difficulties.

- Girls were:
  – twice as likely to leave school without qualifications;
  – twice as likely to become teenage mothers;
  – four times more likely to marry before the age of 20, setting up for the next generation the increased likelihood of repeating the cycle of marriage breakdown and divorce.

For divorce, it is now clear, *will mark a child for life. They do not 'get over it' like measles or mumps.* A symposium of the British Psychological Society on marriage breakdown in 1991 heard the same story of young people failing at school, leaving home early, marrying young, and making families before they were 23. As children, the offspring of divorce are more prone to bedwetting, nightmares and speech problems. As adults, they are more liable to emotional and psychological problems severe enough to need treatment, particularly in their mid-30s, and particularly if they are women. At the age of 36, both men and women have a greater chance of being unemployed. By their early 40s, they are more likely to have lost touch with their parents, even the parent who brought them up.

In the nature of things, that parent is more likely to be a mother than a father, with major implications of further damage to the child. Particularly worrying in today's climate of increasing resistance to all forms of authority is the seemingly irresistible drift away from the father. A British government study carried out by the Family Policy Studies Centre in 1991, showed that only half of absent parents stayed in contact with their children. In Britain alone that means 750,000 children of divorce who never see their father. 'Too often the separation of men and women also means the effective "divorce" of children from their father,' comments Malcolm Wicks, Director of the Centre. 'These are truly the innocent victims. *A child has the right to maintain contact with both parents.*'

In today's epidemic of divorce, it is clear that this right is now far more honoured in the breach than the observance. But when children's rights are being so copiously violated, what is one more or less? When parents split up, many children are denied even the basic right of information, told little or nothing of what is going on. 'I had to ask where Daddy was after he had left,' says James Lyons, a London banker. They may also be actively deceived: 'For me, there was a string of stories, Daddy was on business, he had to go and look after Granny (his mother), he was opening a new factory, he was abroad,' says Samantha Jenkins, now a computer clerk. 'And all along he was living in a bed and breakfast only about a mile from our front door.'

Other children of divorce suffer this crucial disruption at a key point of their own lives, as Angharad Almark relates:

> The day before my first A-level exam I found out there were problems in my parents' marriage. I remember lying in bed that night knowing that Dad hadn't come back. The next morning it turned out that he had spent the night with another woman – someone incidentally who I knew. My mother immediately left to stay with a friend. I can remember meeting her with my brother three days later – it was one of the worst experiences of my life. She couldn't come home in case Dad was there so we sat on a bench in a shopping centre on a dreary blustery afternoon. I kept saying that Dad would come back, that he didn't mean what he'd done, that he loved us really. I completely believed it myself . . . I still wonder why he was able to leave me as well as Mum. I'd always been daddy's little girl and I couldn't see what I'd done to make him want to leave.

Not surprisingly, Angharad has little faith in relationships now, feeling 'it'll all end in tears'. She is sure that she will never marry:

> It's an outmoded institution, which judging by statistics, doesn't work very well. You wouldn't go on a flight which had a one in three chance of crashing, so why walk down the aisle against the same odds?

• • •

Emotional abuse is universal.

John Bradshaw, *Healing the Shame That Binds You* (1988)

• • •

'Divorce, far from clarifying things, makes marriage even more problematical,' observes Phyllis Rose in her study of five Victorian marriages, *Parallel Lives*. The techniques by which the child victims of divorce struggle to cope with the destruction of their lives makes poignant reading. 'I kept my head down at school and tried desperately hard to please, I was terrified they would turn against me too,' says Debbie Grindley, now a catering manager. 'I just hated it, it was like being ill, I felt sick all the time. Everything I did was to get my father's approval – I thought that would get him back. Even going into catering – which I've never enjoyed – was because he's a chef.'

Girls and boys tend to react differently to the absence of a father in these crucial years of their lives. 'I didn't feel angry with him for leaving,' reports James Lyons, 'but I took it out on the old girl quite a bit – I had to punish someone.' In fact the person being punished was James himself: 'At one point I started thinking about suicide I was so depressed.' It says a great deal about his parents that noticing James's state of mind, they refused to give him an air rifle he asked for as a present, for fear that he would shoot *them*.

All this is small beer in comparison with what can befall the hapless child victim of parents truly bent on making each other suffer, and careless of the cost to the child. When Christian Brando stood trial for the murder of his sister's fiancé in 1991, allegedly in defence of the pregnant girl, the more famous Marlon was in court every day at Christian's side. Good stuff, said the world: MARLON STANDS BY BRANDO JR., BRANDO STANDS BY KILLER SON.

But where was Marlon during the much longer trial that had been his son's earlier life? Christian's childhood years were scarred by endless custody battles between Brando and his warring wife, actress Anna Kashfi. Repeatedly kidnapped by one parent or the other, molested by the kidnappers en route and abused by his alcoholic, mentally ill mother between times, Christian finally arrived at the safety of his father's home aged 13, only to spend the rest of his youth in the care of maids and bodyguards. And as Brando's remorseful presence now acknowledged, parental absence is the most basic form of abuse.

The annals of showbiz are stacked with similarly abused boys and abandoned girls, off screen and on, from Charlie Chaplin to Marilyn Monroe. Monroe, modelling herself on Jean Harlow, another abused child-blonde, like Harlow picked up on and was picked up by a series of father figures in her endless search for the one man she could trust. For such women, repeated disappointment, no matter how severe, can never quite defeat the desperate hope that one day they will at last find the love that they have lacked . . . *somewhere, over the rainbow* . . .

'When Daddy is always distant, he's always shining like a star,' explains family therapist Donald Bourne. 'He can never lose his lustre in the eyes of a deprived daughter. She will spend her life looking for him.' Like Judy Garland and Edith Piaf. Like Jane Fonda and Sinead O'Connor. Like hundreds and thousands more, whose names could fill this book.

These women at least found in the adoration of their fans some pale shadow of the love that was their due. Others have to live on in the knowledge that what was brutally taken away, their faith in the adult world, will never come back again. For like child abuse, divorce forces children to confront the weakness or wickedness of those who should be protecting them: it robs them of their childhood, and precipitates them into an alien world before their time. For divorce and, more particularly, remarriage tend to show the least attractive aspects of the adult world to children as they grow. The most common cause of marriage break-up is adultery, which adults tend to feel is 'legitimated' if they go on to marry the object of their illicit amour. They rarely reckon with the conviction of their children that infidelity is the betrayal that should never have happened in the first place.

· · ·

Divorce is the sacrament of adultery.

French proverb

· · ·

It is one story, divorce victims say, when Daddy (for father is the parent who usually leaves or is compelled to go) simply makes himself scarce, reappearing in the lives of his children to reap the maximum adulation with minimum effort. It is quite another when he sets up a new home with a replacement wife, and expects everything to be fine. The son of 'Sunny', the 11th Duke of Marlborough, his young heir James, was presented with not only one but two stepmothers, first the exotic Tina Onassis, former wife of Aristotle, and second the beautiful Swede Rosita, the mother of James's stepsiblings Lord Edward and Lady Alexandra.

Now Marquis of Blandford and heir to the famous dukedom, James has never ceased to blame his afflictions and derelictions, from a ten-year addiction to heroin and cocaine to the habit of bilking creditors and refusing maintenance to his wife and child, on the unhappiness he suffered when his parents divorced. These claims have aroused scant sympathy for the heir to the Blenheim Palace fortune and estate, from a press and public who wish that they had half his misfortunes. In the wave of derision, no one ever pauses to think that the unloved and unlovely Blandford might have a point.

For just as with the crushing sadness and lifelong impact of divorce itself, it seems likely that the effect on children of their parents' remarriage has been grossly underestimated. 'Children don't choose to have a new person in their parent's life,' points out the author Deborah Moggach. 'Home is their own territory and even an alien pair of shoes in the hallway can seem like an intrusion.' As for the adults:

> Nobody approves of the way other people bring up their children: married couples quarrel about it all the time. Second time around it's even worse. In fact, it's a nest of vipers. For the new person is not the parent – they are not even a replacement parent – and they shouldn't try to behave like one.

Yet even trying to behave like a parent, however misguidedly, must be preferable to the insensitivity, hostility, or even cruelty that some step-parents are capable of. 'I felt like a second-class citizen,' says London salesman Charles Coleman of his stepmother. 'I was always the last to be served at dinner. Every time we had a row, I wished she was dead. I thought my father always took her side. He says I was spoilt and got my own way because they were bending over backwards to make me happy. I remember exactly the opposite.'

Other children have darker memories still. 'My father never raised his hand to me,' remembers Lindsey, 'but my mother's boyfriend used to hit me all the time when we went to live with him. He used to grab hold of my neck and belt me around the head so hard I thought he was going to kill me. What really hurt me though was that my mother never tried to stop him. She cried and all that, but she never once stood up for me. I just knew that my real dad would never have done that.'

Nor is physical abuse the worst that children may suffer when they are not protected by the biological bond. In the primate world, as researchers have established, the young are constantly at risk from males who are not their father. Hence the importance of pair-bonding, which evolved, anthropologists now argue, not for the male to reserve the sexual services of the female exclusively to himself, but so that he would have reason to protect his own offspring against hostile marauders.

In the absence of such protection, the consequences are quickly seen. When a primate male takes over either the widow of a pair-bonded male or his harem, he will most frequently kill all the infants. By this he ensures that all the attention of the female is directed at himself, and subsequently at his children by her. He can also be sure that he will never have to take care of or fight for a child that is not his own. Something of the same sort of raw competitiveness is observed in many men who live with their new wife or lover in a home shared with her children. At its starkest, this tension betrays itself in the homicide statistics which show that *mortality is 65 times greater among stepchildren, than for children living with their biological parents.*

At worst, the stories behind this statistic read more like the most brutal of ancient folk tales, or the darker broodings of the Brothers Grimm, than anything we expect to happen in the western world today. These old-world echoes are often heard in the outraged press coverage: UNWANTED BOY KEPT IN DUNGEON, STEPMOTHER TREATED GIRL LIKE CINDERELLA. A London stepmother convicted of cruelty in 1991 gave her 8-year-old stepdaughter the food from the cat's bowl to eat, and kept her shut up in a cupboard under the stairs all the time she was not at school. In the first month of 1993, three London stepfathers or common-law husbands were jailed for attacking the young children of their partner's previous family so severely that all three were in hospital, where one was found to be brain-damaged, and one died. Even without such violent abuse, the children of a home which is no longer a home may slide into depression, delinquency or into care: in any of these situations they will suffer the damage that they then may be driven to pass on in ways beyond their control.

•••

> I can and must try to demonstrate to parents the danger of
> the misuse of their power, to sensitise them and sharpen their
> ears to the child's signals.
>
> Alice Miller, Banished Knowledge (1990)

•••

A parent's divorce may plunge a child into emotional misery and
financial distress, foreshortening its childhood, educational prospects
and employment opportunities. Even the death of a parent, research
has established, does not cause a child to suffer such unresolved
grief and mourning as the loss through divorce. In households under
pressure, the simple absence of a father, or the long hours worked
by a single mother, will inevitably deprive the child of the old structures of supervision and control which worked so well in the past
to keep children out of trouble and off the streets.

Within the close nexus of deprivation, poverty, alienation, antisocial behaviour and crime, divorce cannot simply be seen as the or
even a primary precipitating factor: even to suggest this ignores the
millions of products of a broken home who go on to become responsible and valuable members of society. But the adverse effects of
divorce upon so many mean that we can no longer carry on offering
or accepting the soothing cliché that it is a 'fact of life' like bad
weather, or the car breaking down.

For the suffering never stops. *There is no divorce*, said Thomas
Hardy: we can never be cleanly or finally severed from those who
have shared our lives, our homes, our beds. Above all, we can never
be divorced from the misery it leaves behind, a misery so compelling
that even those who have suffered it themselves seem powerless not
to pass it on. The Irish are more honest about relationships than the
English, says the novelist Jennifer Johnston: 'Perhaps we are more
bitterly realistic, and can't dismiss as the English do the terrible flaws
in family life.' For Johnston these flaws were felt as 'pangs' of grief
for her parents' separation and divorce when she was 8. Later she
had vivid memories of being used as a pawn in the ensuing struggles
between them: 'After both my parents were dead it occurred to me
that they had made me a victim.'

Yet none of this prevented Johnston from leaving her own children
when the time came. Her two youngest, aged 12 and 9, remained in

England when she left their father to go to live with her lover in 'the Big House' in County Derry in Ireland:

> I felt ghastly. I used to cry every afternoon at 4.30, the time they would normally be coming home to me. It was a terrible betrayal, but children are amazing. We just settled into a routine when they came to Ireland in the holidays.

Nevertheless, Johnston says, she takes 'the state of innocence' very seriously: 'The loss of that state is what turns us into adults.'

Arguably what turns us into adults is the realization not that we have lost our own innocence, but that we do not have the right to make others who are innocent pay the price of our happiness. Yet who helps those struggling to reconcile these contradictory claims? Mediation services are few and far between, counselling available only to those with money and time. Yet Britain spent an estimated £1.4 *billion* on divorce in 1990, without counting the hidden costs to other services like health and welfare. In financial terms alone, money spent on counselling or reconciliation services is saved many times over in the heavy cost of welfare benefits which automatically accrue to the casualties of a broken marriage, adults or children.

Surely then we could try harder to support couples in difficulty, above all those with children, who will always want their parents to stay together? 'They say, "We were fighting so much, it was better for all of you that we split up", your parents tell you,' said one child of a hostile divorce. 'But they don't understand, you don't want them to split up, you just want them to stop fighting.' Conciliation, even at its most basic level, can have considerable success in preventing couples from continuing their conflict. When this proves impossible, they can also find ways to soften the impact on the children, both in the short and long term.

But the main objective must be to give more support to all marriages, instead of assuming that divorce is automatically the next stage of marriage after getting into difficulties, or worse still, the only way out. For the children of broken families are not the only ones to regret that the juggernaut of separation and divorce, the lawyers' bandwagon and gravy train, was ever set in motion. Surveys from Europe and America show that in the wake of a divorce, over half of all divorced husbands and a third of divorced wives live to regret the split, even if they have remarried. Personal and anecdotal experience also strongly suggests that spouse number 1 is so often a virtual clone of number 2 as to make the first marriage break-up almost redundant. And every divorcé still has to face the future with the knowledge and pain of a marriage break-up as a constant memory, an unchangeable part of the past, which the passage of time may not lessen but increase. 'Ask the mothers and fathers among them 12 years later,' writes the author of *World Changes in Divorce Patterns*, William J. Goode, 'and I suspect that as many women as men, and more of both [than immediate post-divorce statistics show] will wish after all that they could have cut their losses, compromised their pride, and been considerably better (and richer) parents. I know I do.'

To salvage marriages rather than to terminate them makes sense at every level. Yet the state cannot take all responsibility for the behaviour of adults and their individual choices for right or wrong. The most common cause of marriage break-up is adultery, the second, violence in the home. For neither of these should children be expected to pay. The moral is clear: parents should think twice about adultery, and try to find a way to end violence, rather than kill the marriage.

And don't hesitate to help wherever help is needed. As with child abuse, friends and relatives are reluctant to intervene between husband and wife. Warning signs may be ignored, even pleas for help brushed aside in the fear of taking sides. But the policy of detachment has its price, and again it is children who pay, as this brief testament makes clear:

I have had a lifetime to recover from and ponder over the results of my parents' divorce and subsequent remarriages – I am 72. Through the years of my childhood until the divorce – when I was 13 and my sister 5 – we listened to constant shouted arguments in which our parents seemed to forget our presence: we would sit weeping at the dinner table or in the dark at the top of the staircase. From this I began to feel I was the adult having to live with stupid, selfish and thoughtless children – i.e. my parents; but it was still our father, our mother and our family, and we had to learn to live with it.

Second, the most devastating effect of the divorce was the loss of a home which was truly ours (in spite of my quarrelling parents). Afterwards my sister and I lived with grandparents, father and stepmother, and visited mother and stepfather where it was never our home – at best we were merely tolerated. It was many long years before either of us could bear to speak of these events to others for fear of breaking down into tears.

Can it be doubted any longer that *divorce is a form of child abuse*? From the child's-eye view, assurances that Mummy or Daddy still love the children even though they no longer love each other, cut no ice. 'If Daddy loved me, why did he leave me?' is the abandoned child's perennial cry. The parental assurance, 'it's better this way', provokes the child's protest of silent mutiny, *'not for me!'*

If our alienated children learn nothing else from their elders' marriage failures, it will be that nothing lasts, and that nothing can be relied on. In the absence of trust, what can become of feeling? And in the absence of feeling, what is left but sensation – sensation which must be strong enough to fill the void of life?

• • •

> I'm one of the traumatized children of divorce. It certainly did bad things to me.
>
> Penelope Lively

• • •

CHAPTER 11

Legions of the Lost

The zero-parent family?
This is still a high-voltage subject.

Senator Daniel Moynihan

Always new pain.

Günter Grass, *Local Anaesthetic* (1969)

AFTER DIVORCE, what then? In the wake of a marriage break-up, attention almost always focuses on the adults: how do they pick up the pieces? When will they find new love or happiness again? Rarely do we ask the children who now have to live between the two broken halves of what was once a family, how are they doing in the ruins of their life?

In most cases, the true answer must be, *worse than before.* Inevitably, divorce impoverishes: when father goes, he takes his salary with him. The majority of two-parent families in Britain – 89 per cent – rely on one or both parents' earnings. By contrast two-thirds of all single-parent families – 66 per cent – rely on welfare benefits alone.

For divorce is a luxury whose cost few count until it is too late: 'Unless you are earning less than £2,000 a year or more than £50,000, forget it!' says divorce consultant David Lipmann. To live in a mother-led one-parent family almost inevitably condemns a child to less of everything than it used to have, even without the ever-present risk of slipping into genuine poverty with all its deprivations, succumbing to the constant downward pull each step of the way.

Have we lost the will to aid and succour couples in their vital task of sustaining the framework that traditionally creates a safe place for our young? The modern wave of marriage breakdown has not been effectively resisted in any of the industrialized countries of the world. Churchmen lament, traditionalists protest, but governments seem bogged down in nostalgia, fatalism or inertia, powerless to act, or even to respond. In the absence of clear social policies to sustain the old-style family, or even signs of any political will to take up the challenge of change, the fractured marriage, the lone parent, and the routine of split parenting more and more come to represent the family of the future.

At the same time we have seen a rise in the numbers of never-married parents, both the couples who bypass wedlock, live together and then part, and the women who proceed straight to motherhood in the determination to go it alone. Add to these the far greater number of women who are single not by choice, the widowed, the reluctantly divorced or the plain abandoned, and none can doubt the reality of single parenthood as a social revolution that the powers that be have failed to anticipate, failed to recognize, and failed to engage with except at the level of pious rhetoric and hollow bluster.

Meanwhile, the dance goes on. There are now over a million single-parent families in Britain, and their numbers are increasing by 40,000 a year. Government statistics from the Office of Population, Censuses and Surveys show a steep annual rise in the numbers of single parents with more than one dependent child, from 6 per cent of all families in 1961 to 16 per cent 30 years on. In America, too, nearly a third of all children live in a one-parent home. At the last census in 1990, a record 1,165,384 unmarried mothers gave birth that year, a rise of *75 per cent* in the decade since 1980.

Few would now argue that the children of single parents face a different future from that of children with both parents at home. At a 1991 symposium Professor A. H. Halsey of Nuffield College, Oxford, identified a daunting array of disabilities that such children may experience all through their lives. They will tend to:

- suffer more illness;

- have lower levels of nutrition;

- enjoy less 'comfort and conviviality';

- do less well at school;

- experience more unemployment;

- be more prone to deviance and crime;

- repeat the cycle of unstable parenting from which they themselves have come.

And at the end of it all, they will of course die younger.

•••

If you're poor and black, your dreams are always the wrong colour.

Shanice Dellahaye, teenage mother in Washington DC

•••

Nearly a third of the half-million children living in inner London come from lone-parent families, it was recorded in the 1991 British census. In the borough with the highest concentration of conventional families, Newham, only just over a fifth conformed to the traditional structure of two parents caring for their own dependent children. In the lowest, Westminster, the figure was only just over a tenth (11 per cent). What colour they were, the Office of Population, Censuses and Surveys declined to inquire.

Other countries have long since given up the luxury of colour-blindness. In the US, government statistics show that 66 per cent of all black babies are born to single women, as opposed to 16 per cent to white mothers. 'Government does not know how to get people to conceive only those children for whom they plan to provide stable homes,' comments the Washington columnist George F. Will. 'This aspect of the urban crisis results from a general fraying of the culture.'

Fraying of the culture? Black families everywhere, it is agreed, tend to be poorer and lower down the social system than any other group. For some commentators, however, the malaise runs far deeper than this. 'I must be the first to admit that the black family unit is in ruins: it is our first and basic weakness,' wrote the black activist and thinker George Jackson before his untimely death in 1971:

> This fact may contribute much to our difficulty in uniting as a people. But to say that it is slowly eroding because of poverty and social injustice is to completely mistake the depths of the issue. Three historical factors have produced the present state. First, the family unit was destroyed during chattel slavery. Second, our cultural institutions and customs, without which cohesiveness can never exist, were destroyed and never replaced. Third, our change in status from an article of property to untrained misfits on the labour market was not, as most think, a change to freedom from slavery but merely to *a different kind of slavery*.

Jackson's bleak analysis is supported by the black professor Thomas Sowell in his influential study of the 1980s, *Ethnic America*. To Sowell, the black family, already crushed by slavery, suffered another grievous onslaught in the huge economic migration of the 1920s and onwards, in which the males were lured or forced from the South to the North, only able to work if they left their wives and children behind. Sooner or later these women were forced to turn to welfare: their children then were born into the cycle of welfare dependency still being seen today.

Enter the 'single mother', troublesome mainstay of the troubling modern 'underclass' as defined by the US political scientist Charles Murray, horror-heroines of the welfare-guzzling workshy, the new terror of the Right. In this scenario, 'responsible society' is being held to ransom by gangs of girls who want to be wedded to welfare not to a man, and who see children as no more than bargaining counters in the demand-game of their life. Pregnancy then becomes a deliberate ploy of calculating female fraudsters who obtain free housing, cash, hospital treatment or social benefits through the unscrupulous use of their uteruses in their war against mainstream society and all its virtuous tax-payers, those who pick up the tab.

Or if the unmarried mother is not this kind of feckless, hopeless, amoral child, as much of today's news coverage would suggest, then she is a fanatical feminist using her womb as a weapon in the great crusade to create a world without men. Assisted by other feminists/ lesbians/man-haters, she is pledged to undermine 'traditional values', bringing up her young to value nothing, least of all themselves. One way or another, the 'single mum' or 'woman out of wedlock' has been made to take the blame for countless social problems, especially those of children, as the undisputed star of hot press topics ranging from poverty to crime.

Yet these lurid stereotypes will not stand up even to cursory examination. For the nightmare figure of single motherhood, the wilful teenage fuckwit, prime example of the undeserving poor determined to screw the welfare system as they feel they have been screwed, is more apparent in media hysteria than in statistical reality. In Britain, government statistics showed 895,000 single parents on income support in 1991, both men and women. Of these *only 5 per cent* were girls between the ages of 16 and 19, and *of those*, only 12 per cent had deliberately planned to get pregnant. American figures show a very similar picture: of the total number of American children,

65,093,000, only 8 per cent lived with a female parent who had never married.

Equally, a close look at the real life of even one of these women will show the level of confusion and disinformation that pervades this issue, blurring the categories to treat each new case as an excuse for new moralizing and fresh outrage. Fern is a London hairdresser, pregnant at 19. It is true that the arrival of her baby will antedate her marriage to Albie, a plumber, by some time: 'We can't afford it now.' But as they always assumed they'd have children anyway, it doesn't matter, says Fern. There was no question of her getting pregnant to get state benefit, or to get a council house – both have good jobs and somewhere to live, and 'it just happened'. Albie's Dad told him if you go with a girl, it happens. Not to worry, just both do your best for the kiddy. Dad's giving them a home till they can get a place of their own, and that's when they'll get married.

Another teenage pregnancy then, but not another social-problem 'single mum': Fern has a job, a partner, somewhere to live and plans for the future. As do most mothers, whether married or single. Indeed today's 'single mothers' should arguably be seen not as the chief culprits of our social decline, but as a product of it, responding to, not causing, the social strains for whch they have been blamed. On this view these are not women out of control, but individuals taking the only control they can.

For it is no coincidence that the single mother has arisen in the wake of two of the great stresses of our times, the divorce epidemic and the recession. In both these crises of the breakdown of old certainties, motherhood can offer a young woman what the adult world has signally failed to provide, a role and function, and a place to go. For the children of divorce, having a baby may present itself as the only opportunity to repair or replace the ruined family of their childhood by creating one of their own. Alice Miller outlines some of the psychological mechanisms that lie behind this urge to have a baby, and which run far deeper than any conscious decision:

This means: 'I want to have somebody whom I can completely possess, and whom I can control (my mother always withdrew from me); somebody who will stay with me all the time ... [It means] right now I am nobody, but as a mother I should be somebody, and others would value me more than they do now

I have no children.' Or it may mean 'I want to give a child everything I had to do without, he should be free, not have to deny himself, be able to develop freely. I want to give this chance to another human being.'

In the same way today's female casualties of the recession, the girls without employment and women without jobs, may be thrown back upon the only work left open to them and them alone, the task of reproduction that only women can perform, in the search to give structure and meaning to their lives. This feeling, too, will run far deeper than any imputed desire to milk the welfare state for all it is worth. For what used to be the great female disaster, bearing a child out of wedlock, may now offer a clear advantage to a woman, if it supplies a sense of direction, a useful occupation, or, at least, something to do.

This, suggests the feminist writer Beatrix Campbell, is the central and unpalatable truth behind the rising number of births to young and very young unmarried women in recent years, the founding mothers of the so-called 'underclass'. It is also, Campbell suggests, the reason why official counter-attacks are doomed to fail. 'The rate of teenage conceptions [in Britain] increased during the Eighties from 56 per thousand to nearly 68,' Campbell explains. 'And the government suddenly introduced a commitment to *halve* the rate of teenage pregnancy by the year 2000.'

Without understanding and without insight, in Campbell's view. For teenage pregnancy will not be tackled by educational campaigns alone:

> In regions starved of waged work, young people are eternally infantilised. Teenage motherhood guarantees the metamorphosis from childhood to adulthood: it is a girl's passport into the community of women ... The strongest correlation therefore is not between teenage pregnancy and education, but between teenage pregnancy and a locale's economy. Teenage pregnancy is most likely to be reduced by creating employment.

By giving women economic power and genuine independence, in short, by ensuring to each an income and an autonomy that they would value and seek to preserve, rather than hasten to throw away. *And until we empower all women, from the age of puberty, to make*

*pregnancy a positive choice among a number of good options, then
we shall continue the degrading downward spiral of those still virtually children bearing more children to live in poverty and die in
defeat: the children no one deserves.*

Yet still these are a minority of all single-parent homes. Most
women do not choose to bring up children all alone, without a man:
most indeed embarked on motherhood with the opposite expectations and hopes. It is true that one-parent families have risen in
Britain from 570,000 in 1971 to the record level of 1,225,000 in
1990: true, almost all of these are women. Yet *less than a third of
all single parents are unmarried women*, and this third consisted of
women of all childbearing ages, not simply teenagers. Allowing
for single fathers, who composed less than a tenth of the British
total in 1990, the majority of one-parent families are led by
women who have been separated, divorced or widowed: on the
whole, then, *manless not by choice*, and certainly not when they
set out.

• • •

> Why does it seem so difficult for men? It's still women who
> stay with the children, being a father seems so hard. It's harder
> for men because they don't change as easily as women. But
> they don't want to change. I don't feel optimistic.
>
> Adam Jukes

• • •

Manless women, and fatherless kids: from North to South, in Britain,
in America and almost every other industrialized country of the
world, above all in the dying hearts of inner cities, we are confronting
what the Deputy Director of the Institute for Policy Research in
Britain, Patricia Hewitt, has called 'the extraordinary absence of
men'. And not only in Britain. One quarter of all American children,
over 15 million in all, are now growing up without a father.
Nearly half, as a result of desertion or divorce, will spend some
time in a single-mother home, without the man who authored
their existence.

It's a wise father that knows his own child, as absentee father
William Shakespeare famously wrote in London, while his grass
widow Anne Hathaway reared their three children in Stratford-upon-
Avon. It must be an even wiser child who gets to know its father in

the teeth of the blind selfishness, simple desertion or panic flight from the family that can pass for fatherhood these days.

'Their father?' Jilly, a Liverpool machinist living not far from the Merseyside estate where James Bulger met his death, glances at her three children and looks away. 'Doesn't know, doesn't care, doesn't pay!' She is surprised I am even interested. It's old news now, half the women in her street are in the same boat. More and more men are simply on the lam, running away from fatherhood and all that it implies.

'In the old days,' comments the feminist writer Angela Phillips, '[men] could take refuge in a role that was clearly defined, providing the means by which their wives could do the caring. Love could be left till later, when the child was old enough to play cricket. Today there is no clearly defined role to hide behind, and men are confronted by their own fear of entrapment.'

So they run away, Phillips says, most often departing to the arms of another woman who will lick their wounds and not ask too much in return. The writer A. N. Wilson, leaving his wife after five years of marriage, admits that he was 'pretty selfish' to do it while his children were still so young, but protests, 'All I want is for them to be happy.' He is now married to a woman ten years his junior, and describes himself as 'a poor little person just trying to pay his mortgage'.

Those who stay physically may run away emotionally, hiding behind too much work or constant play, days on the booze or nights with the boys, leaving their women feeling unsupported, angry and resentful. They then have even more to avoid at home, dodging and weaving to duck their partner's exhaustion and resentment, always trying to stay ahead of the trouble they know must come, both in the marriage and in the lives of their children and themselves. But one way or another, they run.

And not because of women: not by any choice except their own. It is essential that we understand this massive, international dereliction of the male for what it is, not for what the media make of it, civil rights campaigner Patricia Hewitt insists:

The absence of fathers is not an invention of feminism or the later 20th century, nor a creation of women who choose to have children on their own. It is essentially a phenomenon of patriarchy, one side of the division of labour in the nuclear family between breadwinner husband and nurturing wife. Now, though, changes in the role of women are forcing new thinking about the role of men ... *We can no longer confine fatherhood to finance* [italics inserted]. Male unemployment and above all female employment mean that most families now have two breadwinners. What children need most from their fathers now is emotional engagement.

With the mothers as well as with their children, it seems, and even more with society at large. For over the last twenty years or so, the revaluation of the relations between men and women, taken with the rocketing rate of divorce, means that women no longer look to men to be their 'Mr Right', the pivot of all their hopes and plans and the linchpin of family life. 'A young woman may start a relationship with high hopes of everlasting love, but that conceals a profound lack of faith in marriage and partnership,' says Angela Phillips. 'Young women are growing up with a new message: *don't put your faith in Prince Charming. Learn to drive your own carriage.*' Deprived of that automatic role of the past, the young husband and father may well find that nothing else tempers the wind to the shorn lamb.

Losing the role, today's father has also lost much of his economic power. 'Some of those who insist that marriage should be the alternative to welfare motherhood seem not to have understood what is happening to young men,' observes Hewitt drily. In the poorer sections of society in particular, unemployment has meant that yesterday's 'good catch', the marriageable young man intent on settling down and raising a family, may be as rare a breed today as the good housewife contentedly scrubbing floors.

Among young black men above all, the US sociologist William Julius Wilson has argued that rates of unemployment, especially if taken with the levels of imprisonment and early death in the same group, mean that, economically at least, there are precious few 'Mr Rights' even worth considering. Yet the marriage rate among black men with jobs in the US has dropped faster than among their unemployed brothers, the *Washington Post* reports. Meanwhile young women bring up their children on their own, with the help of their mothers and grandmothers. 'Prince Charming?' Phillips imagines a modern-day heroine demanding. '*Haven't seen him for ages.*'

•••

Wandering between two worlds, one dead,
The other powerless to be born.

Matthew Arnold, *The Grande Chartreuse*

Make ... the Daddies ... pay!

US Senator Daniel Patrick Moynihan

•••

The majority of people on both sides of the Atlantic would agree
with this prescription of Senator Moynihan that fathers should take
financial responsibility for their offspring. Yet all the economists,
social scientists and strategists of the governments of Britain and
America have yet to come up with a workable formula for achieving
this, or any machinery for enforcing it. And without any such sanctions, 'the daddies' play away and stay away, with incalculable results
for their children.

Yet men matter, and never more so, when the task of redeeming
our alienated children bulks so large. To fulfil its potential, even to
have the expectation of a normal life as society defines it, *a child
needs two parents*. Single motherhood is not simply an alternative
lifestyle, it is a deprivation, psychological, social, and above all
financial. For a woman on her own does not even earn as much as
the equivalent man would in her place, let alone get enough money
to make her one salary serve as well as two.

And children cost money, as we have seen, more and more as they
get older. But the damage done by the runaway father is far more
than merely financial. An exceptionally high proportion of violent
or criminal children have fathers who were absent, or abusive or
both. And both absence and abuse take many forms.

Yet one of the most difficult things for any child to accept is the
idea that the derelictions of an admired or loved father can come
under the heading of 'abuse'. 'I see these articles [on child abuse]
and feel a little foolish for my anger,' writes Travis Simkins from his
cell in the Fulton County Jail in Atlanta, Georgia, where he is await-
ing trial for armed robbery. 'My father was neither abusive, nor
alcoholic. He was simply absent.' Yet what can we call this behaviour
of Simkins senior, if not abuse?

I was only 2 when Dad left, saying he needed to 'stretch his wings' ... He used to fly in at a moment's notice, he drove flashy rental cars, wore expensive suits, took me to top-dollar restaurants ... I recently asked Mom how many child-support payments he made in all those years of absence [and] she said she could probably count them on the fingers of one hand ... When he called a few weeks after Christmas or my birthday and told me the package I had never received must have gotten lost in the mail, I was afraid to mail a letter in case the same fate would befall it ...

For Simkins, there ensued a long struggle to give up the image of his father as 'my hero', 'the king of the world'. Yet desertion, insists psychotherapist Adam Jukes, is in fact 'the most basic form of abuse': 'It's about men refusing to take responsibility, refusing to stop being children, because it's only as children that we can have that primary love that's too good to give up.'

How many deserting males, from Cecil Parkinson to Mick Jagger, are ever seen as abusive? Yet the self-absorption of such men can have painful consequences for the child whose father is never, ever there, and never plans to be. Among such fathers, the prime contender in recent years must be the priapic prelate and most religious hypocrite the Very Reverend Dr Eamonn Casey, Roman Catholic bishop of Galway in Ireland. Casey, later described as a 'flamboyant 65-year-old', in his mid-forties fathered a child on a woman 21 years younger than himself, stood aside in her pregnancy while she was browbeaten by nuns and clerics for compromising his position, refused to acknowledge the existence of his son for seventeen years, and then 'borrowed' £70,000 from church funds to pay the mother off.

After the story was exposed in the media, Casey was reported to be seeking a reconciliation with his son, and praying twice daily for his welfare. The abandoned son Peter had a different story. 'The fact is that my father shunned me completely to this point,' he told reporters in 1992. 'He lacks the basic decencies.' On the one occasion the two ever met, when Peter was 15, the bishop spent '3 or 4 minutes' asking him how he was doing at college. 'Then he walked into another room and asked the attorney to get me to sign a release saying I would never speak to him or bother him again.'

•••

Alone, alone, about the dreadful wood
Of conscious evil runs a lost mankind
Dreading to find its Father.

W. H. Auden, 'For The Time Being'

•••

Nor is this the end. As divorce moves seamlessly from the unthinkable to the unstoppable, even with the futuristic scenario of marriages breaking down at the rate of one in two, we still have not reached the limits of tolerance. The ongoing collapse of families has an irreversible domino effect into the next generation. Children without parents are already out on a limb. When these children become parents in their turn, they can have no reliable models, no assistance and no back-up. And when their bough breaks, all those concerned will fall.

Hence the newest of the social problems with which our problem-ridden age is beset. The stage beyond the single-parent family is the family *with no parents at all*: once almost unthinkable, like divorce, or sex outside marriage, or the single-parent family itself, the recent emergence of what the US has called 'zero-parent families' is already giving professionals cause for acute concern. From a figure of 6.7 per cent of all US families in 1970, the numbers of children living in households not headed by either parent rose to 8.3 per cent in 1980, and had hit nearly 10 per cent by 1990. 'The zero-parent family is replacing the single-parent family as the emblem of social distress,' commented a front-page lead article in the *New York Times* during March 1993. 'And in all categories, *their numbers are growing.*'

Few professionals in the field would question this. 'There's a whole bunch of them out there, the kids whose parents have split up or were never together in the first place, people who've lost the battle, been jailed or institutionalized, or just drifted off,' says Leroy B. Payne, who works in an inner-city housing project in Detroit. 'These kids are the new orphans. They may have grandparents, other relations, or foster homes or schools that care about them. But as far as they're concerned, their only home is somewhere else, like out there, on the streets.'

Substantially an urban development, the problem of children

without parents is not confined to the 'mean streets'. 'You could use expressions like "it's mushrooming" or "growing exponentially", but these words aren't strong enough,' says former Judge Lois G. Forer of Philadelphia, who is on record as calling for the return of orphanages to deal with the situation. 'It's everywhere – New York, Los Angeles, Chicago, Detroit, you name it.'

And the rise of the no-parent family is inevitably creating a juvenile underclass a generation younger than the 'underclass' of feckless young parents already supposed to be causing all the trouble in the first place. 'These are the 12- and 14-year-old children of the 20-something parents who had them at their age,' comments economist Howard Steiner. 'They're the next generation of the unaccountable – only this time, they're starting out even earlier than their parents did.'

• • •

The figures show that 50 per cent of girls have had sex
before they are 16, the legal age of consent.

US Family Policy Studies Centre Review (1990)

• • •

The children of children – children without parents – this post-nuclear vision of the family presents a challenge of nightmare pro-portions to a society still almost exclusively geared to the old-time vision of Mom and Dad at home with the demographically correct 2.1 offspring, the respectable suburban family with its perfect pair of kids. In the wake of Western experience of the one-parent family, the prospects for any real initiative to combat this new development do not look good.

Detroit may be a long way from Dover, Düsseldorf or Madrid. But where America leads the rest will follow, and Jackson's measured words have a resonance for the whole of the 'advanced' world. When we permit 'the family' to be destroyed, in industrialized societies by the economic slavery that began with and has outlasted the Industrial Revolution, we take away the central prop of any civilized society. And as the family is the first and most important site for absorbing 'cultural institutions and customs', without which, as Jackson warns, 'cohesiveness can never exist', when we abandon the family, we aban-don our children to that peculiar limbo of the disengaged, in which they are doomed to drift and float like astronauts condemned for ever to walk in space and never get to earth.

...

This is the game that moves as you play.

Brett Easton Ellis, *Less Than Zero* (1985)

...

If the single- or zero-parent family is the global measure of social distress, what is the individual barometer? 'All it comes down to,' writes Brett Easton Ellis in the brief opening cadenza of his grimly apocalyptic novel of alienated youth, *Less Than Zero*, 'is that I'm a boy coming home for a month, and *people are afraid to merge.*'

As children emerge from their early years into young adulthood, any stress or damage within the family will inevitably make itself felt. The teen years provide the last great chance of growth into a healthy adult life. With discouragement, the girl or boy may drift imperceptibly into disappointment and dejection, taking a downward path from which they may not recover in their later life.

Like the unrecognized pain that children may suffer in silence, the more generalized distress which so many go through afterwards seems to be something that the adult world prefers not to see, even when parents are around to take notice. One or two children in every hundred succumb to depression, says Israel Kolvin, Professor of Child and Family Mental Heath at the Royal Free Hospital School of Medicine: many thousands, then, are suffering at any one time. But a 1991 survey in Britain into the prevalence of this illness among children in the community was, astonishingly, the first of its kind.

Depression in children is markedly under-diagnosed by doctors, Professor Kolvin observes, who are also unaware of its differing effect on the two sexes: girls are twice as likely to be sufferers as boys. These figures were confirmed by research in the 1991 study: out of 400 girls surveyed at three schools, the head of the project, Dr Ian Goodyer, Professor of Developmental Psychiatry at Cambridge University, discovered 28 cases of undetected and untreated clinical depression. Goodyer's findings indicate that 4 per cent of all 11–16-year-olds had serious depression at the time of his study. Additionally, more than 10 per cent had had major depressive symptoms, including feelings of worthlessness and the desire to die, *during the previous month.*

As scandalous as British ignorance and complacency about these children's suffering, is the lack of provision for any kind of help.

Too often their symptoms go unrecognized or wrongly treated – even serious disturbances may be dismissed by GPs as 'something they'll grow out of', while another of Goodyer's patients had had a succession of operations on her tonsils, adenoids, nose and throat for the severe headaches which disappeared once she received treatment for depression.

Yet if doctors were unaware, so too were parents. While adult society is quick to pick up on infringements of its rules or any inconvenience to itself, the plight of the child sliding slowly into the morass of self-doubt and despair can escape the notice of even the most apparently caring families. Often the adult world may not realize the burden it is placing on young and untried shoulders. Or perhaps it may not care, more involved in its own world than in the feelings of the child.

Sometimes the parents' disregard of the child begins at birth. Sappho Durrell, daughter of the author of the enormously successful *Alexandria Quartet*, felt weighed down from childhood by the name her father Lawrence chose for her. From her birth, her mother Eve was depressed – 'she had become frightened of his violence and had decided to leave', Sappho later wrote in her journal – but her only departure was to a mental hospital when Sappho was 2. When Eve recovered, the little girl was forced to choose between her mother on the one side and her father and the grandmother who had looked after her on the other, a cruel choice for any under-three-year-old.

As she grew, the young child was praised for being 'very quiet, very self-contained', in effect commended for repressing her feelings. At school, it was observed that she thought continually about death, a common symptom of depression at any age. All her schoolgirl heroines, Emily Brontë, Sylvia Plath, Virginia Woolf, had died young or in tragic circumstances. As an adult, Sappho struggled to win the approval of her virulently self-regarding father by essaying the one thing he respected, the life of a writer. Yet when she tried to write, he taunted her with 'trying to grow a prick'. Few were surprised when like her admired Plath and Woolf, Sappho killed herself.

Since her death, Sappho's account of Durrell's vicious abuse has taken an even uglier turn with the revelation of his incestuous rape of his daughter from her childhood on. What did Durrell want? Did he even know? And how could any child find her way through this? As Alice Miller points out, children can easily be lost in the wilderness of an adult's unacknowledged and unvoiced but not unacted desires:

Many people suffer all their lives from this oppressive feeling of guilt, the sense of not living up to their parents' expectations. This feeling is stronger than any intellectual insight that it is not the child's task or duty to satisfy his parent's narcissistic needs. No argument can overcome these guilt feelings, for they have their beginnings in life's earliest period, and from that they derive their intensity and obduracy.

The intensity of these childhood feelings can bring unhappy children to the verge of madness, often without the adults in the family even noticing the distress of the child. The novelist Lucy Ellman, daughter of Richard, the biographer of Wilde and Joyce, and Mary, author of the seminal feminist text *Talking About Women* (1968), was uprooted from her home in America to move to Oxford when her father became a professor there. At the same time, her mother had a brain haemorrhage, and Lucy gradually 'withdrew into misery' in what became 'the worst of times':

> I lay on my bed a lot, hoping I would die in my sleep . . . My mother sort of disappeared from my life; she was still barely able to speak. My father . . . was at the hospital all the time and had no time for us . . . I wore a coat and hat all the time, I did it to cover up my body which was ballooning under the effects of the English cuisine . . .

A longed-for return back home simply showed that a place left behind soon becomes a foreign country, and that a six-month separation can be terminal in a relationship between 13-year-olds. The boyfriend Ellman had pined for pretended that they 'hardly knew each other':

> That was real bad . . . I went back to Oxford with no further hope for myself. I became energyless, the effort of getting dressed and undressed was too much to bear, so eventually I took to sleeping in my school uniform. I started cutting my wrists to see if my parents might notice, but I was too scared to cut too deeply. No one noticed anyway. I was just lost . . .

Eventually Ellman's distress could no longer be contained:

I was caught for shoplifting some makeup – and I never wore makeup, I did it just to show off. It did cure me of stealing, it was so humiliating. I was sentenced to two years' probation and psychiatric care, and the court made me go to a shrink until I grew myself sane . . .

• • •

Show me a sane man, and I will cure him for you.

Carl Jung

• • •

Until I grew myself sane?

What was the secret of that?

Many do not find it, and in the search for alternatives can 'grow' themselves far worse. Today's legions of lost boys and wounded girls are never far from apparent consolations and instant distractions, and even the youngest may reach for a starkly adult solution to their distress. Statistics from agencies on both sides of the Atlantic indicate the size and scale of the problem. In Britain alone:

- 30 per cent of people under 20 have taken cannabis.

- 12 per cent have used hallucinogenic mushrooms.

- 7 per cent have taken LSD.

- 3 per cent have taken cocaine.

- 32 per cent of all registered drug addicts are under 25.

- 45 per cent of all new addicts since 1990 have been drawn from this age group.

The softer, more acceptable and more readily available 'social' drugs are even more widely used: nicotine, alcohol and solvents, mind-altering drugs from hash on up, are now a feature of the lives of large numbers of the troubled young, most of whom will find that what starts as a temporary recourse may have consequences for the rest of their lives. Tina is 16, and has been drinking since she was 12:

It began when I was still a little kid, I'd wake up after a party while Mum and Dad were still asleep, too hung over to get up and take care of us. All the glasses would still be there, so I'd mess around trying all the left-overs and I just got the taste for it. I liked how it made me feel, all floppy and sloppy. Then it was a kind of cool thing, you know? – to get the boys. Not that they were hard to get when I was completely legless and laughing at everything they said and they could do anything they wanted to me.

As this shows, the cycle of self-abuse may not stop with one substance, one sensation: the hollowest children flit from one thing to another, combining or permutating the available diversions in pursuit of the ever-receding 'ultimate high'. Like Tina, many begin through some apparently normal or even negligible act of careless adulthood. Sharon started smoking her father's pot when she was 12, as she told the writer Leonie Jamieson: 'I noticed he smiled when he smoked it, so I thought I would see if it made me smile too.'

Is it so hard for today's children to smile that they need drugs to do it? Yet with disturbances at home and difficulties at school, the disaffected young insist that they have little to smile about. 'Often they say they are looking for "a laugh" or "a few laughs",' comments family therapist Tom Snowden. 'In reality young people in trouble are usually low on the "feeling scale" because they simply dare not feel or allow themselves to know what is really happening to them.'

To fill the void of unknowing, Snowden says, hundreds and thousands of young people go on 'sensation-jags', periodic outbursts of behaviour designed to provide a sensation of some sort. Dr Douglas Carroll of Glasgow Polytechnic, researching teenage addiction to gaming machines, found that the tension is stoked by the child's urge to win pitched against the virtual certainty of loss. 'The machine delivers a lot of near-wins,' he explains. 'A cash trail builds up until the punter has almost won, then it dissolves.' The experience of playing these machines, the sense of being in control with the inevitable promise of something better just ahead, a promise which builds up and then explodes in a starburst of disappointment, in fact simply repeats and intensifies the painful rhythms of disillusion the child is seeking to escape in the first place.

And the pseudo-sensation does not end there. Poignantly but predictably, child gamblers at this level may become as addicted to the machines themselves as to the activity they supply. Psychologist Mark Griffiths who has worked with child machine gamblers observes that the young addicts liked to 'humanize their machines': 'they speak to them, swear at them, and treat them as a friend.'

This 'relationship', Griffiths believes, germinates long before the child sees his (for it usually is 'his') first fruit machine: amusement machine addiction can begin with early television watching. Attracted, even addicted to the bland glitter of the silver screen, the child who then discovers the power to manipulate the images himself, who thereby has the heady illusion of entering, even controlling the world he has previously observed only from outside, may well become addicted indeed.

Griffiths also warns of the scale of the problem, which he sees as going hand-in-hand with widespread adult neglect and deliberate lack of concern: 'If there was a disease that was affecting one in a hundred children, the Government would start immunizing them: *but nobody wants to acknowledge that help is needed.*'

• • •

I am: but what I am, none cares or knows.

John Clare

• • •

Help is needed . . .

The machine-players, it is recognized, the compulsive arcade stalkers will be mainly boys. But girls have their own ways of trying to shut out a world they fear, and do not understand. Did our age invent anorexia? historians have wondered, pondering the self-starved, self-styled saints of the convents of the Middle Ages, the spidery skeletons of Giacometti and the saw-boned starvelings of Egon Schiele. Or has it simply been left to the cruelty and perversity of our *fin de siècle* to translate a perennial female tendency into an epidemic?

An epidemic of the young, and getting younger, it seems. In Britain, this life-denying disease is now being diagnosed in girls as young as 10, warns consultant child psychiatrist Dr Richard Williams: in some cases, it will be well estabished even before puberty. Even among girls who cannot be called full-blown anorexics, around one-fifth of all British schoolgirls between 11 and 16 will be dieting at any one time. By the age of 15, anorexia is confirmed in one out of every 150 girls of this age. And once confirmed, the young anorexic will be in and out of the abusive war between her appetite and her body for a very long time to come.

Even if she wins, she may never know the reason for it all. 'I can recall and explain my horror at the sight of a meal, the guilt of swallowing a mouthful of potato, but as to why it started or how it could have been prevented, I am none the wiser,' says Jennai Cox, survivor of a three-year battle with her 'mystery obsession'.

To an equally mystified outside world, anorexia seems as ugly, pointless and destructive as any of the other 'sensation-seeking/evasion' tactics of the lost young things. Sensation there is in abundance, as anorexics report: the feeling of control, of defeating pain and conflict, of meeting a challenge and so winning esteem and self-esteem, and even the reward of the magic ever-elusive 'high'. 'People started saying how good I looked,' says Susan Scott, who went from nine to five stone in the course of her bout of the disease:

> Within a month I was eating practically nothing. A few grapes one day, apples or grapefruit the next. And the less I ate, the more energy I had. It gave me an amazing feeling of euphoria. Within three months I had lost more than two stones . . . losing weight had become a challenge and I wanted to see how far I could go. Sometimes I'd go into a shop and try on clothes designed for a 12-year-old and feel elated that I could fit into them.

When she finally sought therapy, Scott found the focus on her background 'pointless', because she had had 'such a happy childhood'. She could pinpoint the moment when that safe childhood world collapsed, leaving her unprepared for what lay ahead:

> One night we all went off to the pub and a pilot I knew called Ross was there. At closing time I went back with him to a friend's house, and before I knew it, we had gone all the way. There was no forcing and it wasn't horrible, but it wasn't exactly what I'd dreamed of. I suppose I had thought my first time would be wonderful . . . From the moment I woke up the next morning, things started going wrong.

After years of therapy, Scott remains true to her original conviction that the trigger for her anorexia was her unhappy welcome to the world of womanhood: 'I think it started because I was getting serious attention from men for the first time, and it developed as a protection against the pressures of sexual relationships.'

Undoubtedly some of the young will manage the transition from girl to woman with confidence and verve, even a feisty good humour, as 13-year-old Jamie Harges of Santa Monica, California, told *People* magazine in a round-up of her brushes with the opposite sex:

> This kid told my friend that you could land a plane on her chest. I called him an asshole, and he said 'Fuck you'. I said, 'You're definitely not that lucky, and I'm definitely not that depressed.'

But for the damaged children, wounds become wounds with an almost Old Testament implacability: the pain is passed on. As the children of alcoholics become alcoholic, as the children of the divorced themselves get divorced with twice the frequency of other couples, the force of the biblical pronouncement that 'the sins of the fathers shall be visited upon the children' comes home with a terrible force.

Nor is it always as neatly schematized as alcohol-alcohol, divorce-divorce. A study for the *American Journal of Psychiatry* in May 1993 found that the children of 'problem drinkers' were more likely to have a range of marital and psychiatric problems for the rest of their lives than the children of non-drinkers. Personal instability and matrimonial intolerance were the perpetual legacy of parents who clearly never thought for a moment of the impact of their behaviour on the present of their children, let alone on their future.

This cycle of abuse is no respecter of person, place, or class. The supremely snobbish mother of Hollywood 'Rat Pack' film star Peter Lawford married his father for his title, looked down on the popular and successful Kennedy clan as 'bogtrotters' and 'Irish peasants', and insisted that her son was brought up with every ounce of her own sense of gentility and aristocratic disdain. But so entrenched was her alcoholism that a family servant predicted Lawford's own descent into alcohol addiction when the child was only 7. Later, in a quite literal illustration of Larkin's grim prediction 'man hands on misery to man', Lawford became a father who proudly presented his own son with cocaine as a 21st birthday present.

Lawford grew up to be the ultimate hollow man, handsome, admired, fêted for his film performances and, by more than one woman, deeply and passionately loved. Yet it was never enough. His

cold, abusive life, as he tacitly acknowledged to close friends towards
the end of it, was responsible for a trail of emotional carnage among
the women he mistreated and betrayed, including Marilyn Monroe,
whom he virtually prostituted to his important friends Jack and
Bobby Kennedy, with no thought of the cost to her. Over a lifetime
of petty viciousness, only his social position, his money and his contacts kept him out of jail.

Others are not so lucky. Some children fall at the first hurdle, and
there is no safety net of money, power or privilege to catch them
when they fall. Such were the boys young James Bulger blundered
into on his last fatal walk. There was no saving him, because there
was no saving them. None of that trio met what they deserved. But
for some lost souls, it is truly too late.

• • •

> If one wants to seek out evil people, the simplest way to do
> so is to trace them from their victims. The best place to look
> is among the parents of emotionally disturbed children or
> adolescents.
>
> Scott Peck

• • •

CHAPTER 12

Bad Girls and Devil Boys

If as youngsters some discipline had been imposed upon
you at home, at school, or through the courts, you might
not now be standing here for this dreadful offence.

Mr Justice Scott Baker, judge of Maria Rossi and
Christina Molloy in the Phillips case

SHERIFF   What are you rebelling against?
JOHNNY   What have you got?

Marlon Brando as Johnny, leader of a gang of
motorcyclists who terrorize a small American town in
The Wild One (1954)

HERMAN DUTTON was 12 and his brother Druie 15 when one
of them held a hunting rifle to their father's head at their home in
Oklahoma in June 1993, and the other pulled the trigger. Philip
Barber and Paul Chapman were both a year below the legal age of
majority when they broke into the Reigate home of a 76-year-old
spinster in May the same year, beat her until they had broken most
of her ribs, stabbed her in the face, neck and body with a carving
fork, and as she lay dying, raped her on the floor.

Maria Rossi and Christine Molloy were also both 17 in July 1992
when they tortured and battered a 71-year-old spinster to death in
South Wales. And at 11 years and 4 months, the Yorkshire babysitter
who severely battered an 18-month-old boy in her charge later that
same year, and then suffocated him by pinching his nose and mouth,
was too young even to be named at her trial.

Are these the children we deserve?

If they are, what have we done to deserve them?

• • •

You young women are evil products of the modern age.
Your lives seem to be a story of providing for your own
immediate desires above all else.

Mr Justice Scott Baker

• • •

What can the stories of these children tell us? Is there any detail of these atrocities that can hold out any grain of comfort for the future, any hope of change? Or does each one represent an unheralded explosion of evil, unique, exceptional, and beyond understanding, even belief?

Edna Phillips, the pensioner murdered by the two girls, had lived next door to the Rossi family on a sprawling estate in South Wales since the eldest daughter, Maria, was a baby. But relations between the neighbours had deteriorated after the partially-blind spinster complained about the Rossi family's drunkenness and loud late-night music.

Maria developed an irrational hatred of the old woman, screaming obscenities at her in the street, stoning her dog. The outraged Edna called in the police, and a vendetta began. Excrement was smeared on the old lady's house and her belongings vandalized. In the words of the prosecutor, she was soon reduced to a 'life in hell'.

One long hot summer evening Maria and her friend Christine from the estate began to drink with Mrs Rossi: they consumed about three litres of alcohol, and a good deal else. High on rough cider and an unknown quantity of drugs, the two 17-year-olds rolled out of doors and chanced to meet Edna returning home.

Bundling her indoors, they tried to strangle her with her own dog's chain. They then played noughts and crosses on her face with a Stanley knife, stabbed her repeatedly in the chest with a pair of scissors, carved at her body with a piece of broken glass, smashed eggs on her as she lay dying, and finally tried to scalp her. Then they ran back next door, Maria Rossi calling to her mother, 'I've done it, I've killed Edna.' The next morning she was heard singing this refrain to the tune of 'The Wizard of Oz'.

In Maria Rossi's defence, her counsel said that she was the product of a broken home, and her mother claimed to have no control over her. Maria had begun absconding when she was 12, and had moved on to drink and drugs at 14. That year and the next, she had suffered miscarriages. By the time of the murder she had convictions for theft, burglary and possession of drugs. Her friend Christine, too, had been on drugs since she was 11 and she too had a previous record of assault. But she had nothing against Edna Phillips, never having met the old woman before the day of her death.

What can link this act of violence with any other? In particular, does anything connect the death of Edna Phillips with that other random killing, the now-notorious act of cruelty in Liverpool? Wherever spirits walk, do the ghosts of Edna Phillips and James Bulger shake their heads in silent communion at what brought them both to their last Calvary, the place of death?

•••

> James Bulger's murder was a watershed for the country: it made people wake up to the fact that the young people at the margins of society are out of control.
>
> Masud Hoghughi

•••

Out of control – how and when does this happen? Earlier, much earlier in most cases than we are ready to accept. Children whose actions lead them to be branded as bad girls and devil boys do not come out of nowhere like evil demons. And adult society, which then feels so ill-used by what they do, will rarely question its own part in creating this phenomenon, or ask how it might have been prevented. The truth is that many of the young who freak out in violent activity in their teens have in fact been out of control for many years before that. To Professor Masud Hoghuhi, former Director of the Aycliffe Centre for disturbed and delinquent children, the reason is clear:

> Everything which gives us a sense of self-worth is deteriorating. We are creating a society of envy where the prevailing value is how much money you have, not your worth as an individual. At Aycliffe we have children so disturbed they can't even integrate with other disturbed children ... cases I've never come across before – children who are suffering such abuse and neglect they're exhibiting an even greater range of bizarre and disturbed behaviour.

Certainly in a 'grab it and run' society, many of the problem children have today been left far behind in the list of what counts. Unlike the 'have-nots' of earlier generations, too, they are surrounded by images of what they are missing, what they have not got. Yet, unlike adults who can strive for what they want, children have no way to get a piece of the action, a share of the goodies trailed before them in every advertisement, every TV film, every dream of the good life.

And in a world where full employment is a vanished dream, once expelled from childhood and turned out of school, they are refused entry to an adult life, the world of work, with all that that implies. 'They don't have that step up from school to work where you are rewarded for what you do,' says Professor Terence Morris of the Mannheim Centre for Criminology and Criminal Justice at the London School of Economics. 'You don't have to do anything for your dole cheque, so you don't have that sense of achievement or purpose.'

In this limbo, this social void, antisocial activity perversely substitutes for employment as the only opportunity for challenge and stimulus, action and reward. 'If we can't find something legal for them to do, inevitably they'll become outlaws if not outcasts,' says a senior police officer. 'If they've got no stake in their own town, their street, their place of work, what's to stop them tearing it apart?' The stolen cars and burned-out vans found week by week in every town vividly underline the officer's analysis and the crime sheets behind it: areas famed for car theft and 'joy-riding' have on average youth unemployment figures of around 25 per cent, twice as high as the worst of other regional black spots.

One anonymous youth worker on a large urban estate plagued by car crime proposed a radical solution to the problem:

> Give them jobs or buy them cars. I'm serious. It would pay the insurance companies to give these kids vehicles. It costs them about £50,000 a week for this area alone. I'd rather they gave us the money to redistribute to the kids.

Yet is car theft and high-speed road racing entirely about being poor versus the thrill of having a car? The police are not so sure. 'This isn't a fun thing, it's purely for mindless kicks,' comments the same policeman, veteran of many years on motorized patrol. 'And people should understand that there's no "joy" in "joy-riding", it's just another form of search and destroy. Most of these cars finish up torched, completely gutted, did you know that? I could understand a kid nicking a car he's eating his heart out for, and can't afford to buy. It's the bloody horribleness of what they do that gets me.'

And like every other form of juvenile crime, the 'horribleness' is on the increase. In Britain the number of juvenile arson attacks on vehicles has increased fivefold since 1981, with a 60 per cent leap between 1990 and 1991. Arson itself has shown a similar rise in the same period, again in the same youth group: of the 4,000 or so prosecutions in Britain for fire-raising every year, almost half were boys between 10 and 16.

Rarely girls, it seems. The typical school arsonist will be male, psychologists explain, and often less than 10 years old. He may be a jobless ex-pupil bearing a grudge against the school, or a student with one special enemy among the teachers. Between them, child fire-raisers are now causing more than 3,000 school fires a year, more than 40 a week, costing the taxpayer more than £300 million a year. This amounts to *more than three times the annual total spent on books, paper, pencils and equipment.*

What is this rage to burn, break and destroy, and where will it end? In recent years police in Britain have detected an escalation in car-related crime. Working in teams, young car thieves in all the major cities now pull off increasingly sophisticated operations designed to draw police cars into a pre-set trap, where other cars will be waiting either to hit them head on, or to 'roll' them off bridges, down embankments or into rivers. Commenting on one such ambush laid for his men, Detective Chief Superintendent Philip Jones of the South Wales CID said, *'This is attempted murder'*:

They lured the officers into a trap and then deliberately and cynically put them off the road. They do not care what pain or injury they inflict on others, they are devoid of human emotion. It is beyond my comprehension how anyone can do this. Five years ago it would have been unheard of.

• • •

There is nothing to escape from
And nothing to escape to:
One is always alone.

T. S. Eliot, *The Cocktail Party* (1949)

• • •

At the individual level, 'joy-riders' as young as 12 and 10 show themselves capable of crashing the legal, social and mental barriers that restrain adults of twice and four times their age. At a group level, today's problem young can degenerate with terrifying speed into a tribal savagery reminiscent of the barbarians of old. For the ancient Romans at the fall of their empire, the depravity of the Vandals, Huns and Visigoths was apparent from their brutal readiness to assault and kill the aged. Almost 2,000 years of human progress later, an elderly and disabled Cardiff steelworker, on his way home in 1992 after a drink with a friend, rebuked a gang of vandals attacking a road sign, and was kicked to death.

They're getting away with murder – this gut feeling was picked up in headlines across Britain when a 19-year-old youth was found not guilty of the murder of a man he had stabbed after a night of drugs and alcohol, tyre-slashing and assault. Again the victim, a 40-year-old music teacher and father of three, had tried to take issue with a gang engaged in vandalizing parked cars. Again the killer seemed unsatisfied with a single act of vengeance, but continued to attack the dying man as he lay on the ground cradled by his wife.

Car theft and arson, murder and mayhem – in all the anger and confusion, pain and fear, some themes come through with urgent clarity:

- Children becoming adults without roots or attachments, spinning faster and faster out of control.

- Sensation-seekers oblivious to the distress or pain of others.

- A hard core unsatisfied with the 'mere' sensation to be had from drugs or 'wilding', deliberately seeking the sensation of causing another's pain.

And there are other alarming developments, too. Violent assault and death have been for centuries a male preoccupation, with few if any women alongside men in the annals of crime. But just as first-time offenders are steadily getting younger until boys and children are now killing like men, so the girls are entering this horror-movie world. No longer content with the bedroom culture of mutual grooming and My Little Pony, girls are taking to the streets along with their brothers, and like them learning the lessons of today's insatiable violence in the search for ever-stronger stimulation. Only days after the British public was forced to confront the truth of James Bulger's 10-year-old killers, the two girl murderers Rossi and Molloy committed the crime that the British press united to brand 'evil beyond belief'.

In contrast to the killing of James, this was no random encounter of opportunistic attackers with an unknown victim. Rossi at least had hated her victim enough to kill, Molloy had loved the act of killing enough to become a willing accomplice. Yet once it was over, neither girl showed the slightest remorse, or any sense of the horror of what they had done.

In the same vein, the unnamed 11-year-old babysitter who killed the child in her charge seemed quite unaware that she had done anything to be ashamed of. In custody she was unabashed, loud, manipulative and demanding, and continued to show an unnerving interest in other young children at every opportunity. Psychiatric examination revealed a mini-adult who was self-involved, uncaring and pathologically cold. Even after being found guilty and committed to custody, the girl continued to question why she was imprisoned: 'I don't *understand*,' she protested. She had done nothing wrong. When would she be released? She had babysitting commmitments for other mothers and she wanted to go.

At her trial, her defence counsel submitted that her mother had three times been admitted to hospital for psychiatric help. The girl scarcely knew her father, and had also been subjected to 'violence in the family'.

•••

> There is no such thing as a problem child. The problem is with the adult.
>
> Jean 'Nanny' Smith, author of
> *Nanny Knows Best* (1993)

•••

Can it be doubted that the children who go wrong must themselves have suffered wrong? And it will not, cannot end there. Professionals in the field of child abuse are now encountering the grim phenomenon of next-generation suffering as children abuse children: a 1990 British government survey showed a substantial number of boys under 9 now sexually abusing younger ones, passing on what they have learned at the hands of abusers.

Christina Robinson heads a National Children's Home project designed to cater for the children who abuse, a complex challenge when unlike adults they may not know that they are doing wrong. For violent and perverted activities, however extreme, are part of their lives:

It may also be that the abuse reflects a child's anger that has not been dealt with. A child who has been abused and not received adequate help may deal with it by doing it to someone else. Some say that they want to experience the excitement of power and secrecy. Some say they need to touch younger children to relieve unbearable feelings of worthlessness.

Yet whatever the child's motivation, whether its drives are acted out or its actions understood, abuse can never simply go away. We cannot overstate this: *abuse is for life*. Children are changed by it, and its effects will inevitably recur in some form or another. Surveying the cases of all British children held for violent assault or murder, Dr Gwyneth Boswell of the University of East Anglia found that 50 per cent of the offenders had been abused themselves, possibly even more: 'I suspect that the figure is higher, more like 90 per cent – but we don't have the hard facts yet.' The staff who know them, familiar as they are with the signs of abuse, suggest that the true figure may be twice as high as the records show. But there can be no doubt of the reality of the cycle of abuse, says Dr Boswell: 'Many of these children are just reproducing the violence perpetrated on them.'

For abuse is always passed on, even though the victims of later violence may have little or no connection with the original assault. In a 1987 survey by the Professional Association of Teachers, it emerged that one-third of the members had been assaulted by a pupil. Two years later, the largest enquiry ever instituted into classroom violence in Britain found that 800 teachers suffered 'physical aggression' from their pupils every week.

Attacks on staff have now reached such a level, unions say, that members are advised not to await police procedures, but to bring their own private prosecutions. When they do, the results do not encourage others to follow their example. In one case of 1993, a woman teacher, punched in the face by an ex-pupil while out shopping, saw her attacker given a conditional discharge. In another, a middle-aged male teacher was beaten up by two pupils of 15 and 13, one of whom was discharged on payment of £20 compensation, while the second was given sixteen hours at an attendance centre and ordered to pay £100.

Is this enough? Or is it, as observers often feel, too little and too late? Judges are fond of noting that a thug of 20 has been a thug for at least ten years: rather late to get him out of it now. By the same token, a thug of 13 has been practising for a good many more years than is likely to have been acknowledged: where was the help, for him and for his victims, when there was still time to make a difference?

And as the wheel turns, so the victim becomes the victimizer, driven to repeat the past in ways that seem to convey the power so desperately lacked before. As an unhappy child of the great Farrow tribe, never more lonely than when in the group, Mia openly expressed her sense of deprivation with the plea, *'a child needs more love and affection than you can get in a large family.'* Yet as an adult who snapped up children from around the globe, she insisted that 'the benefits of a large family are enormous', her whole life becoming one long hymn to her own brand of triumphant tribalism.

Psychologist Oliver James decodes the buried meaning of these contradictory signs. 'Between her teens and her adulthood [Mia's] feelings of deprivation had become unconscious, but were still dominating her life':

So she 'bought' children from the Third World (at about $8000 each) and put them into a family circumstance which unconsciously she knew all too well would deprive. It meant that she could relive her deprivation by identifying with it in her traumatized offspring, all the while feeling that she was virtuously saving them from her childhood trauma.

Farrow had set herself, James argues, an impossible task, to create a new 'happy family' out of all the old dysfunctional materials. 'Somewhere along the way,' he muses to Mia, 'you blanked out what it was to be lost in a crowd of siblings.' Yet all the evidence would seem to show that Farrow's earlier misgivings were right:

The offspring of families with five or more children are significantly more likely to be delinquent (in 1991 two of Farrow's adopted children, Lark and Daisy, both then in their teens, were arrested for shop-lifting) and to suffer mental illness ... it's especially likely to produce boys who symbolically try to steal what they feel they haven't been given emotionally. And girls who use their young bodies to get undivided adoration from men old enough to be their father – girls like Soon-Yi (the

adopted daughter now living with Woody Allen) amd the con-
spicuously child-like Mia Farrow herself.

'All of us have bad experiences as well as good, as children, and as
parents we swear not to repeat the mistakes,' James concludes
sombrely. *'It's not as easy as that.'*

• • •

> If God were suddenly condemned to live the life he has
> inflicted on human beings, he would kill himself.
>
> Alexandre Dumas

• • •

We swear not to repeat our parents' mistakes . . .
Is this the first of their high hopes and good intentions that all
parents break? In the huge task of parenting, it is so hard to get it
right, so easy to go wrong, so tempting to act without listening or
thinking, so attractive to dwell on what we think we deserve, so
demanding to focus on what children may demand. Nor is it any
easier to rectify our mistakes, even when they come clamorously to
light. Most child offenders have in any case run the gamut of most
adult strategies and penalties long before their problems become
serious, for themselves and others.

When the abused become abusers, how can we deal with them?
Difficult and disturbed children, so professionals say, are not respon-
sive to 'discipline' nor to any of the normal adult controls, because
they are already hardened to both pain and punishment. Equally,
threats rarely work: children like these cannot now believe that things
can get any worse for them, since they have already been so bad for
so long. 'If you have been badly damaged as a child,' asks Masud
Hoghughi, 'what is going to frighten you? Not very much, not the
police, not the law. Some of these children have been brought up
without moral parameters, and have no internal conscience. They
[also] have no external fear.'

After the first death, said Dylan Thomas, there is no other. Even so,
how can they do it? How could the Liverpool children take a 2-year-
old boy and beat him to death? We all could, Hoghughi insists:

> All human beings have the potential to kill. What stops a child is
> that they are small, they are not powerful, they are not normally

capable of forming such hostile cognitive maps in their heads. But we know that children as young as 4 have killed ... Some children remain primitive morally. They cannot distinguish right from wrong.

What then can be done? In severe cases, commonsense attitudes are of no avail, and may even hinder the child's reclamation or recovery. Children who lie, steal, destroy and kill are not simply being 'naughty', nor will they obligingly 'turn over a new leaf' when they know adults disapprove. Harsh handling and strict punishment may satisfy society's demand for retribution and keep the offender off the streets for a time, but they are unlikely to change attitudes that have been forming in the child all its life. 'You wouldn't expect a right-wing chap like me to say this,' opined the mayor of Crewkerne, a Somerset town wrestling with unemployment, vandalism, violence and theft, 'but I don't think compulsion is desirable, nor is it an easy panacea.'

Yet if a hard line will not serve the purpose, does soft treatment work? Faced with these children and their injuries, it is naïve to think that parents can simply 'kiss it better', heal the wound with liberal poultices of tender loving care. And what happens when the parents are the source of the distress?

It must be recognized that the wounds of childhood call for trained, sustained professional help, and that goodwill can never be enough. 'Parents must be helped to realize that you cannot love somebody out of an emotional disturbance any more than you can mend a broken leg with love', says child psychotherapist Valerie Sinason. Her fellow-therapist Chriso Andreou would put it even more strongly: 'Things don't go away, you cannot cure such extreme experiences, but we can stop children falling into madness, and help them to tolerate themselves and their pain better.' '*Sanity*', Sinason concludes, '*is simply managing your madness well.*'

In the failure to 'manage their madness well', or indeed at all, the young who do not take it out by attacking schools, cars, children or other people may in the last resort turn their anger on themselves. Fifteen-year-old Kathy, all her friends agreed, 'had everything to live for'. Attractive and intelligent, she planned to get a good job, learn a foreign language, travel, and work in America. When she hanged herself, it made no sense at all.

A police search of her room after her death showed countless drawings of Kathy's parents, who had gone through a furious divorce, so Kathy's mother said, 'fighting all the way'. Nor was there any respite afterwards, as the two continued to do battle over money, access, and most of all over Kathy herself. Kathy's pictures showed her parents at home, on holiday, playing with the dog, a hundred memories of a happier past when they were still a couple. Each one had been torn in two or cut down the middle.

The last picture Kathy drew was of herself. It had been meticulously shredded into tiny strips. 'The situation was literally tearing her apart,' said a policewoman. 'She just couldn't stand it any more.'

Kathy was unlucky in her choice of parents who could not let go of their rage and desire to hurt each other even to save her life. She was also unusual as a girl in pushing through to this last fatal step. By far the majority of young suicides are male: Samaritan organizations estimate that suicides among young men rose by 50 per cent between 1981 and 1991. In Britain, four out of five suicides under 25 are young men, most of whom it seems, had given no sign that anything was wrong: 'Parents think that their kids can talk to them freely about everything, but their kids think they can't talk to them about anything,' comments a social worker.

When girls invade this male turf, as they are doing in increasing numbers, like Kathy's suicide their actions will inevitably trigger deep breast-beating bursts of 'why-oh-why?' On the evidence of the short life and early death of Sally Anne Cattell, the question seems to be 'when-oh-when?'

When will these children get the help they need at the point they need it? At 14, Sally Anne was already in care when she stole a car in March 1993 and crashed it at 70 miles an hour, killing herself and injuring her two passengers. From the time of her parents' divorce four years before, she had become 'difficult' and 'disruptive'. Excluded from school, she oscillated restlessly and often violently between her mother's house, the dwellings of various relatives, and the home where her father lived with his new partner.

By the time of her death, Sally Anne had been in trouble for four years. In care, she was receiving accommodation and some help, but not counselling or control. 'Sally had never been involved in car theft before,' said an official at the time. How did they know? Sally Anne used make-up like a woman, went to the pub, knew how to handle herself. Somewhere too she had learned to drive. But inside the woman's body was still the mind of a child – a lost child, now lost for ever.

•••

They're outgrowing childhood earlier, and are dumped in
an abyss.

Michèle Elliott, Director of Kidscape

•••

Or are they? Are they sad, mad, or simply bad, as some would
insist? After the fury which greeted her tearing up the Pope's
photograph on the US TV show *Saturday Night Live*, the controversial pop star Sinead O'Connor published this poem in the
Irish Times:

> My name is Sinead O'Connor
> I am learning to love myself.
>> I am and always have been carrying a lot of grief for my lost
>> childhood.
>> And for the effects of its horror and violence in my life.
>> I am grieving the loss of my mother and my father.
>> I am grieving the loss of my brothers and sister.
>> The division of my family.
>> The loss of my SELF.
>> My own inner child
> Who is really me.
>> (Remember you do not know me).
>> Who was tortured and abandoned and spat at and abused,
> Who has been beaten naked until she was bruised.

Not everyone responded to O'Connor's appeal in the spirit of sympathy and understanding. 'It is beyond parody,' howled one British
journalist, Peter McKay. 'No satirist, not even Tom Lehrer, could
have composed such a sublime comedy on the inner-child racket. It
can only be a matter of time before the subject is featured in a West
End musical. The comic possibilities seem endless.'

Not, O'Connor might say, if you're an abused child: not if the
joke's on you. But the adult world will always have the last laugh.
McKay quotes approvingly the story of W. C. Fields looking back
on a wretched circus childhood, where he had to carry water for
elephants: 'Got to thinking I'd do something for circus boys if I ever
made a buck or two. Well, I got to Hollywood, made a million

bucks, got around one day to thinking of those poor circus boys carrying water to the elephants, and I thought, "fuck 'em".'

• • •

Those who feel that nobody cares for them, themselves care for nobody.

Anthony Storr

• • •

Who cares? Darren was the unwanted baby of a young woman living with a much older man because she had nowhere else to go. Her partner was violent, frequently assaulting her and anyone else who annoyed him: when Darren was a year old, she walked out and was never seen again. Darren was brought up by his father's mother, who took the same robust attitude to physical violence as her son. Darren, however, is loved in his neighbourhood as 'pure gold' for his cheerful, friendly nature. He did well at school, went on to university, landed himself a good job afterwards, and has just announced his engagement.

Why do some children of disadvantaged homes collapse under the weight of events while others come through and survive triumphantly? 'We have to accept that some people are simply more vulnerable than others,' says Dr Fiona Caldicott. 'There may be a genetic factor involved here, we just don't know. And it is impossible to predict which ones will come through a given trauma, and which won't.'

What this means, then, is that any child in trouble must be detected and watched closely from the onset of any difficulties. From a boy who was still mute at 5 to a self-starving 12-year-old, from a pre-schooler who attacked all her teachers to a 14-year-old who got drunk every night, the distressed children I have known never seemed to get the attention they deserved: rows and recriminations flew thick and fast, but no one seemed to think of turning outside the family for help.

Of course no parent wants to hang a label round a child's neck, as seeking professional advice is sometimes seen. But denial and delay turned Michael, mute at 5, into a non-reader of 10, and left the teenage anorexic Mary with ruined kidneys for life. For any trauma can be progressive, and the worst manifestations may be averted or minimized with early intervention. Without it, the child is likely to become ever more brutalized, withdrawing to the state where any feeling becomes too much to bear.

The emotional apathy of abused or criminal children and their failure to empathize with those they torment in turn, is frequently remarked by all who deal with them: 'He was not afraid of me,' said a police interrogator of one of James Bulger's killers; 'he is not afraid of anyone as far as I can see.' The deviant young and those engaged in antisocial acts will themselves frequently refer to this lack of feeling. They call it being 'bored', and claim that relief of boredom is the reason for their violent or sensation-seeking activities, whose short-term satisfaction then condemns them to an ever-escalating search for the next sensation, the next 'high'.

Why do they do this? Why are the normal childhood activities, interests and excitements not enough? What has become of their natural sensibility, for no child is born with what Keats called 'the feel of not to feel it'? New research from different sources shows that some children suffer from a kind of boredom which will predispose them to acts of violence and crime. An early lack of interest feeds back into an even lower level of interest and attention as the child loses ground. In school, the truant or absentee is unable to connect emotionally or intellectually with what has been missed. Meanwhile others are learning to focus their minds and progressively build up their concentration span.

The children who fail to develop these adult levels of concentration from around the ages of 11 or 12 are vulnerable to distraction, and hence open to the temptations of crime, rebellion, drugs. Paradoxically, adrenalin levels are twice as high as normal in bored children, which can then translate into hostility, aggression or abuse. For some, boredom becomes pathological: psychopaths are generally marked by their lack of engagement, their need for constant stimulation and distraction, poor tolerance of routine work and desire for novelty.

Can children literally be bored to death – to the death of all human or humane fellow-feeling, even to the point of oblivion of their own self-interest, when they commit acts which will bring down on them the gravest penalties that adult society can inflict? Or are we still in danger of demonizing a few offenders, persuading ourselves that these are 'monsters', freaks of nature, exceptionally 'evil' children who have nothing in common with the rest?

Not so, says writer Andrew O'Hagan in a gravely reflective essay for the *London Review of Books*: writing of his own boyhood in the wake of the James Bulger case, O'Hagan suggested that even the 10-year-old killers are no different from other boys. 'At that age we were brimming with nastiness,' he recalls. 'Torture among our kind was fairly commonplace.' As a 6-year-old, O'Hagan remembered day after day tormenting another child by beating him with a rubber strap, 'practically skinning the screaming boy's legs':

Up until the age of ten I'd both taken part in and witnessed many such incidents . . . It's not that any of us were evil: even the more bookish and shy among us were given to a bit of destructive boredom and stupid imagining. Now and then it got out of hand . . . what started out as a game of rounders or crazy golf would end up as a game of clubbing the neighbour's cat to death. A night of camping on the playing fields could usually be turned into an opportunity for the wrecking of vegetable gardens or the killing of frogs and people's pet rabbits. Mindless stuff.

But there was a darker side than even the killing of cats and rabbits, as O'Hagan concedes:

As only the dependent can be, we were full of our own independence . . . most of our games, when I think of it, were predicated on someone else's humiliation or eventual pain. It made us feel strong and untouchable . . . it was the main way that most of the boys I knew used up their spare time.

As to the 'boredom' argument, O'Hagan would not agree:

Bullies who had no aptitude for classwork – who always got 'easily distracted' scribbled in red ink on report cards that never made it home – had unbelievable concentration when it came to torturing minors in the playground or on the way home. For many of the pupils, bullying was a serious game . . . We all took and assigned roles in cruel little dramas of our own devising.

And for some, as O'Hagan admits, these games were the way in which bridges were built between this 'mindless, childish venom' and adult crime.

Is it inevitable, then, that 'boys will be boys', and that increasingly,

girls are condemned to catching up? That some must and will gradu-
ate to adult crime, and that others, propelled out of childhood by
events or desires beyond their ken, will not even wait for their majority but will become boy and girl muggers, thieves and killers before
they can be anything else? That these then will be the media's 'little
devils' and 'monsters', the 'evil children' who can be swept from our
contemplation as 'beyond belief', and hence beyond hope or help?

Yet each of these was a baby once, deserving of the best care and
love that adults can provide. Children cannot be evil unless adults
let them become so, watching them slide out of control and so out
of normal life, out of the reach of love. Some will indeed precipitate
that process in the young or even knowingly accelerate it, initiating
children into thoughts and ways no child should know of, let alone
be forced to share.

We must speak for the children, protecting them as much from
these harsh labels and false condemnations as from the adults who
would make them all that society will condemn. To think otherwise
is to blame them for our failings, to accept the inevitability of damaged and dangerous children, a grim fatalism that in itself insults the
helpless newborn child. If we can put a man on the moon, people
are fond of saying, we can do anything. If we can put a man on the
moon, surely we can do more to save the children here on earth?

•••

> Until we become sensitised to the small child's suffering, this
> wielding of power by adults will continue to be a normal
> aspect of the human condition, for no one pays attention to
> or takes seriously what is regarded as trivial, since the victims
> are 'only children'. *But in twenty years' time these children
> will be adults who will have to pay it all back.*
>
> Alice Miller, *The Drama of Being a Child* (1987)

•••

Conclusion

It is not true that evil, destructiveness and perversion
inevitably form part of human existence, no matter how
often this is maintained. But it is true that we are daily
producing more evil, and with it, an ocean of suffering for
millions that is absolutely avoidable.

Alice Miller, *Banished Knowledge* (1990)

Will others who come after learn from our lives, take from
it the good and avoid our mistakes? ... I wonder ...

Frieda Lawrence, *Not I, But The Wind ...*

EVERY TWENTY YEARS, writes Alice Miller, the children who
do not get what they deserve become the people that no society
deserves, and no individual deserves to be. For some, especially those
born into a world which now seems permanently set to run on fast-
forward, even that time-span is too long. The two boys who led
James Bulger on to the world's TV screens and off to his death were
no more than 10. How had they found the fast track to that murderous maturity, the killing frenzy that others many times their age will
never know?

James Bulger met his death in February 1993. The two boys accused
of murdering him were brought to trial in November that year, and
once again the dreadful story was played out: the child led astray, the
frantic mother and her fruitless search, the days of anguish, the final
loss of hope with the maimed body on the line. This time more details
emerged, each with its added weight of shock and grief: the witnesses
who saw the weeping toddler in the hands of his tormentors and might
have saved him, the brutality of his hours of dreadful suffering, the
pathologist's cold catalogue of his countless wounds.

Yet through it all, one question went unanswered, the great question which seemed to hold the key to all the others the world longed
to know. Not the sad details, not the *how* and *when* and *where*, but

one simple *why?* Why did these two, each one no more than a child himself, seize on this child and torture him to death?

'I want to see them,' said James Bulger's father. 'I just want to look them in the face.' Yet there was nothing in the face of either boy to see. Both those accused of one of the worst murders of the modern age proved to look like any child that any adult would pass by in the street, as many did, even on the fateful day. 'Two ordinary-looking little schoolboys with smart ties and tidy haircuts,' commented one of the reporters in the Crown Court as the boys were brought up from the cells. 'Whatever we had expected, it was not this.'

If the two boys' appearance gave no hint of their mentality or motive, neither did the evidence. The two had been seen the week before returning from the same shopping mall and the same railway line where James was killed, dragging the weeping youngest brother of one of them, suggesting that the murder had been premeditated, or even rehearsed. On the day of James's abduction they had tried to take another child, but when the mother challenged them, they had simply walked away. The same unchildlike coolness had prevailed throughout: even with James weeping and bleeding beside them they had convincingly fobbed off all questions and offers of help, so much so that not one of 26 witnesses had felt able to intervene.

Under police questioning, Boy A and Boy B as they were known by legal direction, repeatedly denied all knowledge of the crime. But blood on their shoes and marks on James's face showed that both had kicked the toddler on the head, and forensic tests linked them both also to the bloody half-bricks found around the child's body, and to the 22-pound iron bar employed to split his skull. Each then steadfastly laid all the blame upon the other, until B's mother begged her son to tell the truth, promising that his parents would always love him no matter what he had done. 'I did kill him,' was the final reply. But A, accused by B of throwing the first brick, insisted to the end that he was no killer, he had left James alive.

Both boys now suffered nightmares, a forensic psychiatrist told the court. Obsessed by the killing, they were subject to intense anxiety, vivid flashbacks and other symptoms of post-traumatic stress disorder, leading to doubt that they could understand the implications of the court procedure or what was happening to them. But there was no question, the evidence continued, that both children were of good or average intelligence at the time of the crime. They knew right from wrong, and knew that it was wrong to take a child away from his mother, hit him and hurt him and leave him on a railway line in the path of a train.

Found guilty, the two boys, identified as Robert Thompson (Boy A) and Jon Venables (Boy B), wept uncontrollably as they were sentenced to indefinite imprisonment for their 'cunning and wicked conduct'. 'How it came about that two mentally normal boys aged ten, of average intelligence, committed this crime is very hard to comprehend,' the judge summed up. Reams of newspaper analysis followed the boys' conviction, without shedding any light on this grave question. Both came from broken homes, both lived with a single mother, and both had been long-established truants and petty thieves in the area where they lived. Just as so many have been, before and since.

But Robert Thompson (A) emerged at last as the prime mover, 'an accomplished manipulator and a seamless liar', as one reporter saw him, 'detached and cold' even when faced with overwhelming proof of his own guilt. The son of a long-departed electrician, fifth of seven children, he had been subject to sustained and deliberate bullying by his older brothers from the time he was born, a campaign of cruelty which only worsened with the departure of his father when he was 5. His mother, left to cope alone, could not prevent him from maltreating his youngest brother in the same way, nor from roaming the streets at all hours, going to school only to make trouble or to find a weaker character to truant with.

Venables (B), by contrast, had a father who remained in touch with his young son, and who had come to pick him up from school on the day of the crime as part of a doomed attempt to stop the truanting that led to James's death. The middle child of a family of three, the boy had learning difficulties but no previous history of violence: both his parents, reconciled in the wake of his arrest, even described him as 'quite a loving, caring little boy'. They denied too that he had ever seen the controversial video *Child's Play 3*, the story of an evil toddler doll battered to death, which had been borrowed by the father shortly before the toddler James met a similar fate. Yet Venables, too, had kicked and stoned and battered little James with the 20-inch-long iron bar: had piled bricks on his face and turned a deaf ear to his cry 'I want my mummy', repeated, so they said, until the child could no longer speak.

And both boys, it was clear from their own words, felt no compunction at the time in killing for sport, in enjoying the child's pain. How had this happened? Was it produced by unhappiness at home, or was it linked in some way with the influence of horror videos?

Both possibilities were raised by the judge in the Crown Court, and subsequently debated to a standstill by both professionals and laity alike. No firm conclusion finally emerged. Many children had been exposed to *Child's Play* and its sequels, if not worse, much worse, without these consequences: many more were products of broken homes and single-mother families, with or without a father on the scene, and had not turned to crime, let alone murder. Both boys were getting individual attention from their head teacher and guidance with their truanting: neither lived in abject misery or poverty or suffered any kind of overt abuse. This was indeed one sombre lesson to be drawn from the whole savage saga, that these boys were no different from a thousand others, no worse than many and much better than some.

'LITTLE DEVILS' ran the headlines after the trial, making up in sound and fury for what they lacked in explanatory power. But they summed up at least part of the truth as A and B passed like devils from the world, each condemned to the blank eternity of his peculiar hell. From their living grave of indefinite imprisonment, they are unlikely now to give voice or account for themselves. So we may never know how or why this killing came to pass: nor how a killer's heart and mind can grow inside the body of a 'normal' human child.

•••

The trial may be over, but their nightmare will not end.

> The solicitor of Ralph and Denise Bulger speaking
> after the verdict in November 1993

•••

Every parent must have felt for the parents of James Bulger, and not a few for the parents of his killers too: the enormity of the devastation left little room for apportioning blame. On all sides the reaction was tinged, too, with a palpable fear: *are these the children of today? How has it come to this?*

Such cases tap straight into the deep sense of modern parents that they are fighting on two fronts, trying to do their best by their own children, and at the same time take account of the dislocated, dangerous young in society at large. Faced with the seemingly unstoppable rise of crime and truancy, the year on year increases in the wave of hopeless girls with babies and angry boys with guns, it is easy to see troubled children as a problem that adult society does not have to answer for, but only needs to eliminate. 'In the Nineties, children became the enemy within,' comments Beatrix Campbell. 'They were the pariahs who patrolled political discourse, producing panic wherever they went sniffing or stealing or suffering.' A hardened handful of these were promoted to the status of the darlings of the tabloids, the bad girls and devil boys we all love to hate.

Yet children everywhere are still far more often victims than villains, more sinned against than sinning. In the recent history of social misery and personal distress, of unemployment, marriage breakdown, crime, when adult society could not even save itself and its own structures of work and family life, children have been exceptionally at risk. 'What happens to a child that has been invaded mentally physically emotionally spiritually sexually sensually,' demanded Sinead O'Connor in the free-flowing sleeve-notes to her 1992 album *Am I Not Your Girl?*:

> made to lie naked on the floor
> beaten spat at kicked scalded starved degraded
> raped humiliated punished for scraping the plate
> or stealing a few peanuts made to beg for mercy
> mocked MURDER the death of self-esteem
> Self-confidence self-love self-respect identity –

And in an era which has seen refuges for battered women, hostels for the homeless, and centres for the addicted or mentally disturbed, one by one closed down for lack of funds, where is there for a wronged child to go but wrong?

Yet most children, even those most grossly maltreated, do not break the law. Of those who do, the majority of young offenders, after a first transgression, never re-offend. They are the flag-wavers of a wider distress which rarely hits the headlines, yet which afflicts thousands, the huge betrayal of children which has been eroding society, and which leaves them not as the enemy but as the prisoners within.

For when all the hype and overheated headlines are set aside, there still remain families who fail, creating fathers in free fall, mothers in want, and children at risk. In 'ordinary' families, too, however overtly 'normal' they may seem, families of couples who stay married and bring up their children, there will be painful, humiliating or destructive experiences which proceed from a different ignorance, another kind of neglect. From round-the-world explorers to stay-at-home model wives, it is amazing how many adults are still trying to prove things to their father or to win their mother's love. Somehow or other they have grown up with the idea that they are not good enough. Can we arrest or reverse this process for those still growing, and for the generations yet to come? Can we learn now to *put the children first?*

For many of them, it may already be too late. For Mary, Shanice, Jean-Paul and Dave, the die is cast – as it was fatally for James Bulger.

For the others, what can be done? What do children need? Time, care, attention, play, in a word love, the love with time to care. When we talk of 'a mother's instinct', of 'a father's pride' or 'family bonds', the very phrases convey the comforting impression of eternal verities like earth and air and water, always there, and always to be relied on. But just as the Western world has been abusing earth and air and water in the name of social progress, so the recent crises in parenthood and family values show that we neglect the nurture of these ties at our deep peril. Parental love and family life are *work*, like married love, needing effort to be sustained. All effort of this sort is just another word for love. And in a world of monetary values, love is deemed worthless because it has no price.

The last ten or twenty years have seen the creation of a global society in which the pursuit of gain has become the organizing principle of individual life. This pursuit, hot and getting hotter, is not merely of financial or career gain, though these are at or near the top of every smart agenda, but of gains in mastery, in fitness, strength, and knowledge, in sophistication, self-reinvention and improvement of all the externals of life from overall 'lifestyle' to the perfect shade of tan. The long slow haul of bringing up a child from birth to adulthood, the endless work, the cost, the fatigue, the small, slow triumphs, the setbacks, the long-delayed rewards, are all at variance with the current 'Me!-Me!-Me!' philosophy of 'I Want It Now'.

At the same time, too many adults have come to look outside the family for most of their adult needs. Not their material wants, for those have been supplied outside the family since industrialization took all the workers, both adults and children, out of the home and away from the land more than two centuries ago. But the needs that make us human, like the desire for recognition, for appreciation, interest and stimulus, and above all for love, both to give and to receive – how many now can say that their home life and family are the prime source, or even a main cause of those good feelings without which human beings cannot truly live?

'To his wife, every man is a king', runs the Sicilian proverb, 'and every woman is the queen of her domain.' Within the circle of close love relationships, we can all be somebody, holding our special position and with it a status that none can emulate and none usurp. In the outside world we must all fight to set foot on the ladder and then jostle constantly for advancement, always struggling for the recognition that we are doing well, tensely aware of the wheel of fortune, which can throw us off as fast as it drew us up: why then do we neglect to claim our simple, uncontested due in love and recognition at home, in the reward and sense of merit freely available on our own hearth, where none can take it from us?

By neglecting to make family life the centre of our efforts, by persuading ourselves that by working fifteen hours a day we are doing our best for children we hardly ever see, we are setting up the bad behaviour that we are then outraged to encounter, feeling that our children are turning against us, when in truth we first turned away from them. For children's bad behaviour is not random nor is it ever inexplicable, though we may choose to think so. It is always purposive, if we can read the signs, although the purpose of it may be buried deep inside the confusion of a child driven to act in ways beyond its ken. But if we are honest, there can be no real surprises in what children do, argues Martin Amis in an unblinking analysis of 'the fuck-it generation':

The mystery is not why the young offend. The mystery is why we let them. The mystery is the general failure of the will. 'Nothing works', we say, when we talk about crime and punishment. Well, nothing works *now*: the horses have already bolted . . . But let us step right back and see what truly defines the contemporary. It is, clearly, an age in which vandalism has taken on a global – even an apocalyptic – aspect. Stoving in a windscreen doesn't feel like much, when your elders and betters have just put a brick through the ozone layer. Violating the innocent is no great violation, in the age of the billion-casualty war plan. Of course, *they* don't know that. The point is not how it affects them: they are children, and will do what they can get away with. The point is how it affects us. Every parent knows that the assertion of authority is a pitiable bluff. 'Because I say so' – what kind of legitimacy is that? You have to mean it: you have to follow it through. They listen to your voice. They always know when your heart's not really in it.

And when an adult's heart is not in the family, not with the children both at home and school, where will it be? More and more in recent years roaming the wastelands of our popular culture, seduced by fictions of heroism and glamour and sexual adventure far removed from what an average life or the quiet of a home can ever provide. The images of super-masculinity or ultra-femininity are indeed intrinsically at war with what children want and need in Dad and Mom, both of whom must learn to set aside, if only for a while, the joy of the rampant ego, the free assertion of unchecked sexuality, and the thrill of the chase. Yet these are the daily lessons, the prescriptions even, the bombardments of mass media, film and TV, newsprint and magazines, even pop music and the jingles of ads.

And amid all the hubbub, one message above all keeps coming through in today's world, one which children take as their cue just as much as they watch and learn from adult behaviour. 'I feel very strongly that too much violence on television is a cause of violence,' says Dr Richard Ryder, a psychologist dealing with disturbed and delinquent teenagers:

> Sexual violence, for instance, and violence which is unprovoked, selfish, cultish, or performed by attractive figures who can be incorporated as hero-figures or role-models by a certain kind of viewer ... people will be violent if they find themselves part of a violent system ... television is a powerful source of macho attitudes and the tabloid press is also nurturing machismo ... some middle way must be found to reduce the constant reinforcement of the link between crude violence and heroism as depicted in the media.

Are we yet ready to accept that we have in the West created a society and an atmosphere which are at their extremes inherently inimical to children's rights and needs? Are we yet ready to concede that children have rights, and that those rights must be protected and extended?

•••

The purpose of power is to give it away.

Aneurin Bevan

•••

After fifteen years of deliberation, the United Nations Convention on the Rights of the Child was finally adopted by the UN on 20 November 1989, guaranteeing every child the right to life, to freedom of mind and body, to health and education, and to all basic human rights as enjoyed by adults (see Appendix for a fuller version of the text). Requiring 20 countries to ratify it before it became law, the Convention met that target and came into force in 1990, and now has 155 'States Parties' or signatories pledged to observe its rules. But unlike the European Convention on Human Rights, there is no judicial machinery to enforce it, and no right of individual complaint. Instead, each country is placed under a duty to publicize the Convention, and to report progress to the UN from time to time.

Commentators have detected an irony in the fact that in the years since its adoption, certain countries with a questionable record on adult human rights, let alone on the rights of children, like Guatemala, Nicaragua, Vietnam and Egypt, have all ratified the Convention where Denmark, Switzerland, Britain and the USA have not. Until more countries, including these and other leading Western and European powers, agree to do so, the Convention has no teeth. But this is still the first attempt in history to invest the children of the world with rights of their own, rights to such basic human needs as the recognition of nationality and freedom from torture, and as such its potential is awesome.

Yet in the nature of things, a Convention such as this can only give a sense of its grand design, the way things could be in the best of all possible worlds. And rights are not needs: the political and social may be far removed from the immediate and personal, the child as a civic being quite another creature from the infant growing up within the family. In the complex of the pressing wants and urges that make up the newborn baby, what might be an informal Charter for the Child?

- **The right to be wanted**: 'every child a wanted child' should become both an agreed philosophy and a social goal, actively pursued by all the nations of the world. 'We thought because our hearts were pure everything would be OK,' says Erica Jong in her new message to women, the novel *Fear of Fifty*. '*We didn't anticipate what children needed.*'

- **The right to a stable home**: active support for the family from every government should be forthcoming in the form of financial incentives and broad-based provision, including full, free child care. Family education should begin in the schools, with programmes designed to inculcate the skills required for lifelong marriage; in churches and register offices with the recognition that marriage is not an end but a beginning; and in employment, with industry, commerce, the professions and the private sector all recognizing the importance of home and family alongside work in the lives of employees.

- **The right to a father**: it must be accepted that the child has a right to two parents, and a right to know its father. We need to reverse the idea that one woman on her own can do the work of a couple, to check the casual arrival and even more casual departure of too many of today's forgotten fathers and disappearing dads, and if not 'make the daddies pay', at least make them count. 'If you have a child with someone, you are with that someone for the rest of your life,' Jong continues, 'whether you get along with them or not.'

- **The right to parents who will behave like mature adults, not itinerants or adolescents**. 'We came to the end of our rainbow,' said one divorced father of four, 'it was time to move on.' Is it too much to ask a couple who have children to agree to try to stay together, putting the welfare and stability of their children above their own 'right to happiness', to 'personal fulfilment', to romantic adventure, sexual escapades, or the dream of vanished youth?

- **The right to grandparents**: in today's marriage holocaust, many children lose their relationships with those in the older generation. Positive contact between children and 'third-agers' must be promoted as indispensable to both sides.

- **The right to information about their bodies from the earliest age.** Children start playing Mummies and Daddies from the time they start to play: only adult hypocrisy prevents us from accepting what Freud taught a hundred years ago. Full education in personal and sexual relationships given from the age of 5 or 7 onwards could reduce the need for dealing with pregnancies of 11-year-olds or doling out condoms to boys of 12 and 13.

- **The right to early detection**: when children are suffering, failing, or falling out of line, they should have the right to prompt diagnosis, sustained attention and assistance. 'If we are going to affect behaviour, from 3 to 6 is the intervention time,' says Dr Fiona Caldicott. Too much of the limited help currently available for troubled children provides too little, too late.

- **The right to protection**: this right should be backed up by vigorous exposure and unfailing prosecution of any who abuse, with no statute of limitations on their crimes. When a retired priest, Father David Holley, was sent to prison in New Mexico in June 1993 for offences against boys carried out 20 years before, his conviction sent a message to child abusers worldwide.

- **The right to reparation**: convicted abusers should be ordered to pay compensation to their victims. The way forward was established in England by a historic High Court judgement of November 1993, when Endre Keleman was ordered to pay his three daughters a total of £39,000 for beating, raping and buggering them from the ages of 7 through to their teens.

- **The right to intervention**: abuse thrives on secrecy. 'I should have done more, but I was a coward,' said the wife of Keleman. Non-intervention always reinforces the abuser's power and underlines the victim's helplessness. *'Because children and most adolescents are unable to help themselves, it is incumbent upon adults who have even an inkling that abuse is occurring to be the child's voice,'* says US child abuse attorney Paul Mones.

- **The right to protection from physical punishment.** The US loves its paddles, the English their canes. Yet countries like Sweden have outlawed corporal punishment for all their children and are no more lawless than the rest of the European world: indeed, homicides on the all-American scale are quite unknown there.

- **The right to help and treatment when they offend, to be dealt with as 'children with problems', not as 'problem children'.** A persistent offender may need to be confined to a secure unit, but should receive there a programme of education, training and development with a view to a better future.

- **The right to a Children's Commissioner**, Ombudsman or official watchdog to oversee children's rights, to influence policy and legislation, to develop a strategy to promote children's interests and to ensure national compliance with the UN Convention on the

Rights of the Child. If we have an Ombudsman to protect the rights of citizens who quarrel with their insurance companies or take issue with local government, should we not give an equal if not greater status to that far more vital concern, the child?

•••

> The child must be protected, must be cared for with due respect for the family as an entity. The child that is hungry must be fed, the orphan and waif must be sheltered and succoured.
>
> Eglantyne Jebb, founder of Save the Children, 1923

•••

For healthy growth, children need constant recognition and endorsement as valuable and useful members of their own small world. Instead, being young and small is equated with having no experience of any value, with having little weight in the adult scheme of things. When children react to their powerlessness, or rebel against it, they are deemed 'difficult' and 'disruptive'. There are four steps, as Alice Miller writes, towards full adult development, without which no child can be other than at odds with life and with itself: being allowed to describe sensations; to experience and express emotions; to query a situation; and to articulate needs. To which we might add, the capacity to have at least some of those needs satisfied.

How is this to be done? For their own children, parents should try to:

- See things always through the eyes of the child.

- Never force the child to do anything simply because the parent wants them to.

- Recognize but not reinforce gender differences: be alert to the fact that girls are more likely to have problems with depression, boys with aggression, but in today's world, it could as easily be the other way round.

- Respect individuality and foster autonomy, never coercing a child into family moulds.

- Avoid all punishments involving pain or humiliation.

- Guard against all violence in the family, especially sibling violence.

- Monitor and control all images of violence, no matter from what source.

- Distract a child from too much TV or video by offering substitute activities.

- Spend time with them, play games with them, walk with them, talk with them.

- Keep up family contacts, make links with the community.

- Take a consistent moral position and stick to it.

- Build the child's self-confidence at every opportunity.

- Have the confidence in children's judgement to work things through co-operatively with them.

- Never fear that children will be spoiled or parental authority undermined through showing love.

- Try at all times not to control children, but to teach them how to control themselves.

The Royal College of Psychiatrists is not the only official body to be concerning itself actively with the welfare of children as the adults of the future. For their future is the future of us all. In the coming decade, well over a quarter of the world's population will be under 16. This figure will rise as high as three-quarters in some developing countries where adult mortality is high.

With an ever-younger world population balancing an increase in the longevity of 'third-agers', we must face up to the universal need for more help for the parents of the generation caught in between. Modern parenthood has now become too demanding to be performed well by two overworked parents struggling alone in nuclear isolation. And modern life is now so far removed from that of even a generation ago that parenting a child calls for far more than simply having been children ourselves.

At its simplest, the case is one of priorities. 'If we can fund undergraduates to ponder on birdsong, we can afford to subsidize people to rescue our children from madness,' comments writer Yasmin Alibhai-Brown. 'The cost-effectiveness is clear. Save a child, early in life, from inner chaos, and you may prevent crime, long-term psychiatric treatment and countless other kinds of damage.' It is a priority we can hardly afford not to observe, Brian Roycroft, former President of the Association of Directors of Social Services, told Alibhai-Brown: 'Of all the services that we provide, the most important should be those that affect the lives of children who have been damaged. To fail to do this is almost criminal irresponsibility by the nation.'

Above all by its women. As the mothers of these and all future children, as the women who have fought for our own freedoms, we must be ready now to take up arms again on behalf of the child. We can begin by trying to ensure that children's mental environment is as unpolluted as we want the food they eat and air they breathe to be, and that means taking a stand against all forms of cruelty, sadism or bullying wherever we may see it. Standing alone if need be, for we may be readier than our men to accept the implicit harm of the culture of violence, since so many men are schooled in it, even sold on it as the price of being a man. Certainly it is easier for women everywhere to question systems and structures without fear of losing face.

But there is no future in simply reacting to what has gone before and finding it wanting. We must be ready to put new systems forward in place of the old, to advance and defend the rights and needs of children in all dealings concerning them. This will inherently involve a challenge to the supreme power of parents, above all to the father, who still retains and still too often claims the remnants of his ancient right of *patria potestas*, patriarchal power. And once again, in standing up for children, feminism must prepare itself to face the same resistance as before, the same accusations of interfering with the course of nature, of disturbing or destroying what is 'natural' and 'normal' when we question the domination of parents over children, just as it happened when the first mothers of the women's movement fought against the male right to rule.

For truly the rights of children are the last frontier in the fight for freedom for us all, their constant oppression the last right that patriarchy still exacts and the last wrong that it inflicts. Until we can rescue children from the age-old silence of acceptance that surrounds their suffering, until we can identify and bring out into the open their 'problem without a name', we shall see an ongoing progress of flying boys becoming wounded men, bright flowers of girls withering into defeated women, with the extreme casualties, the murdered and the murderers, still the victims at every stage.

Perhaps the last word, if there can be one, should lie with one of the fathers of such understanding as we have of the dark motives that beset us all. 'We need more understanding of human nature, because the only real danger that exists is man himself,' said Jung, towards the end of his life. 'We know nothing of man, or far too little. His psyche should be studied because we are the origin of all coming evil.' A contemporary psychologist, Dr Richard Ryder, takes up the point with an optimism on which we can build: *'One of the positive messages of the study of violence is that there is nothing inevitable about it.'*

And each new baby comes to us with that message and that hope: for there is no such thing as a violent newborn child. No words exist to do justice to that power, that beauty, that delight and wonder that the newborn bring, simply by being born: to have seen this even once in a life is a joy which takes a whole life to repay. It is the same for all, all who have children, all who were children once. Now as we stand at the gateway to the new millennium, an era whose children will need us as never before, we must seize the moment, find the way to do things differently. We must start again in a new determination that things must change, that we must change our attitudes, for only this will bring any change in the children we create. Only when we make this transition to a more child-centred world will we start to deserve the joy and privilege of having children, and only then will we be rewarded with the children we deserve.

• • •

> Your children are not your children.
> They are the sons and daughters of life's longing for itself.
> They come through you but not from you,
> And though they are with you, yet they belong not to you.
> You may give them your love but not your thoughts,
> For they have their own thoughts.
> You may house their bodies but not their souls,
> For their souls dwell in the house of tomorrow, which
> You cannot visit, not even in your dreams.

Khalil Gibran

• • •

The UN Convention on the Rights of the Child

THE UN CONVENTION on the Rights of the Child was adopted on 20 November 1989. A shortened version of the official text is printed below. When 20 countries had ratified the agreement, the Convention became international law in 1990, binding on those countries which have signed to comply with its conditions. However, unlike the European Convention on Human Rights, there is no judicial machinery to enforce the law, and no right of individual complaint. Each country is placed under a duty to publicize the Convention's provisions and to report progress towards fulfilling their obligations under it to a specially constituted UN Committee.

THE CONVENTION
Preamble

The States Parties to the present Convention, Considering that in accordance with the principles proclaimed in the Charter of the United Nations, recognition of the inherent dignity and of the equal and inalienable rights of all members of the human family is the foundation of freedom, justice and peace in the world,

Bearing in mind that the peoples of the United Nations have, in the Charter, reaffirmed their faith in fundamental human rights and the dignity and worth of the human person, and have determined to promote social progress and better standards of life in larger freedom,

Recognizing that the United Nations has, in the Universal Declaration of Human Rights and in the International Covenants on Human Rights proclaimed and agreed that everyone is entitled to all the rights and freedoms set forth therein, without distinction of any kind, such as race, colour, sex, language, religion, political or other opinion, national or social origin, property, birth or other status,

Recalling that, in the Universal Declaration of Human Rights, the United Nations has proclaimed that childhood is entitled to special care and assistance,

Convinced that the family, as the fundamental group of society and the natural environment for the growth and well-being of all its members and particularly children, should be afforded the necessary protection and assistance so that it can fully assume its responsibilities within the community,

Recognizing that the child, for the full and harmonious development of his or her personality, should grow up in a family environment, in an atmosphere of happiness, love and understanding,

Considering that the child should be fully prepared to live an individual life in society, and brought up in the spirit of the ideals proclaimed in the Charter of the United Nations, and in particular the spirit of peace, dignity, tolerance, freedom, equality and solidarity,

Bearing in mind that the need for extending particular care to the child has been stated in the Geneva Declaration on the Rights of the Child of 1924 and in the Declaration of the Rights of the Child adopted by the United Nations in 1959 and recognized in the Universal Declaration of Human Rights, in the International Covenant on Civil and Political Rights, in the International Covenant on Economic, Social and Cultural Rights, and in the statutes and relevant instruments of specialized agencies and international organizations concerned with the welfare of children,

Bearing in mind that, as indicated in the Declaration of the Rights of the Child adopted by the General Assembly of the United Nations on 20 November 1959, 'the child, by reasons of his physical and mental immaturity, needs special safeguards and care, including appropriate legal protection, before as well as after birth,'

Recalling the provisions of the Declaration on Social and Legal Principles relating to the Protection and Welfare of Children, with Special Reference to Foster Placement and Adoption Nationally and Internationally,

Recognizing that in all countries of the world there are children living in exceptionally difficult conditions, and that such children need special consideration,

Taking due account of the importance of the traditions and cultural values of each people for the protection and harmonious development of the child,

Recognizing the importance of international cooperation for

improving the living conditions of children in every country, in particular the developing countries,
Have agreed as follows:

Part I

Definition of child
Article 1

For the purposes of the present convention a child means every human being below the age of 18 years unless, under the law applicable to the child, majority is attained earlier.

Non-discrimination
Article 2

1   The States Parties to the present Convention shall respect and ensure the rights set forth in this Convention to each child within their jurisdiction without discrimination of any kind, irrespective of the child's or his or her parent's or legal guardian's race, colour, sex, language, religion, political or other opinion, national, ethnic or social origin, property, disability, birth or other status.

Welfare principle
Article 3

1   In all actions concerning children, whether undertaken by public or private social welfare institutions, courts of law, administrative authorities or legislative bodies, the best interests of the child shall be a primary consideration.

Duties of states
Article 4

States Parties shall undertake all appropriate legislative, administrative, and other measures, for the implementation of the rights recognized in this Convention. In regard to economic, social and cultural rights, States Parties shall undertake such measures to the maximum extent of their available resources and, where needed, within the framework of international cooperation.

Parental role
Article 5

States Parties shall respect the responsibilities, rights, and duties of parents or, where applicable, the members of the extended family or community as provided for by the local custom, legal guardians or other persons legally responsible for the child, to provide, in a manner consistent with the evolving capacities of the child, appropriate direction and guidance in the exercise by the child of the rights recognized in the present Convention.

Right to life
Article 6

1 States Parties recognize that every child has the inherent right to life.
2 States Parties shall ensure to the maximum extent possible the survival and development of the child.

Nationality
Article 7

1 The child shall be registered immediately after birth and shall have the right from birth to a name, the right to acquire a nationality, and, as far as possible, the right to know and be cared for by his or her parents.

Identity
Article 8

1 States Parties undertake to respect the right of the child to preserve his or her identity, including nationality, name and family relations, as recognized by law without unlawful interference.

Family life
Article 9

1 States Parties shall ensure that a child shall not be separated from his or her parents against their will, except when competent authorities subject to judicial review determine, in accordance with

applicable law and procedures that such separation is necessary for the best interests of the child. Such determination may be necessary in a particular case such as one involving abuse or neglect of the child by the parents, or one where the parents are living separately and a decision must be made as to the child's place of residence.

2   States Parties shall respect the right of the child who is separated from one or both parents to maintain personal relations and direct contact with both parents on a regular basis, except if it is contrary to the child's best interests.

Family reunification
Article 10

1   Applications by a child or his or her parents to enter or leave a State Party for the purpose of family unification shall be dealt with by States Parties in a positive, humane and expeditious manner. States Parties shall further ensure that the submission of such a request shall entail no adverse consequences for the applicants and the members of their family.

Child abduction
Article 11

1   States Parties shall take measures to combat the illicit transfer and non-return of children abroad.

Child's wishes
Article 12

1   States Parties shall assure to the child who is capable of forming his or her own views the right to express those views freely in all matters affecting the child.

Freedom of expression
Article 13

1   The child shall have the right to freedom of expression, this right shall include freedom to seek, receive and impart information and ideas of all kinds, eiither orally, in writing or in print, in the form of art, or through any other media of the child's choice.

Freedom of thought
Article 14

1 States parties shall respect the right of the child to freedom of thought, conscience and religion.

Freedom of association
Article 15

1 States Parties shall recognize the rights of the child to freedom of association and to freedom of peaceful assembly.

Privacy
Article 16

1 No child shall be subject to arbitrary or unlawful interference with his or her privacy, family, home or correspondence, nor to unlawful attacks on his or her honour and reputation.

Access to information
Article 17

1 States Parties recognize the important function performed by the mass media and shall ensure that the child has access to information and material from a diversity of national and international sources, especially those aimed at the promotion of his or her social, spiritual, and moral well-being and physical and mental health.

Parental support
Article 18

1 States Parties shall use their best efforts to ensure recognition of the principle that both parents have common responsibilities for the upbringing and development of the child.

Protection from abuse
Article 19

1 States Parties shall take all appropriate legislative, administrative, social and educational measures to protect the child from all forms

of physical or mental violence, injury or abuse, neglect or negligent treatment, maltreatment or exploitation including sexual abuse.

Adoption
Article 21

1   States Parties which recognize and/or permit the system of adoption shall ensure that the best interests of the child shall be the paramount consideration.

Health
Article 24

1   States Parties recognize the right of the child to the enjoyment of the highest attainable standard of health, and to facilities for the treatment of illness.

Right to education
Article 28

1   States Parties recognize the right of the child to education.

Employment
Article 32

1   States Parties recognize the right of the child to be protected from economic exploitation and from performing any work that is likely to be hazardous or to interfere with the child's education or to be harmful to the child's health or physical, mental, spiritual, social or moral development.

Drugs
Article 33

1   States Parties shall take all appropriate measures including legislative, administrative, social and educational measures, to protect children from the illicit use of narcotic drugs and psychotropic substances as defined in the relevant international treaties and to prevent the use of children in the illicit production and trafficking of such substances.

Sexual exploitation
Article 34

1 States Parties undertake to protect the child from all forms of sexual exploitation and sexual abuse.

Traffic in children
Article 35

States Parties shall take all appropriate national, bilateral, and multinational measures to prevent the sale of or traffic in children for any purpose or in any form.

Child victims
Article 39

States Parties shall take all appropriate measures to promote physical and psychological recovery and social reintegration of a child victim of any form of neglect, exploitation or abuse, torture, or any other form of cruel, inhuman or degrading treatment or punishment, or armed conflicts. Such recovery and reintegration shall take place in an environment which fosters the health, self-respect and dignity of the child.

Penal issues
Article 40

States Parties recognize the right of every child alleged as, accused of, or recognized as having infringed the penal law to be treated in a manner consistent with the promotion of the child's sense of dignity and worth, which reinforces the child's respect for the human rights and fundamental freedoms of others, and which takes into account the child's age and the desirability of promoting the child's reintegration and the child's assuming a constructive role in society.

Notes and references

INTRODUCTION

p. 1 The murder of James Bulger in February 1993 and the trial and conviction nine months later of the two boys who abducted and killed him were widely reported in all the news media of Britain and elsewhere. Specific accounts which have been drawn on are: Robert Porter, 'Liverpool's Murder', *Sunday Telegraph*, 21.2.93; Jonathan Margolis, 'Are Our Children Out of Control?', *Sunday Times*, 21.2.93; Christina Hardyment, 'The Finger Points at Parents', *Sunday Telegraph*, 21.2.93; Masud Hoghughi, 'The Horrors of Crime', *Independent*, 1.3.93; Ann McFerran, 'A Life in the Day of . . . Masud Hoghughi', *Sunday Times Magazine*, 18.4.93.

p. 3 Masud Hoghughi, 'A Life in the Day of', as above.

p. 3 Statistics for crime, drug addiction, illegitimacy and abortion in Britain are taken from Ronald Spark, 'The Moral Cure for a Sick Society', *Mail on Sunday*, 21.3.93; 'More Children Live in Poverty', *Independent*, 22.3.93. US statistics are taken from the US Bureau of the Census, Statistical Abstract of the US 1992 (112th edition), Washington DC (1993); Michelle Healy, 'The Quality of Life Falls for US Kids', *USA Today*, 23.3.92.

p. 4 New York data, Charles Bremner, 'Pistol-packing in the Nursery', *The Times*, 7.12.90; Charles Laurence, 'City's Killers Are Children and So Are the Victims', *Daily Telegraph*, 4.6.92.

p. 4 Masud Hoghughi, 'The Horrors of Crime', as above.

p. 5 Beatrix Campbell, 'When In Doubt, Blame the Children', *Independent*, 24.3.93.

p. 6 British crime and divorce statistics supplied by government departments, US statistics from the US Bureau of the Census, as above. See also Celia Hall, 'One Quarter of Britons "Are Living Below Poverty Line"', *Independent*, 1.9.93; 'Children in Psychiatric Care', news report, *Independent on Sunday*, 4.4.94; 'US Children "Fat Suicidal and Murderous"', news report, *Guardian*, 3.1.92.

p. 7 'Barbara' is quoted from Paul Mones, *When a Child Kills: Abused Children Who Kill Their Parents*, New York, Pocket Books, 1991.

p. 7 Judith H. Weitz was speaking to the *New York Times*, 'Report Says Children Got Poorer in 1980's', 24.3.93.

p. 8 For Dr Spock, see Sue Woodman, 'Thumb-sucking is Healthy, the Family Is Not', *Independent*, 18.5.92.

1 TO BE OR NOT TO BE

p. 13 Statistics on world birth are taken from the US Bureau of the Census Statistical Abstract as before. See also Roger Highfield, 'Curb Births to Save the World', *Daily Telegraph*, 28.10.93, and Jay Rayner, 'It's Getting Mighty Crowded', *Cosmopolitan*, March 1992.

p. 13 For the Rio de Janeiro Earth Summit, see 'Britain Heads for Rio Clash on Birth Control', *Sunday Times*, 31.5.92

p. 15 For the details of *Veritatis Splendor*, see Ann Knowles, 'Guiding Light or Back to the Dark Ages', and Robert Nowell, 'Desperate Clampdown on Voices of Dissent', *Sunday Times*, 8.8.93; Michael Walsh, 'Blunders That Started With Original Sin', *Independent*, 24.9.93; James Brown, 'Pope Wants a Basic Morality Enforced', *New York Times*, 3.10.93; Bruce Johnson and Damian Thompson, 'Pope Orders Unswerving Obedience', *Daily Telegraph*, 2.8.93.

p. 16 China's population policy was reported in 'Chinese Enforce Abortion', Reuter, *Independent*, 5.3.91.

p. 17 Caroline Lees, 'Oxfam Stars Demand Birth Control Drive', *Sunday Times*, 13.1.91.

p. 17 For Poland's birth control debate, see Patricia Clough, 'Polish Bishops Step Up Fight Against Abortion', *Independent*, 5.3.91.

p. 17 For the Irish Family Planning Association case, see Olivia Timbs, 'Condom Criminals', *Independent*, 5.3.91.

p. 19 Desmond Morris, *Babywatching*, London, Cape, 1991, and see 'Babywatching', *Sunday Times Magazine*, 10.11.91.

p. 24 Dr Eleanor Barnes was talking to Denise Winn, 'The Price of Miracles', *Sunday Times Magazine*, 24.4.91.

p. 26 British and US statistics, source as before. See too David Fletcher, 'Baby Death Rate Highest in "deprived" Greenwich', *Daily Telegraph*, 4.3.93. For suicide of US children, see Washington DC news report 'Fat, Suicidal and Murderous', as above. For British children in psychiatric care, see news report, 'Children in Psychiatric Care', as above.

2 MOMMIE DEAREST

p. 30 Statistics on infertility are taken from the US Bureau of the Census Statistical Abstract as before.

p. 31 The quotation from the Quran is taken from Allen Edwardes, *The Jewel in the Lotus: A Historical Survey of the Sexual Culture of the East*, London, Allen & Unwin, 1965, p. 50.

p. 31 Anne Boleyn's comment is taken from W.J. Abbot, *Notable Women in History*, London, Greening, 1913, p. 64.

p. 32 The report of the Sixth World Congress on In Vitro Fertilisation is taken from Varda Burstyn, 'Breeding Discontent', *Saturday Night Magazine*, (Canada), June 1993.

p. 32 The comment of the husband on hospital infertility investigations is taken from the anonymous report 'A Husband: I Want Her to Know the Sacrifice I'm Making', *Independent*, 12.5.93.

p. 33 Tricia Lewis, 'My Heartache Over a Baby that Never Comes', Independent, 12.5.93.

p. 35 For an account of the impact of Truby King's teaching on the mothers of his time, and for the extracts in succeeding pages, see Steve Humphries and Pamela Gordon, *A Labour of Love: The Experience of Parenthood in Britain 1900–1950*, London, Sidgwick & Jackson, 1993.

p. 37 For an analysis of 'bonding', see Diane E. Eyer, *Mother-Infant Bonding: A Scientific Fiction*, London, Yale, 1993, and Laura Shapiro, 'It Doesn't Come Naturally', *New York Times*, 19.11.92.

p. 39 For a full discussion of cot deaths worldwide see Margarette Driscoll, 'The Tragic Cost of Breaking a Golden Rule', *Sunday Times*, 13.6.93. Further statistics are taken from Celia Hall, 'Campaign Seeks Reason for 55 per cent Fall in Cot Deaths', *Independent*, 30.3.93.

p. 40 Alice Miller, *The Drama of Being a Child*, p. 4.

p. 40 The words of Macaulay are taken from G. O. Trevelyan, *The Life and Letters of Lord Macaulay*, London, Longman Green, 1881, p. 186.

p. 40 Auberon Waugh describes his childhood in *Will This Do? The First Fifty Years of Auberon Waugh*, London, Arrow Books, 1992. Christina Crawford writes of her mother Joan in *Mommie Dearest*, London, Hart-Davis MacGibbon, 1979. For Nancy Reagan, see Kitty Kelley, *Nancy Reagan, The Unauthorised Biography*, London, Bantam Books, 1991.

p. 41 Alice Miller, *Banished Knowledge: Facing Childhood Injuries*, London, Virago, (1990) p. 6. For an account of Maureen O'Sullivan's treatment of Mia Farrow, see Sharon Churcher, 'Mia, Still Haunted by Nightmares from her *Own* Childhood', *Mail on Sunday*, 23.8.93.

p. 42 Gail Godwin's comment is to be found in the anthology *Motherhood*, Philadelphia, Running Press, 1991 (no author or editor).

p. 43 Washington Irving's summary of mother love is taken from *The Works of Washington Irving*, London, Henry G. Bohn, 1859, p. 199.

p. 43 For Laurie Lee, see *Cider With Rosie*, London, Hogarth Press, 1959.

p. 43 The Lancaster University survey of entrepreneurs was reported to the British Psychological Society Conference in April 1991: see David Fletcher, 'With a Pearl of a Mother the World Is Your Oyster', *Daily Telegraph*, 15.4.91.

p. 44 George Davis and his mother told their story to Nicola Tyrer, 'Behind a Successful Man', *Daily Telegraph*, 17.4.91.

p. 44 Barbra Streisand was talking to Jerry Watson in Hollywood, 'Tears As Streisand Breaks Down On TV', *Evening Standard*, 25.11.91.

p. 45 The Duchess of Beaufort and her daughter Lady Anne Somerset were talking to Richard Rosenfeld, *Sunday Times Magazine*, 16.8.92.

p. 45 Alice Miller

p. 46 John Carey, 'Elizabeth Smart: Rebel Without a Clue', *Sunday Times*, 27.10.93.

p. 46 Sally Trench and her son Nik were talking to Marina Cantacuzino, *Sunday Times Magazine*, 24.3.91.

p. 47 Lee Langley's story was taken from Danny Danziger, 'A Few Pink Gins and Then Things Would Go Wrong', *Independent*, 29.3.93.

p. 48 Nora Ephron was talking to Reggie Nadelson, 'The Lives of Nora Ephron', *Independent*, 26.11.92

3 FATHER ALMIGHTY

p. 52 The A. E. Housman quotation is taken from *A Shropshire Lad* XL, 'Into my heart an air that kills . . .'

p. 53 Irma Kurtz's comment comes from *Motherhood* (above).

p. 53 The University of Minnesota survey of post-natal sexual experience was reported in the *Independent* Health Update, 23.3.91.

p. 55 The comments of Michael Kimmel and the poetic homily cited are taken from Professor Kimmel's book *Changing Men: New Directions in Research into Men and Masculinity*, Newbury Park, California, Sage Publications, 1987, p. 85.

p. 56 The Muhsen law case and its circumstances were detailed in John Vincent, 'Woman Sues Father Over Her Marriage to Yemeni', *The Times*, 25.3.91.

p. 57 For Sean French on fatherhood, see 'What Is a Father Really For?', *Evening Standard*, 23.2.93.

p. 57 The judge's assessment of Woody Allen as a father was reported in the *Independent Magazine*, 19.6.93.

p. 60 Auberon Waugh as above.

p. 60 John McVicar, 'Like Father', *Sunday Times* Style and Travel, 11.7.93.

p. 61 For details of John Farrow's parenting, see above, Chapter 2.

p. 62 John Harvey-Jones described his boyhood to Lynn Barber, 'Looking for Trouble', *Independent on Sunday*, 14.4.91. Tessa Dahl was talking to Cassandra Jardine, 'Last Chapter of a Love Story', *Daily Telegraph*, 8.5.91.

p. 62 Ronald Segal and his daughter Miriam were talking to Leila Farrah, 'Playing Up To Father', *Sunday Times Magazine*, 5.5.91.

p. 63 Letty Cottin Pogrebin writes about her childhood in *Deborah, Golda and Me: Being Female and Jewish in America*, New York, Crown Publishers, 1991, p. 43.

p. 63 William Miller describes his father Jonathan in Richard Rosenfeld, 'Angry Young Men', *Sunday Times Magazine*, 3.1.93.

p. 64 The details of Sarah Churchill's unhappy relationship with her father are given by John Pearson in *Citadel of the Heart*, London, Macmillan, 1991.

4 HAPPY FAMILIES

p. 67 Arminta Wallace, 'The Family That Frays Together . . .', *Irish Times*, 16.4.93.

p. 70 The story of Russell Moore was told by Isabel Hilton in 'James Savage Will Never Go Home', *Independent* Weekend, 16.11.91. For Mia Farrow and her family, see Reggie Nadelson, 'Want a Happy Ending? Go See a Movie', *Independent* Weekend, 17.5.93, and Glenys Roberts, 'Trial Separation', *Daily Telegraph* Weekend, 10.4.93.

p. 72 For the story of Joel Steinberg and Hedda Nussbaum, see Joyce Johnson, 'This Was Not Done By One Of Us', *Independent*, 19.3.93.

p. 73 American adoption statistics are detailed in Desda Moss, 'Tangled, Troubled Adoptions Spur Reform Call', The Nation, *USA Today*, 3.5.93.

p. 74 The story of Angela Andrews is told in Bill Hewitt and Bonnie Bell, 'The Cruelest Hoax', *People* magazine, 10.5.93.

p. 74 The deBoer–Clausen adoption battle is outlined in Rupert Cornwell, 'Toddler Loses in Adoption Tug of War', *Independent* International Miscellany, 28.7.93, and Matthew Hoffman, 'Tug of Love That Became a Bitter Legal Battle for Baby Clausen', *Independent*, 23.7.93. See also Nigel Housby-Smith, 'Could Jessica's Story Happen Here?' *Independent*, 5.8.93. US reaction is taken from *Time* magazine, 3.5.93.

p. 76 For 'adoption divorce', see 'Our Adopted Son Was an Angel. What Turned Him Into a Devil?', Femail Testimony, *Daily Mail*, 18.3.93. See also Stephen Ward, 'Abused Boy's Legacy of Heartache and Despair', *Independent*, 22.2.93.

p. 78 The research of Dr McWhinnie into adoption is reported by Liza Donaldson in 'Two Mums and Dads Are a Set of Parents Too Many', *Independent*, 22.6.93.

p. 80 For Dr Ron Ericsson, see Barbara Altounyan, 'Would You Make a Baby With the Sperm Firm?' *Independent*, 7.11.91. Sex selection statistics are taken from David Fletcher, 'Legal Loophole Frees Sex Selection

Clinics', Colin Randall, 'A Biochemist Playing God from a Quiet Corner of Suburbia', Roger Highfield, 'Sperm Race Separates Boys From the Girls' and 'Operating a Scam?', all in the *Daily Telegraph*, 23.1.93. See also Libby Purves, 'Fair Play For The Fair Sex', *The Times*, 5.3.93.

p. 81 For female infanticide worldwide, see Jay Rayner, 'Who Is Killing Baby Girls?', *Cosmopolitan*, November 1993, and for China, Anna Pukas, 'Dying Room: The Proof: The Truth About Those Tragic Baby Girls', *Daily Mail*, 17.12.93.

p. 81 The British Medical Association response to sex selection was reported by Judy Jones, 'Doctors Reject Right to Choose Babies' Gender', *Independent*, 30.6.93.

p. 82 Liz Hopkinson, 'Dangers of Selecting Sex in Quest for a Perfect Family', *Sunday Times*, 24.1.93.

5 ENOUGH IS GOOD ENOUGH

p. 85 The Parent-Child Game was reported by Jerome Burn in 'From Little Monster to Little Angel: It's Kid's Play', *Independent*, 4.5.93.

p. 87 For poverty in Britain, see Terry Kirby, 'Police Put Blame on Effects of Recession', *Independent*, 9.3.93. For the increased poverty of working families in the US, see *New York Times*, 24.3.92, 'Report Says Poor Children Grew Poorer in 1980s'.

p. 88 Dr Johnson, Boswell's *Life of Samuel Johnson*, IV, p. 157.

p. 89 Robin Skynner's prescriptions for the happy family were given in the Royal Society of Arts Lecture 'Life, and How to Survive It', 17.2.93, reported in the *RSA Journal*, Vol. CXLI, No. 5440, June 1993. See also John Cleese and Robin Skynner, *Life and How to Survive It*, London, Methuen, 1993.

p. 90 Frieda Lawrence writes of her life with D. H. Lawrence in *Not I, But the Wind . . .*, London, Granada, 1983.

p. 92 The British Crime Survey of 1991 was reported by Celia Hall, 'Violence Linked to "Confused Discipline"', *Independent*, 2.10.91.

p. 94 Details of the Eastern Michigan University survey into children's happiness are taken from Robert Matthews, 'Gift of Love "Most Precious of All"', *Sunday Telegraph*, 16.12.90.

p. 95 Deborah Jackson, 'Mini-gym, Tumble-tots, Ballet . . . And Burn-Out!', *Independent*, 26.4.93.

p. 97 Samuel Beckett's unhappy childhood is discussed in Alice Miller, *The Drama of Being a Child*, London, Virago, 1987, p. 44.

p. 99 Charlotte Wilson was talking to Cassandra Jardine, 'Steps to End the Nightmare', *Daily Telegraph*, 15.1.91. See also Christine Doyle, 'Answering the Cries in the Dark', same source, and Ted Harrison, 'An End to Those Broken Nights', *Independent*, 26.1.93.

p. 99 The Mintel research survey into patterns of parenting was reported by David Nicholson-Lord, 'Parents Under Pressure', *Independent*, 28.7.93.

p. 99 M.Scott Peck, *The Road Less Travelled: A New Psychology of Love, Traditional Values and Spiritual Growth*, London, Arrow Books, 1983, pp. 131–2.

p. 100 The 'Theory of Mind' is outlined by Karen Gold in 'The Development of Mind-Reading', *Independent on Sunday*, 21.2.93.

p. 101 Alice Miller, *The Drama of Being a Child*, as above, p. 33.

6 LOVE AND NON-LOVE

p. 103 Alice Miller, *Banished Knowledge: Facing Childhood Injuries*, London, Virago, 1990, p. 8.

p. 104 Frances Hegarty was talking to Angela Lambert, 'Violent Tendencies in the Closet', *Independent*, 19.2.91.

p. 105 Arminta Wallace, as above, Chapter 4.

p. 105 Bette Midler, see Richard Meryman, 'Divining Miss M', *Lear's Magazine*, April 1992.

p. 106 Lance Morrow, 'The Shoes of Imelda Marcos', *Time* magazine, 31.3.86.

p. 107 Details of the arrest and trial of Wanda Webb Holloway are taken from AP report 'Mother "Tried To Hire Hit Man"', *Sunday Times*, 3.2.91, and Janet Midwinter, 'How Mother's Pride Led Her to Hire Hit Man', *Mail on Sunday*, 10.2.91.

p. 108 Beverley Davison was talking to Christopher Mowbray, 'With Strings but No Hang-ups', *Independent*, 10.2.93.

p. 109 Recent research into the family systems of dysfunctional families is discussed by Anne-Marie Sapsted, 'Addicts on a String', *Observer Magazine*, 13.1.91.

p. 109 Janet Cohen, 'Not Everyone Needs a Degree', You and Your Family, *Daily Telegraph*, 15.1.93.

p. 110 Jennifer Johnston talking to Penny Perrick, 'A Prisoner of the Big House', *Sunday Times* Books Section, 24.2.91, pp. 6–7.

p. 111 Glenn Close, see Minty Clinch, 'Close Encounter', *Observer Magazine*, 22.9.91.

p. 111 Don Boyd talking to Danny Danziger, 'She Ran After the Plane in Tears', *Independent*, 9.12.91.

p. 112 Frances Fyfield [Hegarty] was talking to Fionnuala McHugh, 'The House Where I Grew Up', *Daily Telegraph Magazine*, 9.10.92.

p. 112 Robin Williams, 'My Daddy Is Dry All Night', Adriaane Pielou, *YOU* magazine, 18.8.91.

p. 112 For Anton Mosimann, see Danny Danziger, 'Black Shoes of a Nightmare Man', *Independent*, 29.4.91.

p. 113 The Schoo family 'home alone' abandonment case was reported in *Time* magazine, 'The Week' news roundup, 3.5.93. See also Felix Sanchez, '"Home-Alone" Cases Rising, Official Says', *Houston Post*, 15.2.93.

p. 114 The British 'home alone' case, the story of Gemma Gibson, was reported by Emma Wilkins, 'Mother of Girl Left Alone to Stay in Spain', *Daily Telegraph*, 16.2.93.

p. 115 'Helen Braid' talked to Paddy Burt, 'Can You Slam the Door on a Semi-Detached Son?' *Independent*, 21.4.93. Helen Braid's own account is published as *Letters to My Semi-Detached Son*, London, Women's Press, 1993.

p. 117 Frances Hegarty, Angela Lambert interview, as above.

p. 117 For sibling rivalry see Sarah Stacey, 'The Lifelong Damage of Sibling Rivalry', *Daily Mail*, 6.10.92.

p. 117 For Michele and Tania Wade, see Fiona Lafferty, 'Tartes for Art's Sake', *Sunday Times Magazine*, 14.3.93.

p. 120 Figures for sibling abuse and violence are taken from Beverley Hopwood and Monique Roffey, 'Is There a Little Monster in Your House?', *Independent*, 19.8.92.

p. 121 For a detailed account of the Kennedy family, see Nigel Hamilton, *JFK: Life and Death of an American President*, Vol.I: *Reckless Youth*, London, Century, 1993. Other details are drawn from R. W. Johnson, 'The Kennedy Boys', *London Review of Books*, 28.1.93.

7 KEEPING IT IN THE FAMILY

p. 128 'It has taken me 22 years . . .' For the story of this and other survivors of incest, see Ellen Bass and Louise Thornton (eds), *I Never Told Anyone: Writings By Women Survivors of Sex Abuse*, New York, Harper Perennial, 1983.

p. 128 The Roman custom of violating virgin girls before executing them is described by Suetonius in 'Tiberius', *The Twelve Caesars*, Harmondsworth, Penguin, 1957.

p. 130 The story of Dr Dod is to be found in Lloyd de Mause, *The History of Childhood: The Untold Story of Child Abuse*, London, Bellew, 1991. See also Lucy Hughes Hallett, 'The Child is Father to the Moan', *Independent on Sunday*, 18.8.81.

p. 131 For the mother whose conviction for attacking her daughter was quashed on appeal, see *Daily Telegraph* news report '"Smacking" mother wins assault case', 20.5.93.

p. 131 The trial of the father who beat his sons was reported by Paul

Stokes, 'Father Who Hit Boys With Leather Belt Cleared of Assault', *Daily Telegraph*, 20.3.93, and Stephen Ward, 'Man Cleared of Beating Sons With Belt', *Independent*, 20.3.93.

p. 133 John Bradshaw, *Healing the Shame that Binds You*, Florida Health Communications Inc., 1988, p. 12.

p. 134 Dr Spock, as above, Introduction.

p. 135 For NSPCC statistics, see the 1992 report *Child Abuse trends in England and Wales 1988–1990, and An Overview 1973–1990*. See also 'NSPCC Warning on Ritual Abuse as Child Sex Cases Increase', *Independent*, 19.3.91, and 'Recession is Linked to an Increase in Child Abuse', 30.9.92.

p. 135 The story of Genie is told by Russ Rymer, *Genie: Esape From a Silent Childhood*, London, Michael Joseph, 1993; see also Natalie Angier, '"Stopit!" She Said. "Nomore!"', *New York Times*, 25.4.93.

p. 137 Robert Blake was talking to Mark Goodman and Craig Tomashoff, *People* magazine, 3.1.93.

p. 138 Alice Miller discusses Freud in *Banished Knowledge*, pp. 54–5.

p. 138 The childhood abuse of Virginia Woolf is recounted in Quentin Bell, *Virginia Woolf*, Vol. I: *Virginia Stephen 1882–1912*, London, Hogarth Press, 1972. Daniel Farson describes Francis Bacon's upbringing in *The Gilded Gutter Life of Francis Bacon*, London, Century, 1993. See also Frances Spalding, 'The Butcher Boy', *Sunday Times*, 18.4.93.

p. 139 The North London University survey into child abuse was reported in *The Times*, 12.12.91.

p. 139 'False Memory Syndrome' is reported by Rosie Waterhouse, 'Families Haunted By Accusations of Childhood Abuse', *Independent*, 24.5.93, Geordie Greg, '"False Memories" Raise Doubts on Child Abuse', *Sunday Times*, 20.6.93, and Anthea Gerrie, 'The Accused', *Options*, June 1993.

p. 140 Scott Peck, *People of the Lie: The Hope for Healing Human Evil*, London, Arrow Books, 1990.

p. 141 NSPCC statistics as above. US statistics as above, Introduction.

p. 141 Adam Jukes, 'Violence, Helplessness, Vulnerability and Male Sexuality', *Free Associations*, Vol. 4, Part 1, No. 29, pp. 25–43.

p. 142 Alice Miller, *The Drama of Being a Child*, p. 68: and p. 143.

p. 143 For female participation in sex abuse, see Susan Young, 'Child Sex Abuse By Women Alarms Welfare Agencies', *Observer*, 1.3.92.

p. 144 The story of the Kilkenny father was reported by Alan Murdoch in Dublin, 'Anger in Dail Over Incest Sentence', *Independent*, 3.4.93.

p. 144 Helena Kennedy, *Eve Was Framed*, London, Virago 1991.

p. 145 For the social workers' arguments in defence of children's accounts of abuse, see 'Exploding Myths of Orkney Case', *Observer*,

24.3.93, and Charles Laurence, '"Allowing a Child to Watch Video Nasties, Is That Child Abuse?"', *Daily Telegraph*, 9.3.93.

p. 145 For Christopher Brown, see Charles Laurence, above.

p. 146 Oprah Winfrey was talking to Vyvyan Mackeson, 'A Life in the Day of', *Sunday Times Magazine*, 8.9.91.

p. 146 The incest survivor's story was reported in *Honey*, June 1982.

8 THE HAPPIEST DAYS OF YOUR LIFE

p. 148 Professor Fred Stone's address to the 1993 Annual Convention of the British Association for the Advancement of Science was noted in the news report 'Delinquency', *Independent*, 3.8.93.

p. 148 George Bernard Shaw's observations on education are to be found in *Everybody's Political What's What* (1944), p. 177.

p. 149 Lord Elton, former Minister at the Home Office, chaired the Home Office enquiry into bullying in schools in Britain in 1989. See also Nick Cohen, 'Half of All Children Victims of Bullying', *Independent*, 31.10.91, and Mark Handscomb, 'He's Always Beating Up the Three-Year-Olds', *Independent*, 14.5.92.

p. 150 Rory Bremner talked to Chrissy Iley, 'Not Wacky but Angry', *Sunday Times*, 3.5.92.

p. 151 For Lord David Cecil's account of the poet Cowper's schooldays see *The Stricken Deer, or, The Life of Cowper*, London, Crown Constable, 1929.

p. 152 Frederick Raphael gave his account of being bullied at school to Danny Danziger, 'The Ball Hit My Face: My Own Side Laughed', *Independent*, 1.3.93.

p. 153 The suicide of Mark Maclagan was reported by Jenny Rees, 'Suicide Boy's Parents Seek Full Enquiry On Bullying', *Daily Telegraph*, 16.2.93. See also Judith Judd, '"Ban Initiations" Call At Suicide School', *Independent*, 19.7.93. The suicide of Stephen Woodhall was reported by Andrew Alderson, 'Hanged Boy Was Bullied For 10p', *Sunday Times*, 7.3.93.

p. 155 Tim Laskey's booklet *How To Beat Bullying* was reported by Mark Handscomb in 'How to Give More Power to the Picked-On', *Independent*, 14.5.92. It is available for a £9.70 cheque or postal order from Health Habit Publications, Glen Road, Grayshott, Hindhead, Surrey GU26 6NB.

p. 156 Professor Stone, as above.

p. 157 Robin Benians, 'Problem Children: Problem Society', *The British Journal of Psychiatry Review of Books*, January 1993.

p. 158 Michèle Elliott was talking to Mark Handscomb, 'He's Always Beating Up the Three-Year-Olds', *Independent*, 14.5.92.

p. 158 For Kate Tyldesley and Delwyn Tattum, see Handscomb, as above.

p. 159 For an account of the Hahn theories of education, the regime at Gordonstoun and Prince Charles's reaction to it, see Penny Junor, *Charles*, London, Sidgwick & Jackson, 1987.

p. 159 Alice Miller, *For Your Own Good: Hidden Cruelty in Child-Rearing and the Roots of Violence*, London, Virago, 1987, pp. 64–5.

p. 160 Auberon Waugh, as above, Chapter 2.

p. 160 The anonymous memoir of the sufferings of the beaten schoolboy, 'Beaten, Humiliated and Scarred for Life', is taken from 'Viewpoint', *Independent*, 31.1.91.

p. 161 The details of the Jeremy Costello-Roberts case and the expected verdict are taken from Bruce Kemble, 'Euro Court Verdict Spells Final Stroke for the Cane', *Evening Standard*, 23.3.93.

p. 161 The regime at the ACE school is reported by Fran Abrams, 'Christian Schools Keep Right to Spank', *Sunday Telegraph*, 23.5.93.

p. 162 The judge passing sentence on the schoolmaster priest was dealing with Brother James Carragher: see news report, 'Monk Jailed for School Sex Attacks', *Independent*, 10.8.93.

p. 163 For the account of Carragher's offences, see note above. The offences of Father Michael Creagh were the subject of the news report 'Housemaster Priest Jailed for Indecent Assaults on Boy, 12', *Daily Telegraph*, 12.8.92.

p. 164 For George Zanucki and other US cases see Peter Pringle, 'US Bishops Open Inquiry Into Sex Abuse By Priests', *Independent*, 1.4.91, and Geordie Greig, 'Sex Abuse By Priests Rocks US Church', *Sunday Times*, 19.7.92.

p. 165 The offences of Paul Burton were outlined in the news report 'Kidnapper of Caravan Girl Is Sent to Broadmoor', *Independent*, 14.2.93.

p. 166 For Ray Wyre's comments, see the news report 'Police Faced Wall of Silence', *Daily Telegraph*, 12.8.92. See also Rebecca Fowler, 'Parents Sue Church Over "Hushed-Up" Child Abuse', *Sunday Times*, 23.5.93.

p. 166 The story of Frank Beck was told by Jack O'Sullivan, 'Head of Children's Homes Jailed for Life, Five Times', *Independent*, 30.11.91.

p. 167 For 'Uncle Bill', see news report 'Major Jailed for Indecency Over 14 Years', *Daily Telegraph*, 15.1.91.

p. 167 Details of the sentence of Patrick Gilbert appear in the news report 'Church Worker Convicted of Molesting Boy', *Independent*, 15.6.93.

p. 168 The comments of convicted abusers are taken from Rosalyn Chissick, 'She Never Said NO', *New Woman*, February 1993, and the anonymous confession of an abuser, 'Why I'm Every Mother's Worst Fear', *Woman's Journal*, August 1992.

p. 169 The story of the persecution of the Jewish family by their community is told by Steve Boggan, 'A Law Unto Themselves', Sunday Review, *Independent on Sunday*, 11.8.91.

9 THE PLACE WHERE VIOLENCE GROWS

p. 171 Arthur Miller addressed a London audience on 26 March 1993 at the Young Vic Theatre, where his play *The Last Yankee* was in performance. The seminar was reported by David Lister, 'Playwright Rules Out Censorship', *Independent*, 27.3.93.

p. 171 David Puttnam was reported by Jonathan Margolis, 'The Movies v. Morality', *Sunday Times*, 14.3.93.

p. 171 The words of Jon Venables' mother are taken from Wendy Holden and Nigel Bunyan, 'Yeah, My Son's a Robber But He's Not a Murderer', *Daily Telegraph*, 25.11.93.

p. 172 Arthur Miller, as above.

p. 172 James Joyce describes the approach of the stranger in 'An Encounter', *Dubliners*, Harmondsworth, Penguin, 1956.

p. 172 Statistics of violence in children's television viewing and the report of the research of Professor Signorelli are taken from Rupert Cornwell, 'TV Moguls Find That Violence Might Not Pay', *Independent*, 26.5.93.

p. 174 Paul Dempsey was talking to Robin Hunt, 'How a Revolution Aimed at the Young Brought Violence into the Home', *Sunday Telegraph*, 28.11.93.

p. 174 John Lyttle, 'Cheap "Gorefest" Videos Have Mellowed With Age', *Independent*, 27.11.93.

p. 175 Michael Fallon was reported by Sarah Johnson, 'Parents Told to Cut Children's Videos', *Sunday Telegraph*, 14.4.91.

p. 175 For Howard Gold and 'The Moderator', see Vikki Orvice, 'The Video Game's Up', *Daily Mail*, 27.10.93.

p. 176 The survey by Barnardo's is detailed by Liz Hunt, 'Children Rely on TV for Aids Education', *Independent*, 11.7.93.

p. 176 For Michael Medved, see Margolis, above.

p. 177 Professor George Comstock's research is reported by Margarette Driscoll, 'How Life Imitates Screen Violence', *Sunday Times*, 14.3.93.

p. 177 Professor Guy Cumberbatch was talking to Heather Mills, 'Link Between Crime and TV "Not Proven"', *Independent*, 9.3.93.

p. 178 For Clive Bourne, see Michael Smith, 'School Bans Pocket Video Game Nasties', *Daily Telegraph*, 28.4.93.

p. 179 Luke Harding, 'The Sega Sickener', *Daily Mail*, 28.4.93.

p. 180 David Holbrook's views are contained in a letter to the *Independent*, 16.3.93.

p. 182 Robin Hunt, as before.

p. 183 Josephine Hart, see Margolis, above.

p. 184 Details of the scheduling patterns designed to lure young viewers and to disregard the 'nine o'clock watershed' are given by William Phillips, 'Soap Cleans Up Children's Viewing', *Independent*, 17.3.93.

p. 184 Catherine Deneuve was talking to E. Jane Dickson, 'View from a Pedestal', *Sunday Times Magazine*, 14.3.93.

p. 185 James Ferman, see Margolis, above.

p. 185 Alice Miller, *Banished Knowledge*, p. 46.

p. 186 The remarks of Mr Justice Morland and Superintendent Albert Kirby were reported by Nigel Bunyan and Wendy Holden, 'Boys Guilty of Bulger Murder', *Daily Telegraph*, 25.11.93.

p. 187 Dr Hemming's views are contained in a letter to the *Independent*, 27.11.93. Dr Reibstein was talking to Angela Neustatter and Liz Hunt, 'Young Offenders Are "Sad Rather Than Bad"', *Independent*, 25.11.93.

p. 188 Barry Norman, see Margolis, above.

10 WHEN THE BOUGH BREAKS

p. 193 Lord Mackay of Clashfern was talking to Patricia Wynn Davies, 'A Man for Moral Dilemmas', *Independent*, 11.12.90.

p. 193 The comments of Martin Amis and his father were reported by Toby Young in 'The Old Devil', *Sunday Times* Style and Travel, 12.8.93.

p. 193 Judith Bardwick, *Women in Transition: How Feminism, Sexual Liberation and the Search for Self-Fulfilment Have Altered Our Lives*, Brighton, Harvester Press, 1980, p. 132.

p. 194 John Bradshaw, as above, Chapter 7.

p. 194 British divorce statistics from the Office of Population Censuses and Surveys; US statistics for divorce from the US Bureau of the Census, as above, Introduction.

p. 195 Cliff Richard was interviewed by Tony Parsons, 'No Sex, No Drugs, Just Rock 'n Roll', *Daily Telegraph*, 16.3.93.

p. 195 Scott Peck, *A World Waiting To Be Born: The Search For Civility*, London, Rider Books, 1993, p. 111.

p. 196 Dr Spock, as above, Introduction.

p. 196 *The Divorce Handbook* by Fiona Shackleton and Olivia Timbs, London, Thorsons, 1992. See also Olivia Timbs, 'Divorce Is Bad For You, Try Again', *Independent*, 1.9.92.

p. 196 Jo Ind, *Fat Is a Spiritual Issue: My Journey*, London, Mowbray, 1993, p. 22.

p. 197 The British survey of the prospects of the children of divorce were reported by Steve Boggan, 'Children Suffer "Heavy Toll" When Parents Remarry', *Independent*, 2.12.91. See also 'Consider the Children', *Independent* leader 3.12.91, and news report 'Divorce Hits Families Harder Than Death', *The Times*, 9.10.93.

p. 198 Statistics for the disadvantages of the children of divorce from the Symposium of the British Psychological Society were reported by Sharon Kingman, 'Children of Divorce Suffer in Adult Life', *Independent*, 15.9.91, and by Peter Pallot, '750,000 Children May Have Lost All Fatherly Contact', *Daily Telegraph*, 11.3.91.

p. 199 Angharad Allmark and James Lyons were talking to Louise France and Justine Hancock, 'Divorce Through the Ages', *Evening Standard*, 3.12.91.

p. 200 Details of the story of Christian Brando are taken from the news report '"Remorseful" Brando Awaits His Sentence', *Independent*, 27.2.91.

p. 201 James Blandford was reported by Nigel Dempster and Geoffrey Levy, 'Poor Little Rich Boy', *Daily Mail*, 9.10.91.

p. 202 Deborah Moggach outlined her views in 'If You All Live Together, It Puts A Terrific Strain On Mother', *Daily Mail*, 25.3.93.

p. 202 Charles Coleman, 'I Was Given Everything Last', as Moggach above.

p. 203 The pair-bonding of primates is reported by Sanjida O'Connell, 'Twosomes that Keep the Kids from Danger', *Independent*, 27.4.72. The mortality statistics for stepchildren are also reported here.

p. 203 'Stepmother Treated Girl "Like Cinderella"', *Daily Telegraph*, 27.2.91.

p. 204 Jennifer Johnston, as above, Chapter 6.

p. 206 William J. Goode, *World Changes in Divorce Patterns*, London, Yale, 1993, and see Christina Hardyment, 'Divorce: How We Must Manage the Damage', *Daily Telegraph*, 27.9.93.

p. 206 The testimony of the child victim of divorce was given by S. J. Sly in a letter to the editor, 'How to End the Suffering of Children in Stepfamilies', *Independent*, 5.12.91.

p. 207 Penelope Lively was talking to Pauline Peters, 'A Romantic in the Ant Heap', *Evening Standard*, 8.4.91.

11 LEGIONS OF THE LOST

p. 208 Senator Daniel Moynihan was talking to Joe Klein, 'Make the Daddies Pay', *Newsweek*, 21.6.93.

p. 209 Numbers of single-parent families in Britain are taken from 'Children in Singular Difficulties', *Independent* leader 3.8.91, also the source for Professor Fred Halsey and his summary of the disadvantages of single parenthood.

p. 210 London statistics for one-parent families are taken from Anthony Bevins, 'Family Structure Collapsing in London', *Independent*, 10.4.93.

p. 210 For US statistics of single mothers, commentary and analysis, see George F. Will, 'Clinton: If He Succeeds It Will Be Despite Himself', *Daily Telegraph*, 12.11.92. See also Darryl Figueroa, 'Data Grim for District Children', *Washington Times*, 24.3.92.

p. 210 George Jackson was quoted in the *Independent* 'Diary', 5.5.92. See also *Soledad Brother: The Prison Letters of George Jackson*, Harmondsworth, Penguin, 1971, and *Blood in My Eye*, London, Cape, 1072.

p. 211 For Thomas Sowell, see 'Racism Is Not the Reason', *Sunday Times* leader, 3.5.92.

p. 211 Charles Murray, 'Keep It in the Family', *Sunday Times*, 14.11.93. For a discussion of Charles Murray and his views, see Beatrix Campbell, 'Life Without Father: It's Easy', *Independent*, 17.11.93.

p. 211 For single parents on income support in Britain, see Rosie Waterhouse, 'Cabinet File Quashes Lone-Parent Stereotype', *Independent*, 20.11.93.

p. 212 Alice Miller, *The Drama of Being a Child*, p. 79.

p. 213 Beatrix Campbell, 'A Teenage Girl's Passport to Womanhood', *Independent*, 12.5.93.

p. 214 The rise in single-parent statistics is taken from Michael Jones, 'Wedded to Welfare: Do They Want to Marry a Man or the State?', *Sunday Times*, 11.7.93.

p. 214 Patricia Hewitt, 'In Search of the Modern Father', *Independent*, 10.5.93.

p. 215 For absentee fathers, see Angela Phillips, 'Prince Charming? Haven't Seen Him For Ages', *Independent*, 12.6.93. See also the same author's 'Just Like What Man?', *Independent*, 17.9.93, and *The Trouble With Boys: Parenting the Men of the Future*, London, Pandora Press, 1993.

p. 215 A. N. Wilson was talking to Hunter Davis, 'In Bed With A. N. Wilson', *Independent*, 12.1.93.

p. 217 For the impoverishment of deserted women, see Celia Hall, 'Failed Marriages Create a Female Underclass', *Independent*, 31.8.93.

p. 217 Travis Simkins writes about his father in 'Growing Up Is Hard To Do', *Newsweek*, 21.6.93.

p. 218 The story of Annie Murphy and Bishop Casey is told by Annie Murphy with Peter de Rosa in *Forbidden Fruit*, London, Little Brown, 1993. See also Liam Clarke, 'Bishop Wants to Be Reunited with Teenage Son of Former Lover', *Sunday Times*, 21.3.93, and Lesley White, 'Sin, Sex and Scandal: The Bishop's Lover's Tale', *Sunday Times*, 14.3.93.

p. 218 Zero-parent families are discussed by Jane Gross in 'Collapse of Inner-City Families Creates America's New Orphans', and in 'Orphans Multiply as Inner-City Families Crumble', *New York Times* national news report, both 29.3.92.

p. 221 Depression in childhood is reported by Mary Braid, 'Burying the Past at the Tender Age of Twelve', *Independent*, 8.8.91.

p. 222 The story of Sappho and Lawrence Durrell was told by Justine Picardie, 'A Father's Shadow', *Independent Magazine*, 28.9.93.

p. 222 Alice Miller, *The Drama of Being a Child*, p. 85.

p. 223 Lucy Ellman was talking to Danny Danziger, 'I Withdrew in Misery into my Coat', *Independent*, 30.9.91.

p. 224 Statistics for substance abusers are taken from David Millward, 'Grim Picture of Homeless and Jobless Young People', *Daily Telegraph*, 10.7.93. See also news reports, 'Teenagers report "Widespread Drinking"', *Independent*, 11.1.91, and 'Teenagers' Biggest Expense is Drink', *Independent*, 22.3.91.

p. 225 Pot-smoking Sharon was interviewed by Leonie Jameson, 'Teenagers Can Be Alcoholics Too', *Independent*, 2.6.93.

p. 225 Dr Douglas Carrol was talking to Oliver Gillie, 'Child Gamblers Get "A Sensation Jag"', *Independent* 17.5.91.

p. 225 The child gamblers were reported by Victoria Macdonald, 'Teenagers Steal to Feed Lure of Fruit Machines', *Sunday Telegraph*, 16.12.90.

p. 226 For Dr Richard Williams, see Alan Massam, 'Girls Under 10 Now Hit By Anorexia', *Evening Standard*, 18.4.92. See also Anthea Hall, 'Fighting Children's Fear of Flab', *Sunday Telegraph*, 29.9.91.

p. 227 Jennai Cox wrote her own account of anorexia, 'Everybody Said I Was Losing Weight But No One Could Talk About Me', *Independent*, 31.5.93.

p. 227 Susan Scott was talking to Katy Macdonald, 'My Brief Fling Turned Me into a Five Stone Anorexic', *Daily Mail*, 1.4.93.

p. 228 Jamie Harges was interviewed in *People Magazine*, 1.3.93.

p. 228 Statistics of the children of alcoholics are taken from the *Washington Post* news report, 'Marital Woes May Await Alcoholics' Children', 3.5.93.

p. 228 For Peter Lawford see James Spada, *Peter Lawford: The Man Who Kept the Secrets*, London, Bantam Press, 1991.

p. 229 M. Scott Peck, *People of the Lie*, p. 121.

12 BAD GIRLS AND DEVIL BOYS

p. 230 The story of Herman and Druie Dutton was told to Susan Ellicott, 'When American Children Kill Dad, the Americans Cheer', *Sunday Times*, 1.8.93.

p. 230 The crime of Philip Barber and Paul Chapman appeared in a *Daily Mirror* news report, 'Devil Boys', 5.5.93.

p. 230 Details of the case of Maria Rossi and Christine Molloy are taken from the *Daily Mail* news report 'Evil Beyond Belief', 9.3.93.

p. 232 Masud Hoghughi interviewed by Ann McFerran, as above, Introduction.

p. 233 Professor Terence Morris and the Youth worker were talking to Fiona Weekley, 'The Crime of their Lives', *Sunday Times* Style and Travel, 13.6.93.

p. 234 Details of car theft, assault and arson are taken from Paul Stokes, 'Police Cars Rammed in Ambush by Teenagers', *Daily Telegraph*, 17.3.93, also the source for the comments of DCI Philip Jones, and Richard Ford, 'Joyriders Blamed for Big Rise in Car Fires', *The Times*, 3.5.93.

p. 235 Maurice Chittenden, 'Getting Away With Murder', *Sunday Times*, 18.7.93.

p. 236 For details of the babysitter killing, see Malcolm Pithers, 'Five Years' Custody For Girl, 12, Who Killed Baby', *Independent*, 30.4.92, and Janine di Giovanni, 'Inside the Mind of a Child Killer', *Sunday Times*, 3.5.92.

p. 236 For children abusing children, see Celia Hall, 'Boys Under 9 Abusing Children', *Independent*, 2.9.90.

p. 236 Christina Robinson was talking to Jack O'Sullivan, 'The Young Victims Who Are Trapped in a Cycle of Abuse', *Independent*, 24.4.92. See also Adam Sage, 'Who Cares? Children's Long History of Neglect', *Independent on Sunday*, 2.6.91.

p. 237 Details of the report of Dr Gwyneth Boswell are taken from Jack O'Sullivan. 'Most Young Offenders "Abused As Children"', *Independent*, 4.12.91.

p. 237 Assaults on teachers are reported in Greg Hadfield and Charles Hymas, 'The Blackboard Jungle', *Sunday Times*, 28.3.93, as are the offences against teachers and the penalties for the offenders. See also *Independent* news report, 'Boy, 15, Detained for Butting Teacher', 17.4.93.

p. 238 For Mia Farrow, see Oliver James, 'Family Circles', *Sunday Times* Style and Travel, 13.6.93.

p. 239 Hoghughi, as above.

p. 240 The mayor of Crewkerne is reported in Peter Dunn, 'Rude Awakening for a Peaceful Town', *Independent*, 2.3.93.

p. 240 Psychotherapists Sinasan and Andreou were talking to Yasmin Alibhai-Brown, 'The Wounds Inflicted on the Inner World of Children', *Observer*, 2.6.91.

p. 241 For young male suicide statistics, see Anne Rankin, 'The Ballad of the Sad Young Men', *Sunday Times*, 1.3.93.

p. 241 The story of Sally Anne Cattell was reported by Tim Butcher, 'Girl, 14, Dies in Police Chase', *Daily Telegraph*, 16.3.93, and Esther Oxford, 'Short Life and Death of an Exile from Society', *Independent*, 20.3.93.

p. 242 Peter McKay was writing about Sinead O'Connor in 'The Poor Little Me Generation', *Sunday Times* Style and Travel, 13.6.93.

p. 243 The remark of Anthony Storr is taken from *The Phoenix Appeal*, the booklet of the Peper Harow Organisation, a residential charity for disturbed children.

p. 244 The research on pathological boredom in children was reported by Raj Persaud, 'Today You're Bored, Tomorrow You're Ill', *Independent*, 30.3.93.

p. 245 Andrew O'Hagan was writing of his childhood in the 'Diary' of the *London Review of Books*, 11.3.93.

CONCLUSION

p. 247 The description of the two defendants at the James Bulger trial was taken from Elizabeth Grice and Nigel Bunyan, 'Accused: Two Little Boys With Ties and Tidy Hair', *Daily Telegraph*, 2.11.93. Other details were taken from: Jonathan Foster, 'James Bulger "Hurt Within Yards of Shopping Centre"', *Independent*, 5.11.93; Howard Foster, Walter Ellis and Margarette Driscoll, 'The Story Britain Could Not Bear To Hear', *Sunday Times*, 7.11.93; Colin Adamson, 'I Nearly Saved Tired James from the Grip of "Boy Kidnappers"', *Evening Standard*, 8.11.93; Jonathan Foster, 'James Bulger Suffered Multiple Fractures', *Independent*, 10.11.93, 'Accused Boys' Nightmares Over Bulger', 12.11.93, 'Bulger Trial Boy Blames His Friend', 13.11.93; news report, 'Boy, 10, Says He "Never Hit" James', *Independent*, 17.11.93; Nigel Bunyan and Wendy Holden, 'Boys Guilty of Bulger Murder', *Daily Telegraph*, 25.11.93; Press Association, 'Jon Was "Fearful, Weak, and He Was Provoked"', and 'Mother Cannot Believe That "Devious Child" Killed', *Independent*, 25.11.93; Terry Kirby and Jonathan Foster, 'Video Link to Bulger Murder Disputed', *Independent*, 26.11.93.

p. 250 Beatrix Campbell, 'Legacy of the Demon Master', *Independent*, 25.8.93.

p. 253 Martin Amis, 'The Fuck-It Generation', *Esquire*, November 1993.

p. 254 Dr Richard Ryder was delivering the Cantor Lecture to the Royal Society of Arts on 10 May 1993, reprinted as 'Violence and Machismo', *RSA Journal*, Vol.CXLI, No. 5443, October 1993, pp. 706–13.

p. 255 The UN Convention on the Rights of the Child is published by the United Nations Human Rights Association, 14 Stratford Place, London W1. See also Caroline Moorhead, 'Child Rights Campaign Starts Timidly', *Independent*, 4.3.91. and the *Observer* Bicentary Lecture, 'A New Charter for the Children of Our World', HRH The Princess Royal, *Observer*, 9.6.91.

p. 255 Erica Jong was talking to Chrissy Iley, 'Stark Staring Fifty', *Sunday Times Magazine*, 19.12.93.

p. 257 The case of Father Holley was reported in *Daily Telegraph* Worldwatch, 5.6.93. The story of the Keleman family was told by Heather Mills, 'Abused Sisters Win Damages from Father', *Independent*, 12.11.93.

p. 257 Paul Mones, as above, Introduction.

p. 258 Eglantyne Jebb's pioneering version of the rights of the child is taken from 'Directions UK', the handbook of the Save the Children Fund.

p. 258 Alice Miller's four steps are taken from *Banished Knowledge*, p. 179.

p. 259 Yasmin Alibhai-Brown, as above.

Select bibliography

Abbot, W.J., *Notable Women in History*, London, Greening & Co., 1913.
'AE', *Collected Poems*, London, Macmillan, 1919.
Arnold, Matthew, *Poetical Works*, London, Macmillan, 1869.
Auden, W. H., *Collected Poems*, London, Faber & Faber, 1991.
Bardwick, Judith M., *Women in Transition: How Feminism, Sexual Liberation and the Search for Self-Fulfilment Have Altered Our Lives*, Brighton, Harvester Press,1980.
Barr, Roseanne, *My Life as a Woman*, Glasgow, Fontana,1989.
Bass, Ellen, and Thornton, Louise, *I Never Told Anyone: Writings by Women Survivors of Child Sex Abuse*, New York, Harper Perennial, 1991.
Beckett, Samuel, *Krapp's Last Tape*, London, Faber & Faber, 1959.
Bell, Quentin, *Virginia Woolf*, Vol.I: *Virginia Stephen 1882–1912*; Vol.II: *Mrs Woolf 1912—1941*, London, Hogarth Press,1972.
Benians, Robin, 'Problem Children: Problem Society', *The British Journal of Psychiatry Review of Books*, January 1993, pp. 12–15.
Blake, William, *Songs of Innocence and of Experience*, London, Folio Society, 1974.
Blyton, Enid, *First Term at Malory Towers*, London, Methuen, 1945.
Boswell, James, *Life of Samuel Johnson* (4 vols), London, T. Cadell and W. Davies, 1811.
Bowlby, John, *Childcare and the Growth of Love*, Harmondsworth, Penguin, 1953.
Bradshaw, John, *Healing the Shame that Binds You*, Florida, Health Communications Inc., 1988.
Braid, Helen (pseud.), *Letters To My Semi-Detached Son*, London, Women's Press, 1993.
Brazil, Angela, *A Popular Schoolgirl*, London, Blackie, 1920.
Brontë, Charlotte, *Jane Eyre*, London, Smith Elder, 1848.
— *The Professor*, London, Dent, 1969.
Campbell, Beatrix, *Unofficial Secrets: Child Sex Abuse – the Cleveland Case*, London, Virago, 1988.
Cecil, Lord David, *The Stricken Deer, or, The Life of Cowper*, London, Constable, 1929.

Cervantes, Miguel de, *The Life and Exploits of the Ingenious Don Quixote de la Mancha*, London, J. & R. Tonson, 1742.

Chang, Jung, *Wild Swans: Three Daughters of China*, London, HarperCollins, 1991.

Child Abuse Trends in England and Wales 1988–1990 and *Child Abuse: An Overview 1973–1990*, both published by NSPSCC, 1991.

Clare, John, *Selected Poems and Prose*, London, Methuen, 1986.

Cleese, John, and Skynner, Robin, *Families and How to Survive Them*, London, Cedar, 1983.

— *Life and How to Survive It*, London, Methuen, 1993.

Cox, Kathleen, *Children and Divorce*, London, Methuen, 1987.

Crawford, Christina, *Mommie Dearest*, London, Hart-Davies, MacGibbon, 1979.

de Mause, Lloyd, *The History of Childhood: The Untold Story of Child Abuse*, London, Bellew, 1993.

Dickens, Charles, *Great Expectations*, London, Chapman & Hall, 3 vols., 1861.

— *Nicholas Nickleby*, Harmondsworth, Penguin, 1978.

— *Oliver Twist*, New York, Turney, James, 1839.

Dryden, John, *Works*, Berkeley, University of California Press, 1987.

Durrell, Lawrence, *The Alexandria Quartet*: *Justine* (1957); *Balthazar* (1958); *Mountolive* (1958); *Clea* (1960), London, Faber & Faber, 1968.

Edison, Thomas, *The Papers of Thomas Edison*, Baltimore, Johns Hopkins University Press, 1991.

Edwardes, Allen, *The Jewel in the Lotus: A Historical Survey of the Sexual Culture of the East*, London, Allen & Unwin, 1965.

Eliot, T. S., *The Cocktail Party*, London, Faber & Faber, 1958.

Ellis, Brett Easton, *Less Than Zero*, New York, Simon & Schuster, 1985.

Ellman, Mary, *Thinking About Women*, London, Virago, 1979.

Eyer, Diane E., *Mother-Infant Bonding: A Scientific Fiction*, London, Yale, 1992.

Farson, Daniel, *The Gilded Gutter Life of Francis Bacon*, London, Century, 1993.

Gibran, Khalil, *A Treasury of Khalil Gibran*, New York, Citadel, 1951.

— *A Second Treasury of Khalil Gibran*, London, Mandarin, 1992.

Goode, William J., *World Changes in Divorce Patterns*, London, Yale, 1993.

Grass, Günter, *Local Anaesthetic*, Harmondsworth, Penguin, 1973.

Hamilton, Nigel, *JFK: Life and Death of an American President*, Vol.I: *Reckless Youth*, London, Century, 1993.

Hampshire, Susan, *Susan's Story*, Bath, Chivers, 1981.

Harcourt, Giles and Melville, *Short Prayers for the Long Day*, London, Collins, 1978.

Hart, Josephine, *Damage*, London, Chatto & Windus, 1991.

Hellman, Lillian, *The Children's Hour*, New York, Dramatist's Play Service Inc., 1953.

Hite, Shere, *The Hite Report on the Family*, London, Bloomsbury, 1994.

Housman, A. E., *Collected Poems*, Harmondsworth, Penguin, 1956.

Hughes-Hallett, Penelope (ed), *Childhood, A Collins Anthology*, London, 1988.

Hugo, Victor, *Les Misérables*, Paris, Hachette, 1982.

Humphries, Steve, and Gordon, Pamela, *A Labour of Love: The Experience of Parenthood in Britain 1900–1950*, London, Sidgwick & Jackson, 1993.

Hunter, Evan, *The Blackboard Jungle*, London, Constable, 1955.

Irving, Washington, *The Works of Washington Irving*, London, Henry G. Bohn, 1859.

Jackson, George L., *Soledad Brother: The Prison Letters of George Jackson*, Harmondsworth, Penguin, 1971.

— *Blood In My Eye*, London, Cape, 1972.

Johnston, Jennifer, *The Invisible Worm*, London, Sinclair Stevenson, 1991.

— *Shadows On Our Skin*, London, Hamish Hamilton, 1977.

Jonson, Ben, *Discoveries: Conversations with William Drummond of Hawthornden, 1619*, London, Bodley Head, 1923.

Joyce, James, 'An Encounter', in *Dubliners*, Harmondsworth, Penguin, 1956.

— *Poems and Shorter Writings*, London, Faber & Faber, 1991.

Jukes, Adam, *Why Men Hate Women*, London, Free Association Books, 1992.

Junor, Penny, *Charles*, London, Sidgwick & Jackson, 1987.

Kelley, Kitty, *Nancy Reagan: The Unauthorized Biography*, London, Bantam, 1991.

Kennedy, Florynce, *Color Me Flo*, Englewood Cliffs, Prentice Hall, 1976.

Kennedy, Helena, *Eve Was Framed*, London, Chatto & Windus, 1992.

Kimmel, Michael S.(ed), *Changing Men: New Directions in Research on Men and Masculinity*, Newbury Park and London, Sage, 1987.

Kincaid, James R., *Child-Loving: The Erotic Child and Victorian Culture*, London, Routledge, 1993.

King, Mary, *Truby King: The Man*, London, Allen & Unwin, 1948.

The Koran, Harmondsworth, Penguin, 1974.

Kurtz, Irma, *Malespeak*, London, Cape, 1986.

Lacan, Jacques, *Ecrits*, London, Tavistock Publications, 1977.

— *The Four Fundamental Concepts of Psychoanalysis*, London, Hogarth Press, 1977.

Langley, Lee, *Changes of Address*, London, Collins, 1987.

— *The Dying Art: A Novel*, London, Heinemann, 1983.

Larkin, Philip, *Collected Poems*, London, Faber & Faber, 1988.

Laskey, Tim, *How to Beat Bullying*, Hindhead, Health Habit Publications, 1993.

Lawrence, D. H., *Selected Poems*, London, Penguin, 1950.

Lawrence, Frieda, *Not I, But The Wind . . .*, London, Granada, 1983.

Lee, Laurie, *Cider With Rosie*, London, Hogarth Press, 1959.

Lindbergh, Anne Morrow, *Gift from the Sea*, London, Hogarth Press, 1985.

Lorca, Federico García, *Yerma*, London, Hodder & Stoughton, 1990.

McWhinnie, Alexina May, *Adopted Children: How They Grow Up*, London, Routledge & Kegan Paul, 1967.

Manguel, Alberto, *News From a Foreign Country Came*, London, HarperCollins, 1991.

Margolis, Jonathan, and Walmsey, Jane, *Hothouse People: Can We Create Superhuman Beings?*, London, Pan, 1987.

Mead, Margaret, *Blackberry Winter: My Earliest Years*, London, Angus & Robertson, 1973.

— *Male and Female: A Study of the Sexes in a Changing World*, New York, Morrow Quill, 1949.

Medved, Michael, *Hollywood vs. America: Popular Culture and the War on Traditional Values*, New York, HarperCollins, 1992.

Miller, Alice, *Banished Knowledge: Facing Childhood Injuries*, London, Virago, 1990.

— *Breaking Down the Wall of Silence: To Join the Waiting Child*, London, Virago, 1991.

— *The Drama of Being a Child and The Search for the True Self*, London, Virago, 1987. (Orig. *Prisoners of Childhood*, later *The Drama of the Gifted Child: How narcissistic parents form and deform the lives of their talented children*, London, Virago 1987.)

— *For Your Own Good: Hidden Cruelty in Child-Rearing*, London, Virago, 1987.

— *Thou Shalt Not Be Aware: Society's Betrayal of the Child*, London, Pluto, 1990.

Mones, Paul, *When a Child Kills: Abused Children Who Kill Their Parents*, New York, Pocket Books, 1991.

Morris, Desmond, *Babywatching*, London, Jonathan Cape, 1991.

Neruda, Pablo, *Selected Poems*, Harmondsworth, Penguin, 1975.

Olivier, Christiane, *Jocasta's Children: The Imprint of the Mother*, London, Routledge, 1989.

Oppenheim, Carey, 'The Cost of a Child', Child Poverty Action Group.

— 'Poverty: the Facts', Child Poverty Action Group, both available from CPAG, 4th floor, 1–5 Bath St, London EC1V 9PY.

Orton, Joe, *Entertaining Mr Sloane*, London, Methuen, 1964.

Orwell, George, 'Such, Such Were the Joys', in *Essays*, Harmondsworth, Penguin, 1993.

Patmore, Angela, *Marge: The Guilt and the Gingerbread*, London, Little, Brown, 1993.

Pearson, John, *Citadel of the Heart*, London, Macmillan, 1991.

Peck, M. Scott, *People of the Lie: The Hope for Healing Human Evil*, London, Arrow Books, 1990

— *The Road Less Travelled: A New Psychology of Love, Traditional Values and Spiritual Growth*, London, Arrow Books, 1983.

— *A World Waiting to be Born: The Search for Civility*, London, Rider Books, 1993.

Pepys, Samuel, *Everybody's Pepys, The Diary of Samual Pepys 1660– 1669*, London, Bell, 1926.

Phillips, Angela, *The Trouble with Boys: Parenting the Men of the Future*, London, Pandora Press, 1993.

Plath, Sylvia, *Collected Poems*, London, Faber & Faber, 1981.

Pogrebin, Lettie Cottin, *Deborah, Golda and Me: Being Female and Jewish in America*, New York, Crown, 1991.

Ponting, Clive, *A Green History of the World*, London, Sinclair Stevenson, 1991.

Quran, see *Koran*.

Report of the Enquiry into Child Abuse in Cleveland, 1987,London, HMSO, 1988.

Richards, Frank, *Billy Bunter of Greyfriars School*, London, Charles Skilton, 1947.

Rose, Phyllis, *Parallel Lives: Five Victorian Marriages*, NewYork, First Vintage Books, 1984.

Roth, Philip, *Portnoy's Complaint*, London, Cape, 1969.

Rymer, Russ, *Genie: Escape from a Silent Childhood*, London, Michael Joseph, 1993.

Searle, Ronald, and Shy, Timothy, *The Terror of St Trinian's*, London, Max Parrish, 1958

Seuss, Dr, *The Cat in the Hat*, New York, Random House, 1957.

— *Green Eggs and Ham*, London, Collins, 1980.

— *One Fish, Two Fish, Red Fish, Blue Fish*, London, HarperCollins, 1990.

Shackleton, Fiona, and Timbs, Olivia, *The Divorce Handbook*, London, Thorsons, 1992.

Shaw, George Bernard, *Everybody's Political What's What*, London, Constable & Company, 1944.

Smart, Elizabeth, *By Grand Central Station I Sat Down and Wept*, London, Paladin, 1991.

Smith, Jean, and Grunvelt, Nina, *Nanny Knows Best*, London, BBC Books, 1993.

Smith, Stevie, *Collected Poems*, London, Allen Lane, 1975.

Sowell, Thomas, *Ethnic America: A History*, New York, Basic Books, 1981.

Somerset, Anne, *Elizabeth I*, London, Weidenfeld & Nicolson, 1991.

Spada, James, *Peter Lawford: The Man Who Kept the Secrets*, London, Bantam Books, 1991.

Spock, Benjamin, *Dr Spock's Baby and Child Care*, London, W. H. Allen, 1969.

— *Parenting*, Harmondsworth, Penguin, 1990.

Stone, Fred, *Child Abuse: The Scottish Experience*, London, British Agencies for Adoption and Fostering, 1989.

Storr, Anthony, *Human Aggression*, Harmondsworth, Penguin, 1968.

Stowe, Harriet Beecher, *Uncle Tom's Cabin: A Tale of Life Among the Lowly*, London, Routledge, 1852.

Suetonius, *Lives of the Twelve Caesars*, ed. Robert Graves, Harmondsworth, Penguin, 1957.

Sullivan, Rosemary, *By Heart: Elizabeth Smart, A Life*, London, Lime Tree, 1991.

Trevelyan, G. O., *The Life and Letters of Lord Macaulay*, London, Longman's Green & Co, 1881.

Turner, Tina, and Loder, Kurt, *I, Tina*, Harmondsworth, Viking, 1986.

US Bureau of the Census, Statistical Abstract of the US 1992, Washington DC, 1993.

Waugh, Auberon, *Will This Do? The first 50 years of Auberon Waugh*, London, Arrow, 1992.

Wilcox, Ella Wheeler, *Poetical Works*, Edinburgh, Nimmo, Hay and Mitchell, 1917.

Wordsworth, William, *Poems*, London, Yale, 1981.

Wyre, Ray, *Women, Men and Rape*, Sevenoaks, Headway, 1990.

Index